Progressive Community Organizing

Progressive Community Organizing

A Critical Approach for a Globalizing World

LORETTA PYLES

Routledge
Taylor & Francis Group
New York   London

Routledge
Taylor & Francis Group
270 Madison Avenue
New York, NY 10016

Routledge
Taylor & Francis Group
2 Park Square
Milton Park, Abingdon
Oxon OX14 4RN

Printed in the United States of America on acid-free paper
10 9 8 7 6 5 4 3 2

International Standard Book Number-13: 978-0-415-95780-9 (Softcover)

Library of Congress Cataloging-in-Publication Data

Pyles, Loretta.
　　Progressive community organizing : the roots of social change / Loretta Pyles.
　　　　p. cm.
　　ISBN 978-0-415-95780-9 (pbk. : alk. paper)
　　1. Community organization. 2. Social action. I. Title.

HM766.P95 2009
361.2--dc22   2008029760

Visit the Taylor & Francis Web site at
http://www.taylorandfrancis.com

and the Routledge Web site at
http://www.routledge.com

Contents

SECTION I *Foundations of Community Organizing*

SECTION II   Tools for Community Organizing

SECTION III   Enduring and Emergent Issues in Organizing

Preface

This book is not a "how-to" manual about community organizing. The world is too complex to offer such a guide. Instead, the goal of the book is to help students, organizers, and educators grapple with the salient philosophical, political, and practical issues involved in community organizing. Organizing requires compassionate, assertive, and, most importantly, reflective individuals to do the work. To that end, the purposes of the book are to: (a) articulate the depth of community organizing by introducing the philosophical, political, sociological, and social work ideas that have historically informed community organizing; (b) impart a sense of the breadth of the field by drawing from the wisdom of various social movements, such as the labor movement, global justice movement, and the disability rights movement; (c) review various skills and lessons learned including guidelines for organizing constituencies, ideas for thinking about work in empowering organizations, considerations for framing issues, and various tactics for social change; and (d) describe and analyze the ongoing debates and controversies that face organizers in a complex, globalizing world.

The goal of the text is to promote an understanding of the intellectual underpinnings of community organizing while also emphasizing the practical and contextual aspects. I draw from scholarly research studies, popular literature, and the writings of grassroots organizers to weave together a tapestry of the important social change work of community organizing. While there is much to be gained from learning about the history of organizing and understanding basic theories and methods, all organizing endeavors call for the ability of practitioners to assess each unique situation based on context, resources, and institutional limits. Toward that end, I offer ongoing analyses of the literature on community organizing, highlighting tensions, and laying out possible solutions to doing progressive social change work.

Progressive Community Organizing consists of three major sections. In Part I, I present theoretical and historical ideas and frameworks that will be useful to students of community organizing. Chapter 1 (Introduction) begins with an overview of key definitions that lay the foundation for a critical approach to progressive organizing in the context of a globalized world. Chapter 2 (The Self-Aware Organizer) argues that there is much personal work that an organizer needs to do to be able to be authentic and successful in her or his work. The perils of organizing are addressed, such as dealing with anger, apathy, burnout, and co-optation. In addition, I discuss the importance of finding meaning and joy in organizing. I offer suggestions as to how organizers might go about doing personal antioppression work by looking into their own internalized racism, homophobia, etc., which all organizers must continually face. Chapter 3 (Theories and Ideas for the Progressive Organizer) addresses philosophical and political ideas and theories that are relevant to community organizing and social change. I discuss Marxist, anarchist, and feminist perspectives as well as explorations of ideas related to participatory democracy and social constructionism. Chapter 4 (Learning from Social Movements) discusses aspects of social movement theory in sociology, highlighting some dimensions of key social movements in history and currently. These movements include labor, women's, LGBT (lesbian, gay, bisexual, transgender), and disability. Chapter 5 (Critical Organizing Frameworks) expands on what I mean by critical organizing frameworks, drawing from important organizers/thinkers such as Alinsky and Freire as well as feminist-oriented approaches.

Part II focuses on the nuts and bolts of organizing. Chapter 6 (Organizing People: Constituencies and Coalitions) explores the practice of base building with individuals and existing groups. Whether one's constituency consists of battered women or residents of a housing project, this chapter seeks to describe mechanisms for organizing people and emphasizing empowerment and relationship building. Emphasis is placed on the importance of building indigenous leadership throughout the process and overcoming barriers to organizing oppressed, isolated, and reluctant communities. Many have argued that the most effective way to mobilize for social change is by doing so within an organization. Thus, Chapter 7 (Toward Empowering Organizations) focuses on internal issues relevant to maintaining an organization that empowers constituents, including decision making and funding. Strategies for continuing to build indigenous leadership within the organization are offered. Chapter 8 (Language Matters: Issue Framing and Communication) centers on the social constructionist framing perspective, discussing ways to think about formulating and communicating issues in the context of campaigns and organizations. Chapter 9 (Tactics for Change) explores a range of strategies that organizers use to achieve needed reforms and effect social change. Discussions focus on policy change, community development approaches, direct-action campaigns, and cultural organizing.

Part III considers enduring and emergent issues and controversies in progressive community organizing. These practices are important for dealing with the difficult issues discussed in Chapter 10 (Toward Solidarity: Understanding Oppression and Working with Identity Politics), which focuses on the possibilities and problems that identity politics have presented in social change endeavors. Models of working with interlocking oppressions and the politics of difference are discussed with case examples from campus organizing and reproductive justice organizing. Chapter 11 (Religious and Spiritual Aspects of Organizing) inquires into the role that spirituality and religion can play in social change. Discussions of faith-based and environmental organizing from Jewish, Christian, Buddhist, Hindu, and other perspectives are addressed. The last, but not least, chapter of the book, Chapter 12 (Global Justice: Organization and Resistance) expands on the negative effects that globalization has on communities and the transnational approaches to address them. Resistance in the form of land-based movements, immigrant-rights organizing, and transnational labor movements is discussed. I discuss how the enhanced social networking aspects of globalization can facilitate enhanced organizing strategies.

Acknowledgments

Writing a book, I've learned, is easier said than done. It is like a birthing of sorts, though without a doctor or midwife. The writing was a natural unfolding, an active expression of something that has been lying dormant and waiting to be written, and a great joy. I have had a tremendous opportunity to learn about myself and clarify ideas and values. I am thankful to Routledge for giving me the opportunity.

It has been difficult to write this in the midst of the social atrocities of the post-Katrina world that is New Orleans these days. The words of social activist and Catholic worker Dorothy Day (1981) capture some of my internal conflicts in this regard:

> The sustained effort of writing, of putting pen to paper so many hours a day when there are human beings around who need me, when there is sickness, and hunger, and sorrow, is a harrowingly painful job. I feel that I have done nothing well. But I have done what I could. (p. 11)

I am appreciative of all of the organizers who I have worked with thus far and learned from over the years, particularly people from Greenpeace, Women's Transitional Care Services, Kansas Coalition Against Sexual and Domestic Violence, the National Coalition Against Domestic Violence, University of Kansas Graduate Teaching Assistant's Coalition (GTAC), New Orleans Food and Farm Network, C3/Hands Off Iberville, and many others. These groups helped form my diverse sensibility about social change and ways of organizing.

I would like to thank Anne Dienethal and Carmen Jones for their assistance with research. I also wish to acknowledge the Tulane Research Enhancement Fund for financial support. Thanks to the many people who supported me by reviewing material, offering ideas, resources, and encouragement—Tulane School of Social Work MSW students Mahasweta Banerjee, Elizabeth Beck, Rebecca Chaisson, Scott Harding, Eileen Ihrig, Rachel Mehl, Dawne Pyles, and Angie Reinking. Thanks to Dana Bliss and Charlotte Roh at Routledge.

My husband, Ted Mehl—teacher, artist, and scholar—has been supportive of this project beyond what words could express. He has emanated the love and stability to make this endeavor a possibility. I really appreciate his editorial assistance as he read chapters of this book.

Section I

Foundations of Community Organizing

1 Introduction

Critical thinking [is] the most important skill for the pursuit of freedom, equality and justice, and the greatest enemy of authoritarianism.

Suzanne Pharr (1996, p. 17)

When the United States Army Corps of Engineers' levees failed after Hurricane Katrina in August 2005, the people who were unable to evacuate New Orleans sought safety and higher ground as flooding ensued. During this desperate time, citizens offered each other support, taking care of their families and neighbors, while waiting for help from the government to arrive. The Federal Emergency Management Agency (FEMA), whose authority had recently been diminished by shifting it from a free-standing governmental agency to one of many agencies under the umbrella of the Department of Homeland Security, was conspicuously absent for days. Most of the people who needed resources at the time, such as water, food, and shelter, were low-income African-American families who waited at the Superdome or at the Convention Center. After several days of waiting, they were eventually bussed or flown out of the city to other parts of the country; many are still trying to get back, and many may never return home.

After this massive flood, people all over the globe began discussing the immediate and long-term material and social justice issues that Gulf Coast and evacuee communities were facing. As the waters receded, New Orleans citizens searched for loved ones—and answers. Evacuees attempted to find each other in shelters as well as to call, text message, and e-mail each other; they surfed the Internet for helpful information, wondering what the next steps were, and whom to hold accountable. Faith-based and other relief organizations descended on New Orleans and evacuee communities to provide help where it seemed to be most needed. As citizens gradually reconnected with each other, they began to advocate collectively for levee board accountability, utility services, insurance payments, FEMA assistance, health-care services, and the right to return to public housing. They did this through informal means, as well as by starting new organizations and reviving dormant neighborhood associations. These resilient people were doing this work for myriad purposes and reasons, in some cases, just to preserve their own homes and protect their previous quality of life. In other cases, it was to hold governmental entities such as the levee boards and the Army Corps of Engineers accountable for the vast devastation of almost an entire city. Still others became involved in order to redress the deep-seated local and global racial and economic injustices exposed in the inadequate hurricane response and rebuilding. For many people, the connection between what was happening in New Orleans and what was happening in the developing world was becoming clear—corporations were receiving governmental subsidies to "boost" economies, while public infrastructure and social welfare were being grossly neglected.

Many of these groups were and still are engaged in classical community organizing and activism—organizing people, getting information, identifying grievances, confronting those in power who have the ability to make decisions, and rebuilding communities. The situation in New Orleans was a galvanizing event that has served to marshal diverse citizens in unprecedented ways. Scholars have pointed out that in order to address injustice and engage in community organizing, citizens must feel that their way of life is being threatened (Kieffer, 1984), and such has been the case in New Orleans.

Since the autumn of 2005, scholars and activists have researched and written about a variety of types and levels of community organizing activity in New Orleans.[1] Some of the courageous organizers had never been involved in their communities prior to Katrina, let alone engaged in progressive or grassroots direct-action organizing. Others are lifelong community leaders with a history of activism and organizing successes. Still others identify as part of an international solidarity movement for human rights. And so, to be sure, a wide spectrum of organizing experience has been a hallmark of the post-Katrina landscape. As an illustration, consider that experienced organizers from local and nationally known community organizations[2] have been working in New Orleans—All Congregations Together (ACT), Association of Community Organizations for Reform Now (ACORN), Incite! Women of Color against Violence, and the People's Hurricane Relief Fund. These groups, which consist of local citizens, activists, and professional organizers, are working to mobilize communities to effect change and achieve needed reforms for people in real time.

There are countless examples of inspired and effective community organizing campaigns in post-Katrina New Orleans. African-American neighborhood members in the Lower Ninth Ward founded an organization called the Ninth Ward Empowerment Neighborhood Association (NENA) with the allied support of Mercy Corps, an international nongovernmental organization (NGO). Mercy Corps had previously worked primarily in countries other than the United States, but helped NENA gut a flooded church and begin a neighborhood association, with a focus on the community-development and social-welfare issues that will face them for years to come.[3] NENA sponsored a powerful vigil near the site of the levee breakage in the Lower Ninth Ward after the storm, which brought important media attention to the issue. Another example is the Vietnamese elders affiliated with a local faith-based community-development corporation, Mary Queen of Vietnam Community Development Corporation, who became a powerful force when they descended upon their targets at city hall after toxic trash from gutted-out homes was being illegally dumped in their neighborhood. The closure of the dump was a key victory for a coalition of faith-based groups in the city. Katrina has created a unique opportunity to build solidarity across racial and class divides due to the fact that everyone in the community was affected at some level. Though citizens were not affected by the disaster equally, the conditions have provided an opening for citizens to understand their linked fates and how social problems affect everyone.

But most community organizing does not happen in the context of an event as highly publicized as Hurricane Katrina. Most injustices happen without media coverage; they are not in full view for the world to see on CNN. In fact, most injustice is masked by a narrative that describes it otherwise. Consider the welfare discourse in the early years following the 1996 Personal Responsibility and Work Opportunity Reconciliation Act (PRWORA), which reduced the amount of time a person could receive public benefits and emphasized a "work first" philosophy (Kilty & Segal, 2003). Many politicians and media stated that welfare reform had been a success. The welfare rolls had been reduced by half; but many people knew another side to the story, particularly the people who are in need of public benefits and are living the reality of poverty in the United States. Some scholars and activists understood that many of the individuals receiving public benefits had no choice but to work $7.00 per hour jobs and had little prospects for increasing their chances of making more money (Cancian, 2001). If the goal of the welfare reform policy had been to reduce the rolls, then indeed maybe it was a success, but the thinking person had to ask whether it was even the right goal in the first place: What about living-wage employment opportunities? What about adequate food, health care, child care, education, and housing? (Jones-DeWeever, 2005; Taliaferro, 2005). Who

---

[1] See, for example: South End Press Collective. (2007). *What lies beneath: Katrina, race and the state of the nation.* Cambridge, MA: South End Press.

[2] Pyles, L. (2007). Community organizing for post-disaster social development: Locating social work. *International Social Work, 50* (3), 321–333.

[3] Axel-Lute, M. (2006). Picking up the pieces. *Shelterforce Online, 145.* Retrieved August 1, 2008, from http://www.nhi.org/online/issues/145/pickinguppieces.html

were the real beneficiaries of welfare reform? It is through the posing of such questions that the work of progressive community organizers begins.

PRIVATIZATION, GLOBALIZATION, AND RESISTANCE

The mid-1970s in the United States denotes the beginnings of the retrenchment of social welfare services, laying the foundation for comprehensive welfare reform (Mink, 2002; Quadagno, 1996). This new federalism has been marked by an emphasis on devolution and privatization (Karger & Stoesz, 2006). Responsibility for social welfare provision has been placed in the hands of states and local entities, and ultimately in the hands of private contractors. Faith-based service providers, social service organizations, and informal citizen networks attempt to coordinate the human welfare needs of citizens with minimal assistance from the government. The idea of "cradle to grave" support for citizens, if it was ever achieved, sometimes seems like a fanciful dream.

These policies evolved from a philosophy of the political economy that emphasizes trickle-down economics, free-market capitalism, and social Darwinism (Karger & Stoesz, 2006). This philosophy is based on a "liberal" approach to the flows of capital, unrestricted by governmental interventions.[1] During the 1980s and 1990s, these neoliberal free markets were ever expanding into global venues. This globalization has been referred to as the most significant restructuring of political and economic arrangements since the Industrial Revolution (Mander, 1996). The term *globalization* is a complex and loaded term, and for some it may refer to the increasing states of interconnectedness across the globe—cultural, environmental, and technological. For others, it is a distinctively economic term referring to cross-national economic transactions between corporations and governments (Streeten, 2001). These definitions are not unrelated, and both are relevant to the task at hand.

Multinational and other corporations from the global North, i.e., "developed countries," have for some time been expanding into new territory, or markets, in the "developing" global South. Unfortunately, when many of these corporations begin hiring local labor, it can often happen without attention to living wages or quality of life of vulnerable citizens and families (Streeten, 2001). Free-trade policies and structural adjustment programs have continued to defy attempts to protect workers' wages and conditions worldwide. Studies have shown that such policies have had deleterious consequences for the environment and the quality of life of workers and poor people throughout the world (Lechner & Boli, 2004). These are the times in which organizers across the globe find themselves, and this is the larger context of this book.

The good news is that just like in New Orleans, there has been resistance to these seemingly insurmountable global and local forces. For many, the Seattle protests of the World Trade Organization (WTO) in 1999 signified the great strength and resistance of the global justice movement. Union workers, environmentalists, and social change activists from all over the world came together to resist these policies using a diverse range of tactics (Katsiaficas, 2004; Klein, 2002). In countries throughout the world, people who are living in a context of privatized or no services and corporate greed and irresponsibility, struggle daily for funding for affordable housing, the rights of immigrants, access to clean water, community mental health, reproductive justice, and other basic human needs. Activists throughout the world have been looking to grassroots struggles in Latin America and Asia for inspiration and guidance about how to resist policies and practices that are negatively affecting human rights. For example, after a major economic collapse in Argentina in 2001, multinational corporations pulled out of the country—literally overnight—boarding up workplaces and leaving workers without jobs. Workers took action and organized themselves, occupying the factories and winning the right to form cooperatives and keep the factories going. This National Movement of Recovered Factories has shown the world how the power of regular people working together can resist globalization and create an alternative model of business where all workers earn

---

[1] This "neoliberal" approach to economics is not to be confused with the political spectrum of liberal and conservative commonly used in the United States.

the same amount of money, eliminating a boss who is paid a grossly disproportionate wage compared to the workers. The last chapter of this book highlights some of the early lessons learned from the global justice movements.

DEFINING COMMUNITY ORGANIZING

Trying to define community organizing is actually much trickier than one would at first think. Most organizations and organizers do not necessarily fall under a strict definition of community organizing. Grassroots and nongovernmental organizations (NGOs), or nonprofits, are variously engaged in social services, advocacy, community organizing, and activism. Trying to force a definition of community organizing and attempting to include some activities and exclude others is difficult and, ultimately, a false construction. Nonetheless, it is clearly worth setting some parameters about community organizing as characterized in this text. Before defining what organizing is, it is useful to define what is meant by community.

WHAT IS COMMUNITY?

Defining the notion of community itself has become more complex in a diverse, globalized, and technological world. The notion of community harkens a wide range of ideas, including trust, mutuality, commitment, and solidarity, as well as the ideas of contestation, conflict, and exclusion (Smith, 2001).

To be sure, people who live in close proximity to each other tend to have some common interests and are representative of this complex idea known as "community." Bourdieu (1984) has pointed out that the types of social spaces that people inhabit, particularly economical and cultural, are related to lifestyles, power levels, and identities. People tend to reside near those who are similar to them, especially with regard to social class and racial or ethnic affiliation. Indeed, theories of social exclusion trace, for example, the ways that social exclusion, in particular racial exclusion, can be manifested in a domain such as housing (Somerville & Steele, 2002). Such complexities in social geography can be understood by further inquiring into policies and practices related to social planning, economic development, and real estate development. It is the case that citizens live in neighborhoods with people who are somewhat like them, and it is also the case that even in the most diverse of neighborhoods, a toxic waste dump can bring dissimilar groups of people together pretty quickly. Thus, geographical propinquity is still a valuable factor for understanding community.

And yet, many people today tend to find that they have more in common with people with whom they are not in physical proximity. Indeed, such extended social networks may define community for many people (Putnam, 2000). Recent sociological theories of identity have opened up a conceptual space for thinking about community in terms of political interests or various forms of cultural identities (Hoggett, 1997).

A community may be united by shared racial, ethnic, gender, cultural, or other identities, though not necessarily sharing of geographic location or all common values. The lesbian-gay-bisexual-transgender (LGBT) community is one such example. Though there is great diversity within the LGBT community, many activists have strategically aligned themselves as a community with common political interests (for example, an interest in the legalization of gay marriage). Thus, the dual notions of place and interest/identity appear to both be of central importance when developing a broad concept of community (Smith, 2001).

The global justice movement represents a community of people across the globe whose members consider themselves oppressed by global free trade and structural adjustment policies. From environmentalists in the Australian outback to European labor organizers to indigenous peoples in Mexico who have lost their land to corporatization, this is indeed a broad conceptualization of community. Due to the expansion of social networks, a result of an increase in technology in a globalized world, it is necessary that the concept of community be considered broadly. Global summits of grassroots organizers such as the World Social Forum, first held in Porto Alegre, Brazil, in 2001, are an indicator that the denotation of community has broadened.

It can be helpful when thinking of community in the context of organizing that, although a group may have strategic, political reasons for aligning themselves, their experiences and values are not always unified (Hartsock, 1996; Stephen, 2005). To be sure, however, community membership has been contested by both insiders and outsiders just as the diversity within a group has been problematized. How can members of a community maintain their individuality and still stand in solidarity with the group? To what degree can allies of a community be considered part of that community? These are important questions that, though they do not have explicit answers, must be considered when thinking about community and organizing. In Chapter 11, I discuss some of the complexities of what some have termed *identity politics* and how organizers can work through the important nuances of community identity in order to achieve the goal of solidarity. In sum, community can be defined as a group of people with a common affiliation, identity, or grievance that may be geographically or nongeographically based.

What Is Organizing?

The illustrious Chicago-based community organizer Saul Alinsky once said that one should never do things for people that they can do for themselves (Alinsky, 1971). This is an interesting notion, particularly when considered by practitioners whose vocation may be to provide material necessities or social services to people who are in crisis or who are otherwise living in poverty. Indeed, serving people or being a "voice for the voiceless" is surely a noble pursuit. What Alinsky tried to communicate, though, is really a key feature of what makes community organizing unique from other types of interventions—helping people help themselves. Frederick Douglass believed, and Saul Alinsky agreed, that "to re-claim power must necessarily make demands" (Alinsky, 1971). These two features—people organizing themselves and confronting power with grievances—are central attributes of organizing (Bobo, Kendall, & Max, 2001). The ultimate task of community organizing is to mobilize disenfranchised people to advocate on their own behalf in relationship to some power structure in order to achieve needed changes. Some would add that building mutually supportive communities is a vital element of community organizing and change work (Murphy & Cunningham, 2003). And still others would add that an additional and critical component of organizing, indeed the real raison d'être is to overcome oppression and achieve liberation (Pharr, 1996). Actually, all of these components are integral to what I call *progressive community organizing*.

To be sure, organizing communities for social change is clearly not a value-neutral endeavor. Indeed, no community work could ever be value-neutral. Although this book does begin with such a strong value orientation, my approach is to offer a critical and balanced view of the theories, perspectives, and practices associated with such progressive social change work.

However, not all progressive organizers will always emphasize these various elements of organizing equally, i.e., self-organization, confronting power, building community, and transforming oppression. For example, some community organizers, including neighborhood organizers, labor organizers, and others, may not focus their work on transforming multiple oppressions such as sexism, racism, and homophobia. Their work may be more utilitarian in nature and focus instead on achieving winnable victories or righting a specific injustice. There is always something to be learned from the diversity of community organizers and frameworks.

Organizing Versus Other Interventions

In order to comprehend just exactly what community organizing is, it may be useful to compare and contrast community organizing to other areas of social welfare intervention—social services, activism, advocacy, and community building. Historically, the field of community organizing has gone to great lengths to distinguish itself from what it appears not to be, namely social service. Saul

Alinsky had a disregard for what he called "do-gooders" who were helping the poor; instead, he believed in helping the poor help themselves (Boyte, 1984). In some sense, however, any work that one does in the name of social justice for all people is a kind of service, a "call to service" (Coles, 1993). But, clearly, community organizing has a unique empowerment and change orientation, and thus it is necessary to make some important distinctions.

Examples of services in the traditional sense are: case management services for people with chronic mental health issues, food banks for the working poor, disaster relief, and assistance with filling out disability applications. While some of these activities can involve case advocacy (for example, a social worker making demands for welfare benefits for which a particular client may be eligible) and may have a strong emphasis on empowerment, they are traditionally viewed as services. And yet, it is possible that such services could be provided with a strong social change, or activist orientation. For example, the Black Panther Party, a progressive, politically oriented civil rights organization active in the 1960s and 1970s, provided services through what was referred to as "survival programs pending revolution," which included medical clinics, free breakfast for children, free clothing, pest control, sickle cell anemia testing, education, and prison support. Another example is services for people with chronic mental health issues that are provided by peers, in ways that attempt to deconstruct the power of social service hierarchies, which tend to uphold strong distinctions between those who provide services and those who receive them. Such consumer-led efforts, as opposed to efforts that may only seek input from consumers, are not forms of community organizing, strictly speaking, but are allied endeavors that are important to progressive organizing agendas. These efforts are important because of the strong emphasis on the empowerment of traditionally marginalized people and a social change agenda that seeks to undo societal power structures that oppress people with mental health issues.

Offering training on racism to social service agencies or providing technical assistance on immigration issues to legal aid clinics are also services in the narrowest sense. However, such training/ services may happen in the context of a larger organizing or social movement campaign, and such ally endeavors by supportive organizations seek, for example, to strengthen the rights of immigrant Latino workers. Kivel (2007) attempts to distinguish between social service and social change: "*Social service work* addresses the needs of individuals reeling from the personal and devastating impact of institutional systems of exploitation and violence. *Social change work* challenges the root causes of exploitation and violence" (p. 129).

Social service work can be done with an activist orientation. Interestingly, in my experience, women and low-income people of color do not often so clearly separate community organizing from service provision because they often do not have the luxury to ignore service and just focus on organizing. Women, in particular, tend to be service providers, the caretakers for communities in crisis, the ones who are forced to pick up the pieces of a society that too often ignores its basic social welfare infrastructure. There is a famous Native American parable of a tribe that comes upon some drowning babies in a river. The group begins taking the babies out of the river to save them, one after the other, trying to bring them back to life. It is very exhausting and seemingly incessant work. Eventually, though, somebody gets the idea to go upstream and find out why the babies are drowning, to get to the bottom of the situation and try to stop it from happening in the first place. And this might be a good way to think about the difference between social service and community organizing work—both are necessary, but ultimately organizing work is the only thing that really can get to the bottom of social issues.

Consider now the practice of advocacy, particularly policy advocacy, which is the practice of influencing legislation, appropriations, or planning processes. This usually implies advocating for or on behalf of a group of people, of being a "voice" for the so-called voiceless. Compare the difference between a small group of people with disabilities testifying on a bill at the state legislature about local building codes and accessibility issues versus an able-bodied paid staff person testifying on the same bill. By organizing a group of marginalized people, particularly if they are led by a person with a disability, their sense of personal empowerment as well as group identity may be strengthened. This empowerment could then be leveraged and sustained for future endeavors. Also, consider the effects on the legislators at the hearing. They may be more moved by and thus more inclined to respond to the stories of people for whom the effects of the policy are real rather than a person whose paid job it is to testify. Advocacy work, while it is often better funded than organizing work, is often engaged in without accountability to a base constituency or with only little input from the base. It should also be noted that advocacy may involve a certain amount of organizing a constituency, just like leaders of grassroots community organizing ventures engage in advocacy; to be sure, the definitions are slippery. Community organizing and advocacy are both important interventions, but organizing the people for whom the issues are most real may be a more effective and sustainable strategy for long-term social change.

Community building, the practice of identifying assets and problems and seeking resources and solutions in a neighborhood, is also often contrasted to community organizing. Again, the distinctions are not completely clear, nor is it necessary that they need to be totally distinct. A community development corporation, for example, may emphasize building leadership and supporting small business ownership for people of color in a depressed community instead of confronting power structures with a demand. Their major focus may be to empower local business owners and support neighborhood economic development, and only rarely, if ever, would they engage in an action that would directly attempt to take back power or transform inequities.

Though policy advocacy and community building have received thorough treatments elsewhere, I do consider components of them in this book, particularly to the extent that they are part of larger organizing campaigns (Jansson, 2007; Kretzmann & McKnight, 1993). Though some consider community organizing to entail only those activities whose primary purpose is to organize constituents and take back power, my belief is that organizing, like the notion of community, should be considered more broadly. Organizers should have a comprehensive understanding of the kinds of allied work that are a part of a progressive organizing agenda. Community organizing always involves regular people who confront or resist power, where power is manifested as governmental institutions, legislators, corporations, media outlets, landlords, etc. There are lessons to be learned from community development work, advocacy groups, and social change–oriented service organizations. The above discussion reveals the slippery nature of historic definitions and the socially constructed nature of social welfare practices.

A CRITICAL APPROACH TO ORGANIZING

The paradigms through which one conceptualizes individuals, families, communities, and institutions—and the interactions among them—are directly related to the ways in which one is inclined to intervene in social problems. If one understands domestic violence to be caused by low self-esteem or learned helplessness in women, then concomitant interventions would focus on building the self-esteem of women. On the other hand, if one understands domestic violence to be a result of a patriarchal society that privileges men and devalues women, then interventions would likely focus on changing the social structure—changing norms, educating young boys, and holding perpetrators accountable. Additionally, if one comprehends the problem of poverty to be a function of people being lazy, then policies will require people on welfare to work at any job or even to do volunteer work. Or, if poverty is understood as a function of low wages, then a living-wage strategy might be pursued. Thus, how one frames social problems is clearly tied to how one attempts to intervene. Such paradigms are tied to one's own standpoint, or positionality, in society, as well as influences from the media, educational systems, and the economic system.

The philosophical and literary movements of postmodernism and post-structuralism, particularly that of social constructionism, offer important and unique ways of thinking about breaking down oppressive narratives, revealing the slippery nature of rhetoric and language. These intellectual movements offer tools for reframing issues in ways that attend to the realities of oppressed people that can be empowering. Gergen (1999) and other social constructionists have posited that individuals do not create language and meaning in isolation; rather, meanings are a function of relationships and agreements among people in society. Reality is, in essence, socially constructed and thus can be deconstructed and subsequently reconstructed in ways that are liberating.

Various accounts of economic globalization often state that expanding markets will solve the world's problems; these markets offer a way to finally develop the developing world (Oxfam, 2004). This idea of "development" is based on the belief that Third World or global South countries, i.e., developing nations, are primitive and need to be modernized (Kaufman, 2003). The argument contends that corporate investment in these countries will make the standard of living for the poorest peoples increase. And yet theses narratives of the global economy are often constructed by the people who are the major beneficiaries of the new arrangements—corporate leaders, their allies in government, and centralized global trade bureaucracies such as the WTO and the International Monetary Fund (IMF) (Mander, 1996). While the phrase *free trade* is often used to advocate for policies such as the North American Free Trade Agreement (NAFTA), a better term might be "deregulated international commerce" (Daly, 1996, p. 230). The concept of freedom that rests in the idea of free trade masks the negative effects of a deregulated economy. When one looks a little more closely at the actual living conditions of people living in "free trade zones," one has to question if the workers and their families are indeed free. While a globalized economy that increases communication and respectful sharing of cultures is something most people could agree on, a globalized economy that displaces people from their homes, removes health-care benefits, and pays people low wages does not seem like such a good idea to many people.

This practice of deconstructing narratives and inquiring further into the empirical circumstances of people's lives, ultimately a kind of critical thinking, is indeed, as Pharr (1996) says, "the most important skill" for social change. This approach, which entails inquiring into the winners and losers of social arrangements, is guided by critical theory. Critical theory, which will be discussed in greater detail in Chapter 3, is grounded in Marxist and neo-Marxist analyses that seek to clarify and interpret the power differentials that exist in society (Kincheloe & McLaren, 2000). While Marx was primarily concerned with class power, critical theorists have come to be concerned with racial, gender, and other forms of power that prohibit people from full inclusion and flourishing in society. Such an approach is grounded in the idea of intersectionality, whereby oppressions, such as racism, sexism, and classism, are understood to be interlocking (Collins, 1999; Kaufman, 2003). Thus, an underlying assumption of this text is that progressive organizers working toward social change must necessarily unravel all aspects of oppression based on an understanding of intersectionality (discussed in further detail in Chapters 3 and 12).

It is clear that one's analysis gives rise to one's methods. If one has no critical thinking skills to observe phenomena and deconstruct them, then one can completely miss the boat, just blindly intervening without understanding the roots of issues or the deep-seated strengths of a community. Because the way one frames or analyzes issues is related to interventions, then it follows that critical thinking skills and the ability to analyze are the foundations of organizing. Engaging in such power analysis is a bedrock of community organizing practice (Sinclair & Russ, 2006). Thus, this critical approach is a principal orientation of this text. In Chapter 7, I talk about the framing perspective, a phenomenon identified by sociologists that emphasizes how the reframing of issues is a critical step that community organizers must engage in before determining what action to take.

THE JOURNEY OF PROGRESSIVE ORGANIZING

There are numerous ways to engage in communities as a practitioner. These ways are often based on a variety of goals and methods. Some ways of engagement have stronger elements of social change and individual empowerment than others. Other methods emphasize changing a particular policy or achieving a victory and may involve lesser degrees of engaging a particular constituency in the process. These different goals and methods may all have their place, but it is important to understand them and know when it is appropriate and feasible to incorporate various strategies.

Understanding the organization a person works for, the ideologies underlying policies, and the funding mechanisms of an organization are all a part of understanding one's location as an organizer. I submit that understanding one's own self, especially one's personal history and values, is also a critical component of organizing work.

Some organizations may believe that they are engaged in social change activities that, unfortunately, may actually be perpetuating current arrangements. Social welfare practices have been "implicated in oppressive processes by fostering relations of dominance that are consistent with supporting the status quo" (Dominelli, 2002, p. 28). Organizations may believe they are promoting citizen empowerment when they are actually doing things *for* their constituency rather than doing the work *with* their constituency. An organization that advocates for the rights of immigrants but that is composed only of white citizen professionals with privilege is not necessarily engaged in progressive organizing work. The ability of such a group to be truly accountable to the constituency is virtually impossible without being driven by immigrant voices. Such a situation can be remedied, but it takes a strong commitment to such things as: giving up power, changing organizational policies and tactics, and being open to critique by those who are marginalized.

Empowerment and Social Change

My experience has been that terms such as *social justice, social change*, and *empowerment* are utilized with regularity among organizers, activists, and social workers. Not only are the definitions of these words often unclear, but the activities that correspond to the words are often incommensurate. For this reason, it may be useful to define a few of these terms. (See Key Terms at the end of this chapter.) Many of these terms are interrelated.

Oppression is a socially constructed situation whereby a dominant group "others" a group deemed to be of lower status (Dominelli, 2002). People acquiesce to domination when societal ideas lead them to believe in the naturalness of the present order of oppression (Kaufman, 2003), the idea that the Italian Marxist thinker Antonio Gramsci called *hegemony*. This hegemony is a social construction dependent upon daily reinforcement in the media, workplace, and educational institutions as well as social welfare institutions. Thus, liberation from such oppression entails a kind of undoing of such social constructions. Breaking through belief systems is the first step toward empowerment.

I define empowerment as increasing the levels of understanding, engagement, and/or personal power of individual citizens. This may happen through consciousness-raising activities, participation in social action, and engagement in leadership roles, to name a few. Empowerment has been an important concept in community organizing practice, social work practice, and community development, rooted in and related to feminist and strengths perspectives (Gutierrez, Parsons, & Cox, 1998; Saleebey, 1997). Empowerment is ultimately a political idea that seeks to develop individual power in order to reshape the environment, a belief that people are capable of making their own choices and have much to offer in shaping society. The role of the organizer, then, is to "nourish, encourage, assist, enable, support, stimulate, and unleash the strengths within people; to illuminate the strengths available to people in their own environments; and to promote equity and justice at all levels of society" (Cowger, 1997, p. 62).

Thinking of empowerment as a metaphor of a ladder is a useful heuristic that emerges from urban planning literature (Arnstein, 1969; Murphy & Cunningham, 2003). Greater degrees of participation and thus empowerment are achieved as one climbs up a ladder. Arnstein's ladder of participation (see Figure 1.1) incorporates the idea of a ladder to convey how some activities on the lowest rungs of the ladder, such as "social service provision" and "therapy," represent low degrees of citizen participation. Activities such as "informing" and "consultation" represent medium degrees and the middle rungs of the ladder. Many national advocacy organizations, such as the Children's Defense Fund or the National Organization for Women, fall into this category. Professional and paid staff members consult with their constituencies to learn about what issues are important to them, as well as to inform them of new campaigns and other relevant policy actions. "Partnership" and

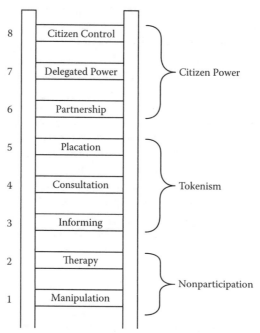

FIGURE 1.1   Arnstein's (1969) Ladder of Participation

"citizen control" are the highest degrees of citizen participation, represented by the highest rungs of the ladder. Thus, empowerment is best achieved on the highest rungs of the ladder and is exemplified in citizen-led organizations such as the Coalition of Immokalee Workers; the Kensington Welfare Rights Union; and the disability rights group, ADAPT.

Bobo et al. (2001) also present a framework for thinking about empowerment as a matter of degrees. Such frameworks are very relevant because they do not succumb to unnecessarily dichotomous thinking that might tend to identify organizing activities as either empowering or disempowering or either just or unjust. Thus, it seems fairly obvious that measuring the degree of empowerment of a social action campaign is fairly complex and only lends itself to such subtle analysis.

Both empowerment and social change are mutually reinforcing concepts. While empowerment is obviously an end unto itself, it also provides fuel for social change. The more individuals feel empowered, the more sustainable organizing campaigns will be over time. Assuming there will always be a need to do social change work, it makes sense to foster the strength and solidarity of groups. It is not uncommon for activists to overstate the amount of empowerment and social change that their activities engender. By thinking about these central elements of organizing as a matter of degree and always in flux, an organizer is better able to be transparent and critical of his or her own practices.

Social change is characterized as concrete alterations of an unequal social structure. This definition rests on the idea that oppression and social injustice such as sexism, racism, ageism, or homophobia are deeply entrenched in society and manifest themselves in manifold ways. Harper (1998) defined social change as "the significant alteration of social structure and cultural patterns through time" (p. 4). Some have argued that the only real social changes that occurred in the 20th century were during the time of the New Deal in the 1930s and during the civil rights struggles of the 1950s and 1960s (Piven & Cloward, 1979). Others may see social change successes as transforming a mental health organization to being consumer driven or securing a living-wage ordinance in a city or municipality.

Papa, Singhal and Papa (2006) offer a definition of the phrase *organizing for social change*: "the process through which a group of individuals orchestrate their skills, resources, and human potential to gain control of their future" (p. 31). I like this definition because it emphasizes organizing for social change as a process and indicates that the goal of such activities is fairly broad, i.e., "to gain control of their future." This phrase has both an empowerment element and a social change element; it leaves open the possibility that the goal may be to pass a piece of legislation and get new programming or funding, or it could be creating a new way of living, a new community, such as a community-based, cooperative business venture that is empowering to previously marginalized populations.

Social change is about creating the kind of world that people want right now, in this moment. It is about challenging a set of practices (Kaufman, 2003). While it is something that occurs over time, it is also something that one can constantly be working on, a way of life. Social change is a process and an outcome. While some may argue that one can only view social change in terms of the long-term outcomes that are engendered, I argue that process is equally important and that the strategies organizers use are an integral component of social change. My assumption is that the seeds that organizers plant and the care that they take with their endeavors will produce the social change outcomes. If one is trying to grow green beans, then it is necessary to plant green bean seeds; it wouldn't make sense to plant squash seeds to grow green beans. If one is trying to grow tomatoes, then the tomatoes should be put in a location that provides them with lots of sunlight; it wouldn't make sense to put them in the shade. All of these acts constitute the act of gardening and growth. And, thus is the case with social change; one must plant the seeds and create the conditions one wants to see in the world. As Gandhi famously said, "You must be the change you wish to see in the world."

To commit to social change work is to commit to a journey. When one embarks on any journey, it is always helpful to try to be prepared—pack a map, tools, and other provisions that one may need over the course. Anything can happen on a journey, however, and thus being open to any eventuality and the new insights that can arise are enormous opportunities. It is when one thinks one knows all the answers to doing social change work that some of these new opportunities can pass one by. Just when one thinks one has arrived at her or his destination, one realizes that the journey is still ongoing. But, how does one simultaneously stay committed to one's ideals and analyses and be open to critical new findings, learning to improvise along the way?

Parton (2007) has argued for what he calls *constructive social work*. Such an approach is based on a postmodernist view of reality that insists on "a critical stance toward taken-for-granted ways of understanding the world, including ourselves" (p. 158). Because the world is the result of social processes, interactions, and negotiated understandings, the basic premise of social constructionism (Gergen, 1999), community organizing practice, can be based on such an understanding. Parton (2007) describes his approach:

> A central emphasis of constructive social work is thus upon process, plurality of both knowledge and voice, and the relational quality of knowledge and language.... Social work is as much, if not more, an art as it is a science, and proceeds on the basis that practice should be understood as much as a *practical–moral* activity as a *rational–technical* one. It is affirmative and reflexive and focuses on dialogue, listening to and talking with the other. An ability to work with ambiguity and uncertainty, both in terms of process and outcomes, is key. The principle of indeterminacy [*sic*] suggests the fluid, recursive, and nondetermined way that social situations unfold (pp. 159–160).

The possibility of engaging in organizing work in a way similar to constructive social work may be a useful way of thinking about a critical approach to progressive community organizing.

Some scholars have articulated a similar approach, arguing that social welfare practices operate in a borderlands space that transcends dichotomies such as art and science (Jackson, 2000; Walter, 2003). Walter (2003) argues that it is like improvisational acting "characterized by creative and spontaneous reflexivity, as well as moment-to-moment decision making in continuous relation to the social context" (p. 320). Writers on the topic have advocated that successful practitioners, like good improvisational actors, attend to the moment, accept ideas and suggestions, and advance the action by adding something to it. Burghardt (1982) has argued for what he calls "tactical self-awareness" in community organizing, which emphasizes that, when one is choosing and engaging in particular organizing tactics, it is helpful to be aware of personal as well as organizing limitations in particular contexts. Rather than succumbing to the idea of a grand theory of organizing, the tactically self-aware person accepts the realities of organizing, including one's own limitations, fears, and concerns.

Sometimes one's ideologies can actually hinder a person on his or her journey. My identity as a "feminist" has actually blinded me from seeing other perspectives or pieces of information that may be relevant. I tell this story by way of illustration of this point. I was working as an advocate for battered women, doing policy work at the statewide level and participating in a working group that was focusing on welfare reform and child support enforcement regulations. One person referred to fathers who owed child support as "deadbeat dads." This was not an uncommon way to refer to men who battered their partners and did not pay their child support. In fact, we often referred to them in even worse terms. It hit me though at that moment that not only was name calling not particularly helpful, but that most of these "deadbeat dads" were struggling economically themselves. They, too, are victims of an economy that favors the rich over the working class and a government that had recently retrenched many social welfare provisions. Many of these men were dealing with the realities of low-paying jobs and unemployment. It became clear that manifesting as a social change activist meant making connections about the multiple ways that power affects regular people. It means speaking out about victim blaming and that one oppression (violence against women) does not necessarily trump another (economic injustice). At this moment, I began to really understand what solidarity means. Though I was not ready to speak up in that moment, the next time that this scenario arose, and it inevitably did, I was able to articulate my concern with the use of such language. Progressive community organizers understand that oppressions are interconnected and interlocking. Organizers must work at maintaining a balance between their ideals and the constantly changing evidence, engaging in a kind of improvisational, dialectical dance of social change work.

Having an understanding of empowerment, social change, and a practice that is flexible and constantly under construction are the key ingredients for a recipe for success as an organizer. Though social systems are indeed formidable, doing one's personal work on the important issues of oppression and clarifying one's own reasons for doing organizing are critical and ongoing steps to social change work. In Chapter 10, I discuss some of the key personal work that organizers can consider doing to be effective and committed for the long haul.

The word *radical* literally means "to the root." To engage in progressive community organizing for social change in a globalized world is indeed radical work; it necessarily involves getting to the root of social issues. Alinsky reminded us, though, that the most effective organizers were always "realistic," i.e., they understood the context and how to achieve their victories. And thus, no matter how one defines oneself—citizen, advocate, social worker, organizer, activist—one should first be a student of history, a student of the political economy, a student of social welfare policy and programs, and a student who understands the various ways that oppression gets played out in people's lives.

QUESTIONS FOR REFLECTION

1. How does globalization affect your life? Describe both positive and negative effects.
2. Describe what barriers you see to doing community organizing, including those barriers that are personal, cultural, and organizational.
3. In what ways is critical thinking encouraged and in what ways has critical thinking been discouraged in our society?
4. What community are you a part of? What communities do you feel an alliance with?

5. Discuss the specific organizations that you work in or have worked in. Do these organizations fit into the categories of social service, advocacy, community organizing, or activist? Why or why not?

SUGGESTIONS FOR FURTHER INQUIRY

BOOKS

Gutierrez, L. M., Parsons, R. J., & Cox, E. O. (Eds.). (1998). *Empowerment in social work practice: A sourcebook*. Pacific Grove, CA: Brooks/Cole.

Moraga, C., & Anzaldua, G. (Eds.). *This bridge called my back: Writings by radical women of color*. Watertown, MA: Persephone Press.

Mander, J., & Goldsmith, E. (Eds.). *The case against the global economy and a turn toward the local*. San Francisco: Sierra Club Books.

South End Press Collective (Ed.). (2007). *What lies beneath: Katrina, race and the state of the nation*. Cambridge, MA: South End Press.

Witkin, S., & Saleebey, D. (Eds.). *Social work dialogues: Transforming the canon in inquiry, practice, and education* (pp. 144–166). Alexandria, VA: CSWE Press.

WEB

ACORN Katrina Survivor's Association. http://acorn.org/index.php?id=10284
Education Center for Community Organizing. http://www.hunter.cuny.edu/socwork/ecco/
The Change Agency. http://www.thechangeagency.org
World Social Forum. http://www.forumsocialmundial.org.br/index.php?cd_language=2&id_menu=
Z Communications. http://www.zmag.org

KEY TERMS

Activism: A general term to cover any number of social-change activities that are political in nature. Activism may include actions done by regular people such as letter writing, political protest, or other forms of consciousness raising. It may also include the work done by paid individuals who work in social-change organizations.

Advocacy: To work on behalf of a marginalized group by working to change policies, secure new programs and funding, or redress some other injustice.

Community development: Efforts to strengthen social networks and a community's capacity for social and economic justice.

Community organizing: Efforts to mobilize people through leadership development to confront power and address issues identified by the constituency.

Progressive community organizing: Community organizing that works toward the liberation of oppressed and marginalized individuals and the transformation of social systems that perpetuate the oppression.

Protest: A moral voice that explicitly criticizes oppressive actions, organizations, and policies. Protest may be exemplified through a variety of means, including the arts and direct action.

Social service: The provision of assistance by relatively formal helping systems, either by a governmental or a nongovernmental organization.

2 The Self-Aware Organizer

We hate our enemies
to provide ourselves in advance
with excuses for possible failure.
Only when we give up
the comforts of pessimism
the luxury of enemies
the sweetness of helplessness
can we see beyond our own doubts.

Paul Williams (1982)

Sociologists and social psychologists have noted that social movements have a transformative effect on people's identities (Yang, 2000). Social change work helps participants break free from certain structural constraints and offers them the power and freedom to reconfigure themselves and society. Identity in this case is not just about personal identity, but it can be also understood as a collective identity, which is an individual's cognitive, moral, and emotional connection to a group or organization. Collective identity is constructed in three ways: (a) through the formation of boundaries that differentiate group members from nongroup members, (b) through the advancement of consciousness as a group with common interests as compared with the larger social order, and (c) through negotiation of novel ways of thinking and acting (Taylor & Whitter, 1992, cited in Staggenborg, 2005). When people are part of a social change organization, they have the opportunity to experience a unique culture and norms that may be distinct from the larger society. This experience of having membership in a social group with shared values can offer organizers a sense of self-definition and solidarity.

Besides addressing the existential aspects of organizing, this chapter focuses on the emotional life of organizers. By inquiring into potential emotional pitfalls that organizers often face, greater clarity about the inner life of organizers can be attained. Here I give special attention to considerations and techniques for working with such emotional and psychical complexity.

THE CALL OF ORGANIZING

People become inspired to organize for a plethora of reasons. These inspirations may include personal or familial experiences with hardship, transformative encounters with organizers, and generalized anger with "the system." What seems to be true for all activists, though, is that social change work gives meaning to their lives. Research has shown that practitioners often engage in social justice work due to their existential commitments (Buchbinder, 2007). Rather than falling into despair and apathy, many people organize out of a sense of hopefulness and sense of responsibility. This meaning is often related to an organizer's identity, which has personal, collective, and spiritual dimensions. In a recent study of community organizers and advocates in post-Katrina New Orleans, I asked these committed practitioners what significance organizing had for them in their lives (Pyles, 2006). They offered a variety of responses that touched on themes related to their individual personalities, quests for social justice, and their own journeys toward self-actualization. Here are some responses that highlight the personal dimension of organizing:

- "I'm the type of person that I would do for others before I do for myself. I always prided myself in as opportunities and doors open for myself that's the reason why they open for me is to open them for someone else. What one of the main reasons why planning and helping the devastated neighborhoods revitalize themselves is that … one of my callings is to help people."
- "My personality I think fits in. I like to do things that are going to benefit somebody. With my agricultural background, with my personality, my comfort in meeting people and explaining—and I guess you would say selling ideas, even—and with media, it fits well for me."

The following quotation reflects the sense of collective identity centered on social justice and freedom and fostered by participation in an organization:

It means freedom, it means justice, it means home and it means community to me. In everything we do, we engage the community. It means community to me, and that's what the community means to me. Being a part of [my organization] means action. You can be a community organizer with anybody but in this organization movement has to occur and it does occur. I'm very appreciative of the fact that it occurs and that it occurs frequently. There's a lot of movement.… It means political freedom. It means that you are no longer bound by what you don't feel can happen. You're not tied up in "It will never happen." Maybe it will take a lot. "I wonder who's going to do it, who's going to do what." That's a cage. That's imprisonment. "I wonder what's going to happen." Just kind of squatting on the sidelines, "I wonder what's going to happen." You're free from that cage of, "I don't know, and I can't affect anything and I'm stuck in this box." That's a tremendous freedom. You're free from the whole stereotypical image of a low to moderate income person. You're free from that, and that's a big freedom. You're free from apathy and free from all of those things. Like I said, that's a little box. If you have to sit and wait for something to happen or wonder what's going to happen or wonder who's going to take action on something, you're imprisoned because you're stuck right in that spot. You can't do anything.

Finally, these quotations highlight an existential or spiritual perspective:

- "We're really transforming the world by engaging in this endeavor.… Abraham Maslow talked about self-actualization. I think the class struggle is where you achieve self-actualization."
- "I'm a very spiritual guy. I'm not a very religious man, but I believe in, you do things on this earth that you're supposed to do, help one another.… And my understanding of Native American culture is that's the way they are. Everything is spirituality. And I think it's pretty fascinating, and that's how I feel about it. I felt a calling. This is what I had to do."

When people think of community organizing, they sometimes have a romantic view that can easily become distorted. Images of extraordinary figures such as Mahatma Gandhi or Nelson Mandela come to mind. Because these are such unique and inspiring people, one may believe that one could never measure up to such standards and thus see community organizing is a path for a different type of person. For this reason, I think it is necessary that one have a more realistic picture of who community organizers are and what it is exactly that they do. We live in a society that practices the worship of heroes, where movie stars, athletes, and religious figures are held in the highest esteem. When we view those heroes as better than us, looking outside of ourselves for strength, we are essentially giving away our personal power. The other problem with such hero worship is that it falsely extricates individuals from their social contexts; it masks the fact that individuals succeed because of a network of individuals around them. This is an extremely important point in community organizing; effective community organizing campaigns and other social change efforts only exist in the context of an activist community of individuals who support each other, vet ideas, and work together to develop and implement plans of action.

Students who first enter the field of community practice are often puzzled and disappointed when they find themselves doing what appear to be mundane tasks—coordinating meetings and events, making phone calls, sending e-mails, creating flyers, collecting surveys, holding focus groups. This work is not nearly as romantic as being in a historic demonstration or speaking to the United Nations, which is often the impression that people have of community organizing. Consider, instead, that the beauty, meaning, and ultimately the success of organizing exists in the seemingly mundane details of everyday organizing practice.

CONNECTING THE PERSONAL AND POLITICAL

When someone's consciousness is first heightened about oppression and the possibilities of liberation, it is a significant moment in a person's life. Many people find that they immediately are compelled to connect this political awareness to situations in their personal lives. They must act a certain way, live a certain lifestyle, spend time with particular people, dress a certain way, ad infinitum. Trying to fit one's life into an ideological framework is not only impossible, but not necessarily even desirable; humans and their social lives are much too contradictory and messy for that. But, nonetheless, a certain awareness and desire for personal change is inevitably and appropriately sparked. Activist Samuel Kass (Berger, Boudin, & Farrow, 2005) had this experience:

> I have found living my life in a way that is consistent with my values to be the most challenging aspect of activism. Our everyday life. Time. Money. Energy. Classes. Groups we participate in. What we read. Clothes we wear. The food we eat. All will not be perfect, and we are often forced to make trade-offs, but we must be aware of and consider every aspect of our life. (p. 188)

For some organizers, the relationship between the personal and political can never be separate. For a lesbian woman who lives in a heteronormative world in a same-sex relationship, her personal reality is always in political dissonance to the mainstream culture. Other organizers proactively seek ways in which they can make their personal lives commensurate with their political leanings. From a transformative organizing perspective, actualizing one's ideals in everyday life is a necessary condition for social change. This can be expressed through a variety of lifestyle choices, such as housing, food, clothing, and transportation. It can also be reflected in the way one chooses to interact with people, emphasizing nonexploitative, horizontal, and compassionate relations.

By choosing to live in a developing country or inner city with limited resources, an activist may consciously create a lifestyle that is in solidarity with people who are suffering the most from damaging economic and social policies and practices. Indeed, historically, living in solidarity with the oppressed has been a social change tactic engaged in by the likes of Mahatma Gandhi, Mother Theresa, Jane Addams, and many others. The Settlement House movement was an attempt to invoke this kind of solidarity as a social change strategy. However, it is important that one not fool oneself into thinking that he or she can completely understand the suffering of a homeless person if one has not personally been homeless. Humans are not all affected equally by everything in the world (Gottlieb, 1999). Most organizers have a warm bed to go home to at night. This is, of course, a good thing because being able to have one's basic needs met is more or less a necessary condition to engage in social change work.

THE PERILS OF ORGANIZING

Community organizing has cognitive, moral, and emotional dimensions; progressive community organizers seek clarity about their inner emotional and moral life. This part of community organizing practice, while often ignored by organizers, may be the most productive work in which an organizer engages. In this section, I identify several potential emotional and moral situations that organizers may at one time or another encounter—anger, fear, despair, burnout, and co-optation. At the end of the chapter, I offer some analysis and remedies for working with them.

ANGER

Anger has always been an emotion that has fueled social movements throughout history. It is a normal feeling that stems from the witnessing of suffering. Upon experiencing suffering, whether personally or by other people, many individuals critically evaluate the suffering and find themselves not just experiencing the emotion of sadness or grief, but feeling outrage at a situation that could be otherwise. Anger and the possibility of confrontation can be scary prospects for many people; indeed, the avoidance of anger seems to be a significant reason why some people do not engage in social change work. People's comfort with scenarios that include tension, hostility, and conflict will likely depend on how anger was expressed in one's family and/or one's cultural or ethnic tradition. Anger also has a gendered component in the sense that society seems to encourage men to experience this emotion (though not necessarily in healthy ways), while, for women, society tends to discourage the expression of anger in any way. Thus, it only makes sense that these and other various dimensions of anger would play themselves out in community organizing practice.

Saul Alinsky believed that discord and confrontation are necessary conditions for social change (Alinsky, 1971). Alinsky and many other organizers have argued that confrontation is a necessary condition for change. This confrontation seems to be accompanied inevitably by anger. When Cortes went through training with the IAF (Industrial Areas Foundation), he gained tremendous insight into himself. He said: "I had a tendency to jump down people's throats, which could intimidate people.... I learned not to allow my anger to get so vociferous, to get more focused.... I learned the value of listening" (in Boyte, 1984, p. 131). Clearly, working with anger in a self-aware manner is a vital practice presenting a tremendous opportunity for progressive community organizers.

Avoiding anger, pretending it does not exist, or being afraid of it will not help organizers. If one avoids anger, then injustices themselves are denied. If one indulges in the anger, one will not be an effective organizer. According to Gottlieb (1999): "It is the inability to be in the presence of our anger, not anger itself, which so often provokes uncontrolled violence, bitter revenge, or the loss of peace of mind" (p. 175). It is tempting to stew in righteous anger. While anger is justified and useful because it stems from an acknowledgment of injustice and propels people to organize, it can also be a hindrance to completely being present and understanding a person, a policy, or a situation.

Anger is nothing to be afraid of, and it can be very useful in certain contexts. In some situations, it might be better to consider delivering messages in creative ways. Sometimes people can hear a message more clearly when it is not presented in a hostile manner; sometimes people only hear the anger and cannot hear the message itself because of their own issues with anger. Because many people do not know how to be with anger and be okay with it, they may avoid the content of a message and only be engaged in the negative energy. A sophisticated organizer has the opportunity to work with these emotions in powerful and transformative ways. Saul Alinsky (1946) once said: "If radicals are stormy and fighting on the outside, inside they possess a rare inner peace. It is that tranquility that can come only from consistency of conscience and conduct."

FEAR

Fear is another emotion that can overwhelm organizers. It is a significant barrier that prevents many people from engaging in organizing. Personal and social change implies a threat to that which is comfortable and familiar, even when the comfortable and familiar is inequitable or unjust. One interfaith community organizer said:

> We all have fears from time to time and anxiety, but you can't be afraid to take a stance. You've got to be clear about your own weaknesses, but you can't feel like anybody, no matter how powerful or smart

they might be, has anything on you. You've got to figure them out and then you can play in that ballpark. Deal with fear in such a way that you can be clear in any situation. (Perkins in Szakos & Szakos, 2007, p. 95)

There are innumerable fears that organizers confront in the course of their work—a fear of speaking in public, a fear of crowds, a fear of angry people, a fear of people in authority. Others may find themselves afraid of engaging in a one-on-one conversation with a constituent and asking her or him to join an organization or participate in an action. These organizers may be afraid of being rejected, judged, or retaliated against. These fears are all normal, and paying attention to them is the most important course of action one can take. In addition, organizers can talk to colleagues, engage in rituals or spiritual practices, and in some cases seek outside professional help.

Despair

The far-reaching impacts of social injustice across the globe can feel overwhelming and can easily propel people into states of despair. Poverty, discrimination, violence, and disease can all seem like too much to bear and certainly too much to do anything about. Feeling and thinking about these issues can engender feelings of powerlessness and despair. Despair can turn into hopelessness and even cynicism. Gottlieb (1999) discusses this phenomenon with regard to the barriers faced by environmental activists:

> Because the engines of environmental destruction are strong, entrenched, and often mighty rich, and because … we carry conflicting obligations, time pressures, and simple fatigue, it often seems easier or safer not to resist. Thus if we are to act, we will need to overcome the temptations of fear or laziness, of complacency and habit. These temptations, as I know very well from my own life, are continual. (p. 166)

Community organizing can be an overwhelming and confusing practice. Krill (1978) discusses how he felt in the 1960s when organizing was heightened across issues including war, poverty, and race. He writes:

> Those years were exciting but also puzzling. If one found some ways to engage in radical protest, one felt some relief. Yet it never quite seemed that one was sufficiently involved, and change efforts too often seemed like some kind of predetermined scenario. Despite dramatic efforts, little seemed to change. When there was a change it appeared that new problems, equally bad, replaced the old ones. One seemed deluged with "shoulds" and "oughts" concerning one's professional mission. Yet one remained bewildered as to what to do, where to start, how far to extend oneself. (p. 175)

Nevertheless, successful organizers have structures and tried-and-true practices for achieving success. In addition, progressive organizers can create spaces to attend to these complex emotions and concerns. The issue of despair, like many of the emotional perils confronted by organizers, is not something that is necessarily addressed at one point in time and then never to be seen again; it is an ongoing component of social change work. Environmental organizer Joanna Macy conducts workshops for activists wanting formal practices that can help them work with this sense of despair. Like any of the emotional perils confronted by organizers, including fear and anger, despair is an emotional and arguably spiritual state that is best attended to rather than ignored or pushed away. Developing a sophisticated understanding of one's own mind can enhance organizers' capacities to work with constituencies; such understanding can enhance empathy and the abilities to move people from inaction to action.

BURNOUT

One of Alice Walker's (1976) early novels, *Meridian*, tells the story of activists in Mississippi during the civil rights movement. Walker recounts personal narratives of organizing work touching on themes such as the racism and sexism within the movement, the physical and psychological toll of organizing, and romantic love between activists. She writes about the emotional effects that organizing has on people's lives:

> Later that summer, after another demonstration, she saw him going down a street that did not lead back to the black part of town. His eyes were swollen and red, his body trembling, and he did not recognize her or even see her. She knew his blankness was battle fatigue. They all had it. She was as weary as anyone, so that she spent a good part of her time in tears ... whatever she was doing—canvassing, talking at rallies, tying her sneakers, laughing. (p. 82)

Organizing can bring up a variety of emotions, ones that may appear in other realms of people's lives and ones that can only emerge from the daily grind of organizing practice. The "battle fatigue" of organizing is experienced by many practitioners and can manifest by negatively impacting people's physical, mental, emotional, and spiritual well-being. Burnout can affect an organizer's intimate relationships with partners, children, family, and friends.

Researchers have noted the differences between burnout and compassion fatigue (Figley, 2002). Compassion fatigue is a condition that is the result of continuous contact with people who are suffering. Burnout happens to practitioners often as the result of environmental, particularly workplace, conditions that are antithetical to well-being. Thus, not only are personal self-care habits important for mediating burnout, organizational mechanisms may be even more important. Organizational mechanisms are value-oriented policies and practices, particularly those that provide organizers the opportunity to have a say in their working conditions.

CO-OPTATION

Organizers are often at great risk for being co-opted by the power of the social structures that they seek to change. When this happens, organizers inadvertently may assimilate into an established group or institution whose interests and values may be at odds with those the organizers were originally struggling for. It is not uncommon for this to happen, and there are a variety of situations that can trigger co-optation. It is easy to see why organizers could succumb to or align with people or policies that support the status quo. Association with the status quo can result in money, prestige, security, and other opportunities for an organization or for the organizer himself or herself.

Of course, this perspective on co-optation assumes that the interests of corporations, social systems, and institutions are separate from those of communities. Based on a Marxist historical analysis, for example, these interests certainly are quite distinct. On the other hand, such conflicts between the oppressed and oppressors are certainly social constructions that could be otherwise. From the perspective of a consensus-oriented approach to organizing, there is always common ground or shared values. But, how does one balance the risk of co-optation and the opportunities to negotiate or reach consensus with the people who hold power? This can be balanced through values-clarification at the personal and organizational level. The final section offers some additional pathways to attend to these and other perils.

AN ORGANIZER'S PATH TO MEANING AND SUCCESS

Community organizing and social change work are practices that have the potential to create tremendous meaning for organizers in addition to the obvious benefits to the most marginalized individuals in society. In this final section, I offer some perspectives on the qualities that can be helpful to an organizer's social change journey. When nurtured, these qualities can enhance not only one's personal power and well-being, but they also can facilitate a community organizing practice that is sustainable over time. While there are many qualities that are important for organizing, I propose three that are most essential to pursue—persistence, clarity, and joy.

PERSISTENCE

If one analyzes major social reform and social change victories in history and across the globe, most organizers would say the secret to their success was persistence. In the face of anger, fear, and despair, the key is not to give up. It is important to recognize that real results always entail a significant commitment of time, energy, and resources. While there certainly are small victories, including moments of opening, consciousness-raising, and empowerment (and these are never to be underestimated or devalued), social change and other reform-oriented victories are fairly elusive. For some organizers, their ultimate goals may never be achieved in their own lifetime. If one is not prepared for this long journey, one may not be prepared to do social change work.

A Zen Buddhist *koan* (a teaching question or paradox) asks: "How do you go straight up a mountain with ninety-nine curves?" (Glassman, 1998). The answer is that one has to take every curve as it comes—every systemic flaw, every victim-blaming legislator, every racist planning commission. Taking every curve includes being present and gentle with one's self and one's colleagues in times of confusion, hopelessness, and apathy. Fostering a persistent community organizing practice requires self-awareness and attention to the rugged terrain of emotional perils. Supportive organizational environments and nurturing self-care plans can enable practitioners to persist through difficulties.

CLARITY

To gain clarity about organizing contexts, it is necessary to pay attention to evidence that is constantly shifting. This clarity is achieved not just by observation, but through critical reflection grounded in a power analysis that questions the social constructions of economic policies, social welfare programs, and institutions. It is necessary to seek this clarity every day. When one gets up in the morning and feels stiff even though one might have done some yoga stretches the day before, one has to begin anew and get the kinks worked out. Just as one might strive for a kind of clarity with one's body every day, so too a community organizing practice requires daily and even moment-to-moment maintenance. Everyone has blind spots or kinks to be worked out. Making the most of supportive resources can facilitate this clarity. These resources include personal resources and resources within communities and organizations, including allies.

The Quaker tradition has developed a process known as the Clearness Committee to enhance clarity in important decision making. The method is based on the idea that everyone has innate wisdom and that this wisdom can be illuminated through the help of a group of people who offer compassionate, undivided attention. This group poses questions to the seeker rather than offering advice. Integrating similar practices can be efficacious for organizations and facilitate clarity about confusing situations that require action.

JOY

Attending to the pain and suffering of the communities in this world can seem like pretty grim work; many organizers may appear to be very serious people. Engaging in liberating practices, though sometimes painful, need not be joyless. Though no one is quite sure whether she actually said it or not, the 20th-century activist Emma Goldman is thought to have proclaimed: "If I can't dance, I don't want to be part of your revolution." Indeed, Goldman was interested in social-change work that was in itself creative and joyous and that also worked toward a world where the creative was valued. She said, "I want freedom, the right to self-expression, everybody's right to beautiful, radiant things."

Sometimes social change work can appear to be quite linear—getting funding, identifying issues, developing a tactical plan, engaging in actions, evaluating actions, and then on to the next issue. This approach can unfortunately block out creative and innovative ideas that can influence organizing. Thus, making space for art and creativity in social change work is very important. Shepard (2005) has highlighted the "interrelations of joy, justice, pleasure and a use of culture as an organizing tool" (p. 435). This creativity and joy has been a hallmark of organizing in post-Katrina New Orleans. The strength of the culture has fueled community redevelopment, including celebrations such as Mardi Gras and second-line parades, neighborhood festivals, and various forms of art such as dance, painting, and street theater.

QUESTIONS FOR REFLECTION

1. What are your personal motivations for engaging in and learning about social change and community organizing?
2. Talk to someone who is doing community organizing as a full-time job. What does a typical day look like? What does he or she love most about the job? What is most challenging about his or her job?
3. Discuss how you have dealt with anger in your life. What are some useful techniques that can help you work with anger when doing social-change work?
4. Why might some people be more vulnerable to burnout in community organizing than other people? What do you think are the factors that can prevent burnout?
5. Discuss the organizer's existential path to meaning and success, i.e., persistence, clarity, and creativity/joy. How might these qualities be relevant to your work? What are some other qualities that might be helpful for organizers to cultivate?

SUGGESTIONS FOR FURTHER INQUIRY

BOOKS

Berger, D., Boudin, C., & Farrow, K. (2005). *Letters from young activists: Today's rebels speak out.* New York: Nation Books.

Dass, R., & Gorman, P. (1985). *How can I help? Stories and reflections on service.* New York: Knopf.

Rosenberg, M. B. (2004). *The heart of social change: How to make a difference in your world.* Encinitas, CA: Puddledancer Press.

Szakos, K. L., & Szakos, J. (2007). *We make change: Community organizers talk about what they do—and why.* Nashville, TN: Vanderbilt University Press.

Zinn, H., & Arnove, H. (2004). *Voices of a people's history.* New York: Seven Stories.

WEB

Idealist.org. http://www.idealist.org
National Organizers Alliance. http://noacentral.org
Re-Evaluation Counseling. http://www.rc.org
Transformation Central. http://www.transformationcentral.org
Wiser Earth. http://www.wiserearth.org

KEY TERMS

Burnout: In contrast to *compassion fatigue* (which happens as a result of bearing witness to suffering), burnout happens to individuals working in organizations and movements that do not attend to an organizer's personal, emotional, and spiritual needs and realities.

Collective identity: The shared emotional, cognitive, and moral connections that organizers experience in relation to other social movement and organizational participants.

Co-optation: A term used in conflict-oriented organizing that explains how organizers can lose their path when tempted by the rewards of allying with those in power.

Existential commitment: The view that organizing represents a person's ongoing individual quest for meaning in life, whereby dedication to social change becomes a way to overcome feelings of personal and social meaninglessness and helplessness.

Personal is political: A term coined during the second wave of the women's movement to emphasize the idea that what happens in a person's personal life, such as intimate partner violence, has political dimensions to it.

3 Theories and Ideas for the Progressive Organizer

Philosophers have only *interpreted* the world, in various ways; the point, however, is to *change* it.

Karl Marx, Eleventh Thesis on Feuerbach, 1845

Some of the most effective social change actors in history have been highly influenced by the work of philosophers, political theorists, and public intellectuals. Indeed, early civil rights organizers were moved by the work of W. E. B. DuBois, feminist advocates by the work of Patricia Hill Collins, and contemporary global-justice activists by Noam Chomsky. Ideas can impart inspiration for change; however, as the philosopher and political organizer Karl Marx noted, they are not the change itself. The relationship between organizers and ideas is often a synergistic one—organizers and grassroots movements are influenced by the ideas of academicians and intellectuals, who are inspired by practitioners, some of whom may be theorizing as they do their work. In some cases, such as that of activist and historian Howard Zinn, being an organizer and intellectual are not separate roles.

The Italian social theorist Antonio Gramsci argued that social theory should always be connected to social movements and oppressed people, believing in what he called "organic intellectuals."[1] In other words, social theory, he would say, should not be separate from social action. Overall, Gramsci emphasized the need for a "battle of ideas" in society before major alterations could occur (Blackburn, 1994).

A progressive organizer is often engaged in just such a "battle of ideas," being concerned with notions about what oppression is, what a vision for liberation might look like, and ideas about how to achieve change. Because ideas form the foundation of economic and social welfare policies, it is within the context of these ideas that modifications to policies and practices can happen. Someone advocating for economic justice issues ought to understand something about capitalist theories and practices and how a living-wage ordinance might threaten such theories and practices. Critical thinking about the various social constructions of ideas, and the policies and practices that follow from them, is the initial and enduring stage of organizing. The purpose of this chapter is to present and explore some of the social change ideas and theories that historically have influenced activists, community organizers, and other political advocates. I will offer summaries and analyses of some of the philosophical perspectives that are relevant to doing empowering, social change work in communities. Such an endeavor could actually fill volumes of philosophy, political science, social work, cultural studies, and sociology books. Indeed, for many of these perspectives, there exist infinite nuances and debates. However, my goal here is to pique the reader's interest in some of these thinkers with the hope that as one travels on one's own social change journey, he or she will continue to explore these concepts. By choosing to engage with some of these ideas, an organizer has the opportunity to grapple with new perspectives, push the horizons of thinking, and clarify his or her values.

---

[1] The relationship between theorists and practitioners is not always equal in terms of power and money, however. Academics who are paid by universities and intellectuals who make money from writing books receive significant amounts of societal prestige, whereas community practitioners and grassroots activists do not often have the prestige and money.

I believe that there are five major schools of thought that are relevant to organizing from a critical perspective—the Marxist tradition, feminist tradition, civil society perspectives, anarchism, and postmodern perspectives. These five intellectual movements certainly do not capture every analytic standpoint or theory relevant to social change and community organizing, nor can they be covered completely in this limited space. Nonetheless, their broad nature can encapsulate a significant portion of the important theoretical trends relevant to progressive community organizers. Introducing these ideas will also serve as the foundation for further discussions in this book that articulate and clarify a critical approach to progressive community organizing practice. I conclude this chapter by offering some ideas about how to apply these ideas to organizing practice.

THE MARXIST TRADITION

Sociologists generally identify three major approaches to understanding the elusive realities of historical social change. These approaches can be understood as linear, cyclical, and dialectical (Harper, 1998). Linear models of change are grounded in the assumption that change is developmental over time; as time progresses, positive change happens. A cyclical model of change can best be understood through the phrase, "The more things change the more things stay the same." Social arrangements do not necessarily ever change, but they do go through cycles. Dialectical change theories emerge from the notion that change happens because of contradictions in society. The Marxist tradition has been the primary exemplification of a dialectical change theory and has been highly influential to social change organizers. Indeed, any discussion of community organizing owes a certain degree of intellectual and political homage to Karl Marx and his legacy.

Karl Marx (1818–1883) was a Prussian radical social theorist and organizer of the working class who lived during the 19th century. He observed that a worker's existence in the factory was unfulfilling because his or her daily life was reduced to meaningless physical activity and rendered him or her a mere arm of capitalist mechanisms. Identifying what he called the alienation of labor, Marx noted that workers (the proletariat) do not experience the products of their labor as their own because the products belong to the capitalist owner (the bourgeoisie). Marx's labor theory of value explained that the specific form of labor characteristic of bourgeois society, wage labor, corresponds to the most profound form of alienation. Since wage workers sell their labor power to earn a living, and the capitalist *owns* the labor process, the product of the workers' labor is in a very real sense *alien* to the worker. It is not his or her product but the product of the capitalist (A. Wood, 2005). Marx was deeply concerned with the ways in which work in a capitalistic framework can suppress the human spirit; he had a particular interest in freedom and human fulfillment (Kaufman, 2003).

Marx was a student of the German dialectical idealist philosopher G. W. F. Hegel. Hegel's dialectical understanding of history offered a view of the world whereby one moment in history appears and eventually ends by contradicting itself. When the contradiction comes (the moment when the logic of the dialectic is fulfilled), history goes on and a new reality will develop that overcomes the previous contradiction. The oppressor/oppressed dialectic is one such historical dialectic. Thus, a dialectical analysis assumes that society is full of internal conflicts, which are by their nature unstable (Kaufman, 2003). Attending to the contradictions and understanding them can help people see the possibilities for change. For example, employees of a private company that provides health-care services may identify that they are not able to afford or do not have access to proper health care themselves. These employees then seek to resolve this contradiction by organizing for greater health-care benefits. Revealing such contradictions in daily reality is central to a dialectical analysis.

Marx espoused a philosophical position known as dialectical materialism, a theory of change that perceives the social world in terms of categories of class as defined by relationships to economic and productive processes. He ultimately believed in the development of society beyond the capitalist phase toward a revolution of the proletariat, culminating in socialism and communism (Marx & Engels, 2004). Marx's theory repudiates the exploitation endemic to private control of productive processes. The Marxist maintains a commitment to the exploited and oppressed classes and to the change that can better their position.

Of course, it may be difficult for the marginalized to understand this situation precisely; Marx refers to this inability to see things, especially social relations and relations of exploitation as they really are, as false consciousness. The state of false consciousness may be the inevitable result of living in a kind of servitude that cannot even perceive its own situation. As an organizer of the working class, Marx distributed his pamphlet, *The Communist Manifesto*, as a way to break through this false consciousness.

Marx predicted that, in the future, social relations would become increasingly commodified. Marx commented that "as money expands,... the social character of the relationship has diminished" (Nash, p. 19; Marx, 1971, p. 157). Influential thinkers such as Adam Smith and Thomas Jefferson agreed with this idea and argued that if corporations amass too much power, it will be a detriment to democratic capitalism (Kaufman, 2003). Thus, today, as global capitalist enterprises expand, private property rights and individual rights to expansion and growth dominate and commodify social relations; these processes are viewed by many as a threat to humanistic values (Nash, 2005). Furthermore, current policies and practices afford corporations more expansive rights than individuals. Under the World Trade Organization (WTO) rules, corporations have the right to "national treatment," which means a corporation operating in El Salvador can demand to be treated like an El Salvadoran firm; of course, an El Salvadoran person cannot come to the United States and demand national treatment (Chomsky, 2000). In the late 1990s, Guatemala attempted to reduce infant mortality rates by regulating the marketing of infant formula by multinational corporations. The governmental proposal was in line with World Health Organization guidelines; however, the Gerber Corporation claimed expropriation, i.e., the action of a government taking away a private business from its owners. The possibility of a WTO complaint by Gerber was enough for Guatemala to withdraw the regulations out of a fear of retaliatory sanctions by the WTO (Chomsky, 2000). The practice of unmasking the power of corporations as veiled through the WTO is an example of the unique contributions of the Marxist legacy.

CRITICAL THEORY

Writing in the Marxist and Hegelian traditions and emerging from what was referred to as the Frankfurt School, critical theorists work dialectically and seek to uncover the contradictions in society. Like the Marxist tradition, critical theory is social theory oriented toward critiquing and changing society as a whole, in contrast to traditional theory oriented only to understanding or explaining it. Critical theory attends to sociohistorical context and issues of differential power (Kincheloe & McLaren, 2000). According to Kincheloe and McLaren, "To seek critical enlightenment is to uncover the winners and losers in particular social arrangements and the processes by which such power plays operate" (p. 281). During the height of the Frankfurt School in the 1930s, theorists were concerned with cultural production and mass communication, arguing that the "culture industry" provided ideological legitimation of capitalist practices and sought to integrate individuals into the capitalist way of life (Kellner, 2004, p. 291). As victims of European fascism, the Frankfurt School was highly sensitized to the ways that instruments of mass culture could be used to produce submission to a particular way of life.

Critical theorists have engaged in philosophical domains beyond political and social theory, focusing on epistemological questions concerning science, objectivity, and reason. Philosopher Jurgen Habermas has questioned the claim that knowledge is value-free and understood that theories are products of social processes. Critical theorists have argued that science embodies values, such as the desirability of the technological domination of nature (Inwood, 2005). This critical perspective can endow organizers with analytical tools for understanding and critiquing social policies grounded in "scientific evidence." For example, advocates can further investigate the research that guides public policy by learning who commissioned the research and what the social standpoints and agendas of the think tank or funding agency are.

An additional contribution of critical theorists is the contestation of the notion of the "consent of the powerless"; instead, they highlight resistance to oppression in their hermeneutics. This aspect of critical theory, which has been bolstered by the work of historians such as Howard Zinn, can be empowering and validating for community activists whose work may be silenced by the larger society. Finally, recent developments in neo-Marxist critical theory have drawn from postmodernist discourses (discussed in more detail later in this chapter). These developments emphasize understanding the social construction of race, gender, and class as a valuable hermeneutic device in critical, social analysis (Kincheloe & McLaren, 2000).

ANALYSIS OF THE MARXIST TRADITION

Marx questioned the fundamental assumptions about the capitalist economic system, a system held in tremendous value by many people throughout the world. It should not be surprising, therefore, that he has been criticized profusely for these radical ideas. For example, he has been accused of economic reductionism, i.e., reducing his explanation of the nature of the world and history itself to economics. Though Marx himself may have been guilty of this, later thinkers have maintained the basic Marxist premise of dialectics and infused categories such as race and gender to extend his theory, drawing more heavily on the concept of power generally. This makes Marxism more applicable to many contemporary social issues. Because race has more than any other place in the world played out in the Americas, American critical race theorists and other neo-Marxist theorists have developed a dialectical analysis that incorporates race along with class (Kaufman, 2003). Multisystem theorists concerned with intersectionality go even further and look at the interrelationships of different types of oppression (e.g., racism, sexism, heterosexism, etc.) (Collins, 1999).

Other evaluations of the Marxist tradition tend to focus on the point that it would seem that Marx is arguing that the progression of history has a certain amount of inevitability to it, a kind of determinism. Marx, however, actually held the belief that "history has no power," meaning people have the potential to be in control of their destiny. For Marx, praxis is central to change and more fundamental than theory; praxis is "connected with genuinely free, self-conscious, authentic activity as opposed to the alienated labour demanded under capitalism" (Blackburn, 1994, p. 298). Although humans clearly do remain objects of historical forces, by understanding that everyday they participate in the social construction of the world, culture, and history, it is then possible to claim their agency and participate in a reconstruction of the world, culture, and history, and their own lives.

It is not necessary to be a revolutionary, communist, or socialist to appreciate the ideas and contributions of Marx. His critique of capitalism and the recognition that it necessitates a working class that tends to be marginalized is a relevant contribution to the world of progressive social ideas. These ideas have been very relevant for union organizers throughout the world for over a century and likely will continue to be relevant in the future.

FEMINIST PERSPECTIVES

Though feminist thought encompasses an extensive scope of philosophical positions, all feminist thinkers surely agree to disagree with the ancient Greek philosopher Aristotle's claim that "the female is a female by virtue of a certain *lack* of qualities; we should regard the female nature as afflicted with a natural defectiveness" (cited in Kreps, 2003, p. 45). This obviously sexist position becomes more complicated to deal with when one begins to consider the origins and context of such a claim, as well as the correct remedies for society. Because feminist thinkers offer such a variety of explanations and solutions, scholars, as they are inclined to do, have consistently divided feminism into various historical waves as well as philosophical camps. Though nuances can be lost and some perspectives silenced, it can be helpful to categorize feminism as a heuristic practice in order to make meaning of a vast amount of rich material.

Feminism has often been divided into liberal, radical, and socialist approaches, where liberal feminism focuses on promoting the equality of women in political and economic spheres (Kaufman, 2003). Liberal feminist thinkers seek to uncover the institutional barriers that have blocked women's access to power and prevented women from fully participating in society. Radical feminist thinkers critique the underlying assumptions of the patriarchal culture itself. The patriarchal paradigm, they argue, which has an enormous sphere of influence, overemphasizes the traditionally masculine values of reason, hierarchy, and competition and undervalues the traditionally feminine virtues of emotion, cooperation, and compassion. Rather than focusing solely on gaining entry into patriarchal society as liberal feminists do, radical feminists seek to critique this society and highlight the strengths of traditionally feminine virtues. Socialist feminism is closely aligned with radical feminism in that it contests the structure of society; however, it tends to critique radical feminism for making a virtue out of the feminine roles assigned by a sexist society. Kaufman differentiates the three approaches by analyzing the common claim, "Men are more rational and women are more emotional":

> Where a liberal feminist might be compelled to argue that women can be just as logical as men, radical feminists are more likely to challenge a value structure that puts reason above emotion. They would re-value the terms and argue for the importance of the female side. Socialist feminists pay more attention to the social structures that force women and men to play their assigned roles. They would support liberal feminists' argument that women can be as rational as men, as well as radical feminists' claim that emotion is something important that needs to be valued. Going beyond these, socialist feminists also look at … what we mean by rationality and how it has come to mean something cold and calculating…. Socialist feminists are interested in the political history that creates these roles and differences. (p. 170)

Historical approaches to feminism have emphasized first-wave, second-wave, and third-wave periods of feminist thought and practice. First-wave feminism tends to be associated with the early work of women suffragists such as Elizabeth Cady Stanton and Susan B. Anthony and political thinkers such as Mary Wollstonecraft. Wollstonecraft's seminal work, *A Vindication on the Rights of Women*, published in 1792, expressed a hope for social arrangements in which all individuals are free from the fallacies of tradition that hold them back. Wollstonecraft argued that "women, deprived of education, taught to defer to men, and appraised according to the double standard of morality, have been prevented from exercising genuine judgment or attaining genuine virtue" (Hornsby, 2005, p. 965).

The theoretical path of second-wave feminism was laid by the publication of Simone de Beauvoir's *The Second Sex* in 1949 and Betty Friedan's *The Feminine Mystique* in 1963 (Rogers, 2005). Simone de Beauvoir was an early feminist philosopher whose book *The Second Sex* maintained that woman has historically functioned as the culturally constructed "other" of man. Friedan's groundbreaking work argued that women's limited roles as housewives and mothers are caused by a false belief system that affects women's loss of their identities. Women's movement activities during this time included the founding of the National Organization of Women (NOW), the attempt to pass the Equal Rights Amendment (ERA), and the Paris student revolution of 1968. In addition, continental philosophers such as Julia Kristeva and Luce Irigaray argued against the Western patriarchal tradition of a rational, disembodied consciousness and articulated a feminist consciousness based on the maternal bond. Carol Gilligan argued against male-centered notions of moral development, which tend to value the separation from other people, objectivity, and the equation of fairness with noninterference, arguing for an ethics grounded in care (Meyers, 1997). Such an ethics of care is based on the idea that people are fundamentally connected, and they see attachment to other people as valuable.

Third-wave feminism began in the 1980s with the publication of *This Bridge Called My Back*, an edited collection of essays and poems highlighting the voices and identities of women of color (Moraga & Anzaldua, 1983). Feminist critics argued that feminism and women had been essentialized to imply only white women by previous thinkers, leaving out the diverse experiences, realities, and locations of women of color and poor women (Zack, 2007). These critiques resulted in a focus on intersectionality, emphasizing the ways that patriarchy perpetuates racism, classism, and sexism in women's lives. The works of Patricia Hill Collins and other African-American feminist authors such as Audre Lorde, bell hooks, and Angela Davis have been central developments in black feminist thought, while the works of Gloria Anzaldua and others have focused on Latina feminist identity issues. The philosophy known as womanism, first articulated by African-American author Alice Walker, represents the perspectives of women of color who have felt silenced by white feminist narratives (Phillips, 2006). In a later chapter, I focus in more detail on the role that such feminist identity politics has played in organizing.

ANALYSIS OF FEMINIST PERSPECTIVES

Antiviolence organizer Andrea Smith (2006) has been critical of attempts to categorize feminism:

> The problems with this approach become clear when acknowledging that the histories of feminism extend beyond these narrow waves. For example, if one were to develop a feminist history centering Native women, feminist history in the country would start in 1492 with the resistance to patriarchal colonization. The insistence on a first, second, and third wave approach to understanding feminism therefore keeps white feminism at the center of our analysis and organizing practice. (p. 66)

The problem identified by Smith is important because it reminds us of the ethnocentric past of much of feminism and the way that women of color and poor women have been silenced by feminist analyses, mistakenly assuming that white women's experiences are equivalent to all women's experiences.

Backlash has always coexisted with feminism. For example, some critics have argued that feminism has been the cause of various social problems, including the breakdown of the nuclear family, pointing out that increasing women's access to the public sphere of work has diverted women from raising children properly. Liberal divorce laws have also been identified as harming children (Kaufman, 2003).

Feminist thought has influenced organizers working on explicitly women's issues such as domestic violence and reproductive health care. Certainly, feminist ideas propelled organizers to achieve monumental victories, including the right of women to vote in the United States, grounded in arguments about the equality of women. The passage of rape and sexual assault laws occurred because advocates argued against the traditional belief that women are not the property of men. Current campaigns to change the Global Gag Rule are based on a framework focusing on women's health and the belief in the democratic principle of full access to information. The Global Gag Rule is a policy passed in 2001 that asserts that no U.S. family planning assistance can be provided to foreign nongovernmental organizations (NGOs) to provide counseling and referral for abortion, nor can they lobby to make abortion legal or more available in other countries; this rule has been shown to be a threat to women's health (http://www.globalgagrule.org).

It is important to note that the influence of the feminist tradition extends beyond such clearly "women's domains." Feminist theories and ideas have been valuable for other aspects of community organizing practice, including issue framing, organizing constituencies, and organizational practice. For example, the feminist philosophy that the "personal is political" and the associated practice of political consciousness-raising about personal issues through group processing represent important contributions to popular education techniques. These ideas will be clarified further in Chapter 5, Critical Organizing Frameworks.

CIVIL SOCIETY PERSPECTIVES

Recently, a proliferation of ideas has emerged in response to the growing perception that life in developed nations has become increasingly individually focused and less focused on community and public life. In addition, observers have noted that citizen political and community participation in the United States and other nations has waned. Many people argue that democracy itself is in peril. Civil society perspectives have differing political and philosophical orientations and include social capital theories, communitarianism, the local participatory democracy movement, and others. These ideas have potential implications for the resurgence of community organizing, other forms of civic engagement, and the revitalization of democracy itself.

Aristotle (1962 version) wrote that humans are by nature "political animals." In other words, our nature as human beings is to live in a political milieu, in the context of a state. During Aristotle's time in ancient Greece, the nascent political system of democracy required most citizens to participate in the functioning of democracy. All citizens (defined in this case as older, male, nonslaves) were obliged to serve as representatives, and thus it was important for everyone to understand the political issues of the day, as well as to develop the skills of critical analysis and rhetoric or oration. Over time, these democratic customs have changed dramatically. For a variety of complex reasons, it seems that citizens' ethical and practical commitments to democratic participation have declined.

When the French count Alexis de Tocqueville visited the United States in 1831, he was particularly impressed with the way that Americans took part in community-based associations and believed that such activity overcame individualism and buttressed democracy. Tocqueville referred to this as "self-interest properly understood" (Fried, 2002, p. 26). Harvard scholar Robert Putnam (2000) and others have noted that civic participation rates of Americans so valued by Tocqueville have declined dramatically since the end of World War II.

Putnam has noted that civic virtue is most influential when it is embedded in a network of reciprocal social relations; he invokes the term *social capital* to conceptualize the connections that exist among individuals and the trust and reciprocity that arise from these connections; these social networks, like other forms of capital, have value in society. Social capital is beneficial to the individuals who are a part of these networks as well as to the larger society as a whole. Putnam and others have researched a variety of aspects of social capital, including political participation, civic participation, religious participation, connections in the workplace, informal social connections, altruism, volunteering and philanthropy, reciprocity, honesty and trust, and social movements (Healy, Hampshire, & Ayres, 2004; Miller, 1997; Tolbert, Lyson, & Irwin, 1998). High amounts of social capital tend to result in better outcomes in education and children's welfare, safe and productive neighborhoods, economic prosperity, health and happiness, participatory democracy, and tolerance. Putnam believes that the erosion of social capital is causally related to the decline of democracy in America generally. He articulates several reasons for the wearing away of this essential resource, including geographic shifts (moving to the suburbs), generational changes (the aging out of the civically active World War II generation), and an increase in television watching.

Closely linked to Putnam's social capital theory is the communitarian perspective, which emphasizes the significance of community over the individual or the state. Whereas liberal political philosophies in the tradition of John Rawls have tended to focus on an abstract and disembodied individual, communitarians emphasize the embedded and embodied status of the individual person, particularly focusing on the social nature of life, identity, relationships, and institutions (Frazer, 2005). The communitarian approach offers a prescription for public life, i.e., that collective and public values guide and construct our lives. According to Frazer:

> A society which understands itself to be constituted by atomistic and autonomous discrete individuals, and which makes that kind of autonomy its highest value, will not work. Similarly, a top-down imposition of values (as in Stalinism) or the attempt completely to subordinate the individual to the state (as in modern fascism) will fail. (p. 151)

Communitarians encompass a wide range of adherents, including those more conservative who emphasize upholding tradition, downplay the importance of individual rights, and reject welfare-state programs (Selznick, 2002). Liberal communitarians critique such a conservative perspective and emphasize community values such as reciprocity, rejecting a society that emphasizes individualism. Critics of communitarian ideas are concerned that individual rights, which have formed the basis of modern Western political theories, have been abandoned in favor of communal rights. At any rate, all communitarians agree on the importance of a strong social fabric (i.e., high rates of social capital) to make democracy work. Communitarians have argued for better work and leave policies so that people can strengthen the social fabric by participating more actively in civic life.

Building community, including global community, and enhancing social networks are central elements of civil society perspectives. Manuel Castells (1999) has argued that the organization of contemporary society is based on networks. This form of organization emerged from the need of transnational corporations to perform transactions at high speeds. According to Castells:

> Networks have always existed in human organization. But only now have they become the most powerful form for organizing instrumentality, rather than expressiveness. The reason is fundamentally technological. The strength of networks is their flexibility, their decentralizing capacity, their variable geometry.... Their fundamental weakness throughout history has been the difficulty of coordination toward a common objective, toward a focused purpose, that requires concentration of resources in space and time within large organizations, like armies, bureaucracies, large factories, vertically organized corporations. With new information and communication technology, the network is, at the same time, centralized and decentralized. It can be co-ordinated without a centre. (p. 6)

Stalder (2006) describes how the flow of information operates, explaining that, through deep flows of information and people along networks that span the globe, ideas travel from their place of origin to where it appeals to people's agendas. In the process, it is adapted and becomes a part of the constitution of the very networks along which it flows. This flow of information is equally relevant to global capitalist production methods and to progressive social movements, to efforts to save the planet as well as attempts to destroy it (Stalder, 2006).

PARTICIPATORY DEMOCRACY

International groups such as the United Nations Educational, Scientific, and Cultural Organization (UNESCO) are particularly concerned with fostering ideas that promote a just notion of global democracy. What makes democracy work is citizen engagement in civil society, where civil society is public space separate from the state, the market, and the family, though to be sure these spheres are not always discrete (Beausang, 2002). Access to socioeconomic resources and the conditions the state creates have enormous implications for the most marginal individuals in society, including people in developing countries. "The existence of civil society groups 'from below' is not sufficient for democracy to work. In fact, civil society can be 'undemocratic' if it is isolated" (Beausang, 2002, p. 5). A strong civil society needs a healthy, functioning state to accomplish goals and provide a stable political context (Beausang, 2002).

Efforts to promote participatory democracy (rather than just a representative democracy) have the potential to engender an active civil society, a socially just economy, and a democracy that serves to channel the interests of the people. The city of Porto Alegre, Brazil, has forged an important path in the participatory democracy movement by implementing a participatory budgeting process for its citizens; cities in Europe and North America also have been developing such processes. A participatory budgeting process has shown promise in more equitable distribution of funds, greater governmental transparency, and increased citizen involvement. Through deliberative decision making about priorities, ordinary citizens decide how to allocate city or municipal funds affecting social policy. Introduced in 1989, this approach to budgeting is based on "civil, not state, governance" (Menegat, 2002, p. 8).

Other thinkers and activists have proposed the idea of transborder participatory democracy (Ichiyo, 1994), a democratization process emphasizing the emancipatory transformation of everyday relationships in the family, community, workplace, and other institutions. This democratization extends beyond social, cultural, and state barriers to reach, influence, and ultimately control the global decision-making mechanisms wherever they are located. This perspective emphasizes that people, especially oppressed people, have a right to criticize, oppose, and prevent the implementation of decisions that affect their lives, arguing that the right permits people to cross borders to carry their struggles to the sources of power that seek to oppress them (Ichiyo, 1994). Such approaches can be especially useful for transnational organizing, which will be discussed in greater detail in Chapter 12, Global Justice: Organization and Resistance.

ANALYSIS OF CIVIL SOCIETY PERSPECTIVES

Calls to reclaim democracy are coming from every direction and across political lines. The fostering of social capital and the revitalization of civil society are clearly necessary conditions for social justice and social change. Nonetheless, the enhancement of social capital does not by itself alleviate social problems or enhance equity. Critics have pointed out Putnam's omission of the realities of the political economy into his concept of social capital (McLean, Schultz, & Steger, 2002). The potential risk when thinking about social capital approaches is the belief that increasing social capital is a panacea for community problems. Without confronting power structures, the practices of building community and strengthening assets may fall short of remedying inequities (Pyles & Cross, forthcoming). The discourse of "social capital" may be silencing other discourses related to power and oppression. Some have questioned why Putnam does not discuss historic, systemic inequalities as well as policy trends such as neoliberal economic policies when theorizing the decline of democratic participation (McLean, Schultz, & Steger, 2002). Other thinkers have argued that the decline of trust in the government has been one of the most significant factors in the decline of participatory democracy, arguing that this dimension has also been silenced in Putnam's work (Boggs, 2002). This decline may be due to factors related to globalized corporatization, particularly the rise of corporate power in the guise of "special-interest groups." Indeed, the recognition that the government may exhibit a corporate agenda over a people-centered agenda quite likely has eroded interest in community participation.

Understanding the way our network society functions can enhance and deepen community organizing practice. Organizers today are able to communicate through the Internet, cell phones, etc., making communication much more rapid, inexpensive, and efficient than in previous generations. By understanding how to strengthen their social capital and how networks operate, organizers are better positioned to be successful in their campaigns.

ANARCHIST THOUGHT

One of the most misunderstood philosophical perspectives relevant to community organizing is that of anarchism. The word often conjures images of chaos and violence, a Hobbesian world of all against all. It does not take much time inquiring into anarchism to realize that this is not at all what it is about; in fact, anarchists consider anarchy to be an ordered way of life. The familiar anarchist symbol consisting of the "A" in a circle is derived from Pierre-Joseph Proudhon's slogan "anarchy is order; government is civil war" (Kinna, 2005).

Anarchism essentially emerged from struggles to liberate working-class individuals. Two key components of anarchism are a critique of the state and an emphasis on the strengths and capacities of individuals and communities for social care. From an anarchist perspective, the very nature of the state tends to be one of manipulation and deception of its people. However, anarchism is not necessarily opposed to social organization or rules, or even to certain forms of governing, as long as it is not coercive or oppressive. "Anarchism maintains that all those who hold authority should exercise it for the benefit of those below them, and if they hold offices of authority they are account-able to those below them and recallable by them" (DeGeorge, 2005, p. 32).

Another key idea of anarchist thought is mutual aid, or reciprocal exchange of resources (Kropotkin, 1919). Creating new alternative structures is a cornerstone of such anarchist approaches. In the weeks following Hurricane Katrina, action medics began a health clinic on the West Bank of New Orleans in Algiers (Benham, 2007). The clinic was started by a network of individual prac-titioners who had been working for many years to meet the unmet health-care needs of people in their communities as well as providing medical support for direct actions. One of the founders of what came to be called the Common Ground Health Clinic, Roger Benham, discusses some of the problems and limitations of such mutual aid activism:

> No matter how hard we worked or how many donations we received, our efforts could never match the lack of effort on the part of the government. It was sometimes easy to become intoxicated with how much was accomplished with so little, but we should be realistic. We cannot perform helicopter rescues, evacuate large numbers of people, or deal with thousands of hospital patients and nursing home resi-dents, as the official response did in the first days of September, however belatedly or badly. We cannot build levees that can withstand storm surges, or restore wetlands that have been lost, which would have provided additional protection. These are all larger social functions that require the mobilization of large-scale resources. (p. 79)

Emma Goldman, one of the most famous anarchists in history, was a labor activist who immi-grated to the United States in 1885 at the age of 16; she lived in New York City and became involved in anarchist causes (McAllister, 1997). She founded a radical monthly periodical called *Mother Earth*, which was censored by the U.S. government in 1917. She organized around labor issues, birth control, and women's rights. In 1919, she was deported to the Soviet Union during the postwar "Red scare." One of her important intellectual contributions was the idea that social transformation should entail living the kind of life one is working toward to whatever extent possible (Kaufman, 2003). This idea would later form the foundation of the progressive social movements of the 1960s, i.e., to create organizational structures that express the compassionate and cooperative world that organizers envisioned. Goldman was committed to the development of individual human potential, which she viewed as thwarted by the constraints of social systems; she was particularly concerned with laws that repressed the expression of one's sexuality.

More than most theoretical perspectives, anarchism consists of a wide range of differing and contradictory views. It may be useful to consider three different groups of contemporary anarchists (Kinna, 2005). The first group considers anarchism to be a political movement working toward liberation of the working class. This group also appeals to women and people of color by connect-ing sexism and racism to economic oppression. The International Workers' Association (IWA), an international federation of labor unions, is one example of such groups. The second group views anarchism as an umbrella movement radicalized by feminists, environmentalists, and gays and lesbians. This group tends to downplay the working-class struggle, viewing anarchism as a com-mitment to a countercultural lifestyle marked by beliefs in interdependence and mutual support. The third group also deemphasizes the working-class struggle, instead embracing the aesthetic dimension of organizing and liberation. This group attempts to overcome the alienation and ennui of consumerism and everyday life by "challenging the system through cultural subversion, creating confusion to highlight the oppressiveness of accepted norms and values" (Kinna, 2005, p. 5). These latter two groups have recently focused more on the individual pursuit of freedom, and are some-times referred to as "lifestyle anarchists" (Bookchin, 1999).

Bookchin (1999) articulates the further complexity and seeming contradictory aspects of anar-chist views:

> At one extreme of anarchism is a liberal ideology that focuses overwhelmingly on the abstract indi-
> vidual (often drawing on bourgeois ideologies), supports personal autonomy, and advances a negative
> rather than a substantive concept of liberty. This anarchism celebrates the notion of *liberty from* rather
> than a fleshed-out concept of *freedom for*. At the other end of the anarchist spectrum is a revolutionary
> libertarian socialism that seeks to create a free society, in which humanity as a whole—and hence the
> individual as well—enjoys the advantages of free political and economic institutions. (p. 160)

Thus, anarchism can include a wide range of ideological perspectives ranging from a socialist anarchism on the left to an individual anarchism on the right.

ANALYSIS OF ANARCHIST THOUGHT

Like thinkers in the Marxist tradition, anarchist thinkers are concerned with excessive accumula-
tions of power in society. Anarchists disagree with Marxists, however, when it comes to the parameters of social institutions (Kaufman, 2003). In other words:

> Many Marxists are content with a situation in which state institutions administer social needs, as long
> as they are administered fairly and in the interest of society. Anarchists oppose the creation of an
> "administered society" and argue for active participation in the creation and re-creation of social forms.
> For them, democracy is one of the most important values. (Kaufman, 2003, p. 242)

Anarchist perspectives also have some similarities with participatory democracy perspectives. Both
perspectives find common ground in the belief that regular people should be empowered to identify
what is of utmost importance to their communities and set the agenda for their lives.

Critiques of anarchism abound, particularly critiques of the so-called lifestyle anarchists who
many perceive to be isolationist. Adherents to anarchist philosophy may tend to ignore electoral
politics and the possibilities that policy reform can offer to people's lives. According to social
critic Noam Chomsky (2005), anarchist projects have met with some success, including the Israeli
Kibbutzim experiments and during the Spanish Revolution of 1936, when the economy was put
under worker control.

Like any philosophy or set of ideas, it is not necessary to embrace all of its implications to appreciate how they may be useful in one's practice. As Gandhi said, "You must be the change you wish
to see in the world." For organizers, this means that campaigns, organizational structures, recruit-
ment strategies, and tactics can all reflect that change. Consider a neighborhood association that is
making a decision about how to hold a city accountable for implementing a sidewalk project that it
promised but is threatening to renege on because a new mayor has deemed it unnecessary. This can
include making a decision about how to act by consensus of a diverse representation of neighbors;
this can help the association avoid the trap that the most enfranchised, privileged neighbors make
the decisions in lieu of those who may have less access to the meetings of the neighborhood. Lower-
income individuals, women, and people of color may have less availability due to work hours.
Facilitating the enfranchisement of the most marginalized in a neighborhood into the structures of
the neighborhood association can create an environment that does not replicate some of the negative, hierarchical practices of the city it is organizing against. Though I will discuss this idea in
greater detail in Chapter 5, Critical Organizing Frameworks, the idea that the means and the ends
of organizing are related offers a powerful and transformative direction for organizers.

POSTMODERN PERSPECTIVES

Postmodernism is an intellectual movement that casts doubt on metaphysical and epistemological
assumptions about reality. Emerging after World War II, thinkers came to question the assumptions
of modernity and the fact that it had resulted in the Holocaust, environmental destruction, and a

variety of oppressions including racism, sexism, and homophobia. This movement has manifested in the disciplines of philosophy, art, architecture, literature, and others; it is also philosophically linked with post-structuralism in psychology and linguistics and post-colonialism in literary theory. Modernism and other traditional views based on objective, scientific approaches to knowing are deconstructed as false impositions on what are actually multiple realities that are constantly in flux (Blackburn, 1994). Postmodernists question the entire politics of knowing, and objectivity is viewed as a mask for various types of power and authority.

Postmodern philosopher Jacques Derrida introduced the idea of the deconstruction of literary and philosophical texts, arguing against essentialism and holding that their meanings are multifold and slippery at best. The fluidity within texts and ideas generally is an argument against traditional modernist metaphysics based on stable opposites. Ideas such as good and evil, black and white, man and woman, and nature and civilization are just some examples of opposites that are imposed in a "violent" way on society. Queer theory, which emerged from the influences of both third-wave feminism and postmodernism, represents a philosophical movement that has critiqued the notion of any kind of fixed sexual identities.

Even ideas such as racism or patriarchy or capitalism, which according to many social change actors should be overthrown, have been misunderstood as essentialist ideas, when in fact they are also slippery notions. It may be more useful for understanding such ideas as a set of practices. "If we analyze capitalism as a system that must be overthrown all at once or not at all, then it isn't clear how it is possible to struggle against it in the present period" (Kaufman, 2003, p. 114). Feminists who pursue reform agendas such as increasing pay for women or prosecuting perpetrators of sexual assault are challenging patriarchal practices. Rather than getting stuck in essentialist ways of thinking and reifying ideas such as capitalism, breaking them down into moments or components of practices can be a useful way of thinking of them.

The significant project of post-structural theorists has been to articulate the diverse identities of persons who have been living under colonialist conditions that are oppressive and silencing. Cultural theorist Gayatri Spivak has been concerned with the "subaltern," who are people who "cannot speak," i.e., cannot be heard by the privileged (Landry & MacLean, 1996). She has advocated for "unlearning," which is to work critically through one's prejudices, history, and instinctual responses (Landry & MacLean, 1996). Landry and MacLean explicate Spivak's view of unlearning one's privilege as one's loss:

> Our privileges, whatever they may be in terms of race, class, nationality, gender, and the like, may have prevented us from gaining a certain kind of Other knowledge: not simply information that we have not yet received, but the knowledge that we are not equipped to understand by reason of our social positions. To unlearn our privileges means, on the one hand, to do our homework, to work hard at gaining some knowledge of the others who occupy those spaces most closed to our privileged view. On the other hand, it means attempting to speak to those others in such a way that they might take us seriously and, most important of all, be able to answer back. (pp. 4–5)

SOCIAL CONSTRUCTIONISM

Social constructionism is a sociological and philosophical perspective that is concerned with how social phenomena come into being. An understanding of the self is one of the central components of a social constructionist viewpoint. Gergen (1999) exemplifies this perspective, arguing that the self is fluid; "who one is depends on the moment-to-moment movements in conversation" (p. 80); thus, the self is an expression of relationship. Philosopher Michel Foucault's ideas about the self are compatible with a social constructionism perspective, arguing that it was historicized and that everyone is captive to what he calls "regimes of truth" or the prevailing norms of a particular society at a particular historical time (Chambon, Irving, & Epstein, 1999; Foucault, 1980). Black feminist thinker bell hooks (1984) writes of how power structures shape individual selves, having historically defined both what it is to be black and what it is to be a woman.

Many constructionist views of the self stem from a critique of the modernist view of the self, which is grounded in the philosopher Rene Descartes's *cogito*, i.e., "I think, therefore I am." The modernist position maintains that what it is to be human and to know something rests on the capacity for inner rational thought. In contrast, through his analysis of language, Gergen (1999) holds a relational view of the self and asserts that it is not reason, but "relationships stand prior to all that is intelligible" (p. 48). Bakhtin (cited in Irving & Young, 2002) holds a similar view, criticizing modernist monological thinking and positing an unfinalizable nature of the self. The self is unfinalizable because it is constantly participating in an open-ended dialogue (Irving & Young, 2002, p. 23).

In addition to understanding the self, an analysis of epistemology, or the study of knowledge, is a key component of the social constructionist agenda. Modernist epistemological views are grounded in the belief that the mind is a mirror to nature. Gergen (1999), like many other postmodern theorists, holds the position that there are multiple ways of knowing reality. He offers the example of looking out a window—a botanist gives one description, a landscape designer another, an artist another, and a real estate agent still another. In his words:

> The individual mind (thought, experience) does not originate meaning, create language, or discover the nature of the world. Meanings are born of coordinations among persons—agreements, negotiations, affirmation.... Nothing exists for us—as an intelligible world of objects and persons—until there are relationships. (Gergen, 1999, p. 48)

Gergen (1999) states that "what we take to be knowledge of the world grows from relationship," and is embedded not within individual minds but within interpretive or communal traditions (p. 122). So, for Gergen, not only does the self emerge from relationship, but knowledge emerges from relationship as well. Literary theorist Mikhail Bakhtin holds a similar view and believes that understanding comes from dialogue. He writes: "Understanding and response are merged and mutually condition each other" (cited in Irving & Young, 2002, p. 24).

Generally speaking, postmodernist and social constructionist thinkers are inclined to believe that democracy is one of the great gifts of otherwise oppressive narratives of modernity. According to Gergen (1999), "To it [modernity], we must largely credit our institutions of democracy, public education, and justice" (p. 102). He states that "the very idea of democracy—each individual endowed with the right to vote—derives from Enlightenment presumptions" (Gergen, 1999, p. 7). As one reconstructs and transforms oneself and unearths subjugated ways of knowing, one can also reconstruct the manner in which democracy proceeds, enfranchising people to become part of the process, people who were often marginalized and oppressed. This enfranchisement can happen, according to Gergen, through the potentials of dialogue.

Bakhtin offers the notion of *carnival*, a metaphor for the freedom from repressive monological structures that are characteristic of modernist thought. Like Gergen, he believes that dialogue and relationship offer a new way of constructing reality. Bakhtin affirms that "carnival is the place for working out a *new mode of interrelationship between individuals* counterposed to the all powerful socio-hierarchical relationships of noncarnival life" (cited in Irving & Young, 2002, p. 26). Writer bell hooks (1984) echoes this sentiment, calling for change that is transformative:

> To restore the revolutionary life force,... women and men must begin to re-think and re-shape its direction ... we must be willing to criticize, re-examine, and begin ... anew, a challenging task because we lack historical precedents.... Our emphasis must be on cultural transformation: destroying dualism, eradicating systems of domination. (p. 163)

ANALYSIS OF POSTMODERN PERSPECTIVES

One common critique of postmodernist viewpoints concerns the philosophical consequences of postmodernism. On the one hand, if reality and knowledge are based on a group or individual's gender or race or socioeconomic location, then skepticism and even nihilism can arise. If there is no objectivity, then how can one say with any certainty that poverty exists or that a particular social policy is detrimental? Doesn't this lead to the idea that everything is true (or that everything is false)? These kinds of philosophical debates are not new and existed in ancient Greek and Indian philosophy. Postmodernists respond to this dilemma by reiterating that the technique of deconstructing practices is a path toward transformative political possibilities (Gergen, 1999; Witkin & Saleebey, 2007). Paulo Freire (1994) calls this a pedagogy of hope.

Postmodernism and social constructionism can be helpful philosophical perspectives for thinking about community organizing for a variety of reasons. First, they are helpful in breaking down the negative metanarratives of the dominant culture. The dominant culture often manifests itself in social welfare institutions (both public and private) and in the policies and programs created by the institutions. In order to evaluate a policy or program and its effects on communities, families, and individuals, it is often necessary to understand the stories about reality that lie behind a policy. Foucault wrote about the social construction of the mental institution beginning with mid-17th century internment houses, responding to the ways that modern policies have silenced and marginalized mental illness. Second, because organizing and advocacy communities obviously have their own narratives as well, it is often useful to have the tools to deconstruct these narratives. For example, a common discourse among organizers is what I call the "us–them" discourse. This is based on the idea that there exists in reality a group of people who "get it" or who are "right," i.e., "us," and that there is another group who does not get it and thus who are "wrong", i.e., "them." Organizers should be cautious when creating new sweeping dichotomies, such as the global justice movement arguably has done with the ideas of the "global North" and the "global South." Finally, community organizing practice can be subject to a kind of textual analysis. This can be done by being transparent about the fact that practice is always grounded in one's socioeconomic location, race/ethnicity, and other individual lenses and experiences.

The relevance of postmodern thought on contemporary activism can also be understood through the lens of the work of Bakhtin. Bakhtin's concept of carnival has opened the way for organizers to consider protest as a form of play that disrupts the rational order (Irving & Young, 2002; Shepard, 2005). Overall, postmodernism is relevant to a variety of aspects of community organizing practice, including consciousness-raising and popular education techniques; organizing constituencies, including working in coalition; and grappling with identity politics. Indigenous Mexican organizers, the Zapatistas, engage in the practice of *encuentro*, a dialogical encounter, and feminists have engaged in the practice of consciousness-raising about oppression. Postmodernism and social constructionism remind us that such democratic discussions of ideas are the center of social change work.

DEVELOPING A CRITICAL APPROACH

The social change ideas discussed here represent a complex amalgamation of critical perspectives on social realities. These ideas are not always compatible with each other; indeed, some even contradict each other. The world is a complex place in which everyone has a limited view; any theory that purports to explain it fully or that reduces reality to a basic concept should be approached with caution. How, then, can community organizers draw from these complex perspectives in their practice in a way that is ultimately beneficial for communities? One must keep in mind that it is not the ideas themselves that are most important, but what the ideas can do for people. Marx employed the notion of praxis (practical application of theory) to emphasize the worth of not just interpreting the world, but of actually transforming it with actions in the real world.

Overall, these perspectives are valuable for understanding and critiquing the underpinnings of social welfare policies and practices, including questioning underlying stories, dichotomies, and frameworks. Practitioners could engage in a critical analysis of a restrictive immigration policy, exposing the contradiction that the histories of many countries, particularly that of the United States, have included immigrants and that many people are descendants of immigrants. A new vision for a progressive immigration policy would incorporate this history and emphasize the strengths of a diverse, multicultural environment.

Parton (2007) has proposed the practice of *constructive social work*, a system that could be of benefit to progressive community organizers. First, social workers develop a critical position toward assumed modes of understanding the world as well as ourselves. Second, the world is seen as the product of social processes. Third, there are many forms of knowledge available; knowledge is a result of historical and cultural processes. Fourth, knowledge comes about as a result of negotiated meanings and relationships. Fifth, relationships are bound within rituals and traditions.

Social change ideas can stimulate envisioning what liberation can look like and how groups can organize themselves in their work. These ideas are central to developing a critical perspective, and working with them always entails questioning fundamental assumptions about policies, programs, and practices. Particular concern about the effect on marginalized people is an essential and continuous task of the organizer. Though I have offered some analysis of the social change ideas that have been presented, it is ultimately up to the practitioner to vet the ideas and determine if they are helpful for a given context.

QUESTIONS FOR REFLECTION

1. Explain your personal understanding of Marxist thought and how it is relevant to social issues today.
2. What would a neo-Marxist or critical theorist say about "work first" welfare reform policies that force low-income individuals into low-wage jobs?
3. Describe the role social capital building can play in effecting social change. What other factors are at play and need to be addressed?
4. What socially constructed dichotomies do you see in community practice contexts? Are these constructions helpful? Why or why not?
5. Discuss what a critical approach to organizing means to you. Is this a useful concept? Why or why not?

SUGGESTIONS FOR FURTHER INQUIRY

BOOKS

Bourdieu, P. (1991). *Language and symbolic power.* Cambridge, MA: Harvard University Press.
Hooks, B. (2000). *Feminist theory: From margin to center.* Cambridge, MA: South End Press.
Horowitz, I. L. (1964). *The anarchists.* New York: Dell Publishing.
Kaufman, C. (2003). *Ideas for action: Relevant theory for radical change.* Cambridge, MA: South End Press.
Norris, P. (2002). *Democratic phoenix: Reinventing political activism.* New York: Cambridge University Press.

WEB

Center for Popular Economics. http://www.populareconomics.org
Liberty Tree Foundation for the Democratic Revolution. http://www.libertytreeFDR.org
Marxists Internet Archive. http://www.marxists.org
The New Rules Project. http://www.newrules.org
The Noam Chomsky Website. http://www.chomsky.info

KEY TERMS

Civil society: The nongovernmental sector of society that includes community organizations working toward social change. Recent writings on civil society have focused on the importance of this sector for moving democracy forward.

Critical theory: A broad philosophical and literary movement grounded in the basic societal analysis offered by Marx concerning class power. Neo-Marxists are concerned with emancipation from a variety of forms of domination (e.g., racism, sexism) in society.

Oppression: Occurs when power is used to silence, marginalize, or subordinate individuals or groups of individuals either directly or via social systems such as economic, educational, or social welfare systems.

Participatory democracy: The movement to actualize the vision of democracy whereby citizens drive governmental processes such as budgeting and other aspects of policy making.

Patriarchy: A term critiqued by feminist and postmodernists that explains the social structure of society that is grounded in male-dominated values and that marginalizes those who do not exemplify such values.

Third-wave feminism: Having its origins in the mid-1980s, this wave of feminist theory and activism emphasizes postmodernist perspectives on femininity, emphasizing the voices of women of color and LGBT women.

4 Learning from Social Movements

And there are those who are called social activists, who are men and women who have been fighting all their lives for exploited people, and they are the same ones who participated in the great strikes and workers' actions, in the great citizens' mobilizations, in the great *campesino* movements, and who suffer great repression, and who, even though some are old now, continue on without surrendering, and they go everywhere, looking for the struggle, seeking justice ... and they are just not quiet and they know a lot because they have seen a lot and lived and struggled.

Zapatista Army of National Liberation (n.d.)

The tactics used by revolutionaries who envisioned a more democratic way of life have been an inspiration for many activists and community organizers (Honey, 2006). Emerging from the circumstances of the American Revolution, the U.S. Declaration of Independence itself expresses a philosophy committed to social transformation to maintain a free society. Indeed, if any form of government becomes destructive of the ends of democracy, it is the right of the people to alter or abolish it (Declaration of Independence). When established political systems do not respond to the needs of people, organizing has historically been a way for citizens to ensure their grievances are heard (Zinn, 2003). In addition to such democratic mandates, organizers across the globe have drawn from human rights frameworks, as well as indigenous or localized legacies of resistance, to inspire them to work for change.

Modern scholars consider a revolution to be "violent, abrupt or radical change," a kind of rupture or innovation within a linear or evolutionary conception of time (Beilharz, 2005, p. 642). However, from the time of the Greeks to the Renaissance, revolution had a more cyclical or circular sense of meaning, indicating a complete or full cycle of seasons, a kind of restoration based on a cyclical sense of time (Beilharz, 2005). One can argue that organizing, particularly social movement organizing, happens with regularity as a normal part of the human social and political cycle, performing the function of the restoration or creation of free and democratic practices.

The second half of the 19th century in Europe and the United States was marked by technological innovations in the production of goods. Iron, steel, steam engines, the telephone, the typewriter—these inventions greatly increased the world of production. And with these innovations also came increased risks to workers. To achieve the ends of faster production required "clever organizers and administrators of the new corporations, a country rich with land and minerals, and a huge supply of human beings to do the back-breaking, unhealthful, and dangerous work" (Zinn, 2003, p. 254). In the 19th and early 20th century, immigrants from Europe and China were exposed to harsh conditions, including long work days, dangerous machinery, the heat, and the cold. Consider that in 1889, the Interstate Commerce Commission showed that 22,000 railroad workers were killed or injured in the course of a single year.

While these workers had much in common in terms of their political and economic situations, their ethnic differences were often emphasized, and thus they were easily pitted against each other, a mechanism that would have the effect of impeding their potential solidarity as workers. During this time, ethnic communities also were subjected to explicit violence due to ethnic hatred—Jews beaten in New York City and Chinese killed in San Francisco (Zinn, 2003). These divisions would be a recurring theme in the history of social movements and community organizing. And yet, these workers found ways to overcome the divides.

The movement for the eight-hour work day was growing in 1886, and in the spring a strike occurred that included 350,000 workers in 11,562 establishments throughout the country:

> In Detroit, 11,000 workers marched in an eight-hour parade. In New York, 25,000 formed a torch-light procession along Broadway, headed by 3,400 members of the Bakers' Union. In Chicago, 40,000 struck, and 45,000 were granted a shorter working day to prevent them from striking. Every railroad in Chicago stopped running, and most of the industries in Chicago were paralyzed. The stockyards were closed down. (Zinn, 2003, p. 270)

The struggle for the eight-hour day would continue and included the infamous Haymarket struggle in Chicago; eventually, workers would achieve victory across ethnic differences on this important labor issue, one that is often taken for granted today.

Even at the time of these labor struggles in the late 19th century, organizing was already a global struggle. The key constituents were immigrants from distant parts of the globe; these groups of people had moved across international borders to escape injustice or to find economic opportunity, an obviously global issue. In addition, labor organizers in Europe were already collaborating with U.S.-based organizers during this time. The global nature of social movements, both historically and contemporarily, cannot be underestimated. Scholars argue that the nature of organizing and movements has changed in this new era of a globalizing world, and indeed, it is changing. Yet, one should keep in mind that the global aspect of social movements has existed for some time. Consider, as well, the critical years of 1848 and 1968, which were heightened times of revolution and social change across the globe. The European revolutions of 1848 occurred in the same year that Karl Marx published *The Communist Manifesto*. The Paris student movement of 1968 was happening at the same time the civil rights and antiwar movements were reaching their heights in the United States. Such significant global social change activity speaks to the importance of communication and alliance-building across national and ethnic boundaries. Today, the contemporary global-justice movement includes people working together in real time from diverse corners of the globe on a range of issues, including health, child welfare, the environment, and other social justice issues.

Social movements and revolutions are not the only contexts where community organizing happens. Indeed, there is a considerable amount of organizing that takes place somewhat in isolation that is not necessarily being conducted and not identified in the context of larger social movements. Nonetheless, an understanding of the history and dynamics of social movements can provide rich insights for organizing work. In this chapter, I define and discuss various dimensions of social movements, particularly as articulated by sociologists. This is followed by an introduction to some historical social movements, including those focused on women's rights, labor issues, LGBT (lesbian, gay, bisexual, transgender) rights, and disability rights. I conclude with a discussion of some of the organizing lessons to be learned from social movement theory and history.

UNDERSTANDING SOCIAL MOVEMENTS

The term *social movement* is a broad one that often encompasses a wide range of definitions. Some may employ a broad description of the term, citing the increased use of digital technology across the globe, e.g., as a social movement. However, a social movement, as defined here, has a fairly narrow definition. According to Jasper (1997), social movements are "conscious, concerted and relatively sustained efforts by organized groups of ordinary people to change some aspect of their society by using extra-institutional means" (p. 5). Two chief elements of social movements, as articulated by Jasper, may be helpful to consider—first, a change in consciousness, and second, a change in behavior. A change in consciousness occurs when people come to believe that social systems are unjust and are losing legitimacy. Many global-justice activists, for example, have ceased to believe in the

promises of free-trade agreements, believing that such agreements hav[...]
to indigenous communities, resulting in displacement of peoples across the [...]
consciousness also means that the system appears as no longer inevitable, and peop[...]
their rights. There is a sense of one's ability to change the situation. A change in behavio[...]
of defiance that may involve violating traditions, laws, and authorities to which people would [...]
mally defer (Jasper, 1997). In the context of a social movement, this change in behavior necessarily
is acted out collectively, as a group, not as individuals. In the case of global-justice activists working
for immigrant rights, for example, some organizers have sought to provide sanctuary to immigrants
who are at risk of being deported, a clear defiance of federal laws.

Other important facets of social movements have been captured by Tarrow (1994), who defines
social movements as "collective challenges by people with common purposes and solidarity in
sustained interaction with elites and authorities" (p. 4), and by Castells (1999), who states that they
are a "purposive collective action whose outcome, in victory as in defeat, transforms the values and
institutions of society" (p. 3). Recalling previous definitions of community organizing articulated
in Chapter 1, it is critical to remember the idea of interaction with elites and authorities, whether
it be social welfare administrators, politicians, or corporate executives; it is necessary to engage
with such key decision makers. In addition, the idea that this interaction is sustained (not fleeting)
is an indicator of a social movement rather than an isolated rebellion or even a one-time organizing
campaign. Finally, Castells's point about the transformation of values and institutions is fundamental. By developing a social analysis or frame through consciousness-raising and popular education
techniques, groups envision and work for the kinds of communities in which they want to live. For
example, organizers in post-Katrina New Orleans have proposed and advocated for a social policy
alternative to the Stafford Act that supports the complex needs of low-income disaster victims who
are displaced from their homes. Such an alternative disaster policy attempts to meet the needs of
everyone in society rather than the current Stafford Act, the benefits of which are primarily geared
toward middle-class homeowners. Such organizing is geared toward a transformation of the institutions that oversee disaster recovery.

DIMENSIONS OF SOCIAL MOVEMENTS

Social movements and social movement organizations can be appreciated through a variety of
dimensions or types. Harper (1998) identified the distinctions between reform/moderate movement
organizations and revolutionary/radical ones. Revolutionary movements are movements that seek
to transform the system itself. These movements tend to focus on fundamental political and economic change, i.e., social change. An example of such a movement is antiwar movements, which,
though they may have an immediate goal of ending a particular war, also uphold longer term goals
of peace by organizing to abolish the mechanisms in society that perpetuate wars and violence.
Reform movements, on the other hand, attempt incremental changes within the existing system. The
welfare rights movement that emerged in the 1960s attempted to work within the existing system
by arguing for better access to state-administered social welfare benefits. Rather than seeking to
abolish capitalism or engage in some other kind of radical change, this movement worked for better
trained caseworkers, simplified application processes, and higher benefit levels for public welfare
recipients. Both revolutionary and reform movements are relevant to the work of progressive community organizing. Changing policies, improving programs, and enhancing economic access for
disenfranchised communities represent reform work and indeed are an important part of progressive social change. The revolutionary work of transforming political and social structures is equally
as important. It is probably most useful to think about these dimensions on a spectrum, with some
organizing campaigns and organizations containing elements of both dimensions.

Another distinction between movements is that of progressive and conservative (Harper, 1998).
Progressive movements, or left-wing movements, are described as forward thinking and often seek
to improve the situation of marginalized groups. The disability rights movement has sought to

.nstitutionalized barriers that people with disabili-
.s may seek to prevent change or resuscitate the past.
.ment, which works to restore what it understands to be
_ht include a call for the resurgence of the nuclear family,
.holds, or attempts to pass state-level constitutional bans of

OF SOCIAL MOVEMENTS

.oncerned with questions such as why social movements come into
. do not join them, and what ultimately makes them effective (Goodwin &
Jasp. .ans, 2001). Clearly, social movements come into being because people are
aggrievc .tice. According to Klandermans: "The transformation of social and cultural
cleavages in. .ctive action frames does not occur by itself. It is a process in which social and
political actors, .nedia, and citizens jointly interpret, define and redefine states of affairs" (p. 272).
He proposes three processes whereby this happens. First, it happens by means of public discourse,
i.e., the interface of media discourse and interpersonal interaction; second, through persuasive communication during mobilization campaigns by movement organizations, their opponents, and coun-
termovement organizations; and third, through consciousness-raising during episodes of collective
action. This is the demand side of social movements.

A major and public injustice can often spur a social movement into action. One such episode
was the murder of Emmett Till, a black Chicago youth who was visiting family in Mississippi in
the 1950s. This young man was brutally murdered by local whites for supposedly ogling a white
woman. The injustice of the murder and the lack of criminal accountability for the perpetrators
spawned outrage among the civil rights community. Recently the case of the Jena 6 has mobilized
the African-American community to protest an unfair criminal justice system, which has served to
revitalize civil rights organizing in a new generation of African-Americans.

Another reason why social movements come into being and why social movement organizations may be successful is because people have the resources to mobilize. This is the supply side of
social movements. According to the resource mobilization approach, the availability of resources
makes the difference. Resources include money, time, technical infrastructure, expertise, and so
on, including the structures and organizations to mobilize and deploy these resources (McCarthy &
Zald, 1973). According to McCarthy and Zald (2003), the resource mobilization approach "exam-
ines the variety of resources that must be mobilized, the linkages of social movements to other
groups, the dependence of movements upon external support for success, and the tactics used by
authorities to control or incorporate movements" (p. 169).

Political opportunity is another facet of the emergence and effectiveness of social movements.
Tarrow (1994) asserts that people engage in movements and that they tend to succeed when political
opportunities open up. Groups with only minor grievances and significant resources may appear,
while those with profound grievances and significant resources, who lack political opportunities,
do not (Tarrow, 1994). "Political opportunities are elements of the political environment that affect
perceptions as to the likelihood that collective action will succeed or fail" (Staggenborg, 2005, p.
754). According to McAdam (cited in Goodwin & Jasper, 2004), political opportunity includes the
degree the institutionalized political system is open or closed, the stability or instability of elite
alignments that tend to undergird a political system, the presence or absence of allies who hold
positions of power, and the state's inclination for repression.

Though many have argued that the focus on political opportunities is one of the greatest deter-
minants of the success of social action, others have argued that such attention to political structures
negates the agency of social movements. Some of the success of the changes during the 1960s
antipoverty movement in the United States can be attributed to the fact that there were favorable
political opportunity structures in place, for example, a Democratic president who was sympathetic

to poverty issues. Besides being influenced by political structures, one should remember that movements create opportunities for themselves (and other social movements) (Staggenborg, 2005). Indeed, women did not obtain the right to vote because the time for it was inevitable; it happened because people organized for it (Kaufman, 2003).

Beck, Dorsey, and Stutters (2003) analyzed the women's suffrage movement through the lens of social movement theory and found several factors operated to influence the movement's success. First, the framing processes that raised consciousness and enhanced collective identity positively influenced the outcome in an ongoing way. Second, a movement community emerged during a protest cycle that was influenced by abolitionist and temperance movements. The movement community included a wide spectrum of organizations, some of which had a radical-flank effect on the outcome. Third, because movement participants consisted primarily of privileged classes of women, external resources steadily flowed into movement activities. Fourth, transnational interactions with international suffrage groups, particularly in England, infused the movement with new ideas that would continue to bolster the movement's effectiveness. Fifth, strong leadership, which framed issues and analyzed the political context, contributed to the effectiveness of the movement.

In addition to a concern with why movements come into being, social movement scholars have asked why people do not participate in social movements. Olson (1965) believed that the reasons for nonparticipation were as follows:

1. Incentives must persuade people to contribute to the collective good.
2. Because movement goals are collective, people will achieve the benefits of the goal even if they do not participate.
3. Because the goal is uncertain, rational actors will often take a "free ride."

Other perspectives on social movements identify the radical-flank effect, arguing that the existence of a "radical flank" can have a range of effects on the outcome of movements. This radical flank is perceived to be threatening to authorities as compared to more moderate participants in a social movement (Goodwin & Jasper, 2003). Authorities can decide to repress the entire movement because of the beliefs or actions of the more radical flank. For example, during the 1999 Seattle protests against the World Trade Organization (WTO), which were almost entirely peaceful on the part of participants, police responded with brute force against peaceful protesters because a few radicals had smashed some windows of businesses in Seattle. The entire group suffered the consequences of the actions of the radical flank. Recent public housing organizing in post-Katrina New Orleans arguably suffered a blow due to the actions of the radical flank. The groups expressing disapproval of the New Orleans City Council's proposal to issue demolition permits of several public housing units were essentially radical ones. These groups only offered a flat-out "no" to the process; no moderate groups were available with which the city council could have negotiated.

Moderate participants often reap positive benefits of a radical-flank effect because the less radical organizers can distance themselves from radical activists, yet they still can obtain the benefits of the actions of radical organizers. According to Goodwin and Jasper (2003), in some cases:

> The radical flank is threatening enough that the forces of order take the movement more seriously, often making concessions. The moderate flank can present itself as a reasonable compromise partner, so that authorities give it power in order to undercut the radicals (although the moderates must distance themselves from the radicals to garner these benefits). (p. 347)

In the case of the women's suffrage movement, the radical work of activists like Alice Paul had a positive effect on the work of more moderate suffragists such as Elizabeth Cady Stanton. While movement organizations employed a wide range of tactics, the actors did not openly condemn the other groups (Beck, Dorsey, & Stutters, 2003).

The recent social movement literature is filled with the complexities of intellectual disputes that focus on the differences between structuralist approaches, which include political opportunity perspectives and resource mobilization approaches, on the one hand, and constructionist approaches, which include a stronger emphasis on culture, meaning, emotions, and identity issues (Goodwin & Jasper, 2004; Polletta, 2004). Stemming from some of the philosophical and literary tensions in postmodern and post-structuralist scholarly trends, these debates can be characterized as occurring between traditional, political process theorists and new social movement theorists who emphasize the roles of culture (Polletta, 2004). Jasper (1997) summarizes these cultural approaches:

> They have begun to write about the social construction of grievances and worldviews. They have described the social-psychological identity formation of activists, often through critiques of rationalist and mobilization approaches. They have refocused their attention on the role of ideas and ideologies in political action. And they have pushed the idea of culture beyond static cognitive grids and into modes of action. (p. 69)

Cultural approaches to studying social movements represent an important way to view movements as not just about the purposive and rational activities of groups, but to include the complexities and social constructions that shape social movement activity. According to Jasper (1997):

> In addition to the other aspects of culture is its creative moment, the active side of construction in which culture meets artfulness. People work out new sensibilities in response to economic, technological, demographic, and other changes. Groups, interacting with each other, breed patterns of friends and foes. Tactical innovations arise from the interplay of protest groups and their opponents. A gifted speaker invents new frames and images that resonate with varied audiences. And so on. Cultural creativity begins with individual idiosyncrasies and spreads from there. (p. 99)

Such a perspective of social movements is commensurate with a community organizing practice that emphasizes organizing as a technical–rational practice, in addition to something that is always being constructed, an artistic or improvisational practice.

A BRIEF HISTORY OF SOCIAL MOVEMENTS

The conditions of industrialization and urbanization in the 19th century set the stage for the early social movements in the United States. Before there were what we understand today to be social movements, groups of individuals displayed subtle, and not so subtle, acts of resistance. During the preindustrial period, which occurred roughly from the Middle Ages until the 19th century, peasants responded to immediate threats to their livelihoods such as grain scarcities, high bread prices, and other attempts to curtail their rights. The responses of these peasants included destroying the homes of tax collectors and confiscating shipments of grain. These actions were local in nature and usually short-lived. The actions tended to target those whom the peasants perceived to have wronged them (Jasper, 1997). By the time of the French Revolution, citizens began to engage in boycotts, mass petitions, and urban rebellions.

Later in the 19th century, citizenship movements emerged (Jasper, 1997). These movements were initiated by the emerging industrial worker class. They were organized by and on behalf of categories of people excluded in some way from full human rights, political participation, or basic economic protections. Such movements tended to be more national and sustained than peasant movements. Working for women's right to vote was an important example of a citizenship movement.

Most recently, postcitizenship movements have surfaced. These so-called new social movements usually comprise people who are already integrated into their society's political, economic, and educational systems. Because they need not demand basic rights for themselves, they often pursue protections or benefits for others. These movements are generally interested in changing the cultural sensibilities of society. Some contemporary authors writing on recent movements are new-movement theorists and emphasize consciousness and culture as vital components to movements. Such movements have expanded globally over the last couple of decades. Whereas previous views have focused on the spatial or locality component of social movements, recently more emphasis has been placed on the common identities of people within movements (Stalder, 2006).

The remainder of this chapter focuses on several key social movements over the course of the last century. Like any retelling of a story, the story will often vary depending on a person's social standpoint and personal perspective. A discussion of the history of social movements is not any different; indeed, the actual movements that are discussed are relative to such a standpoint and are in fact a social construction. My representation of these historical movements is neither exhaustive nor comprehensive. Indeed, I leave out an explicit discussion of the civil rights movement, though I do incorporate many of its influences throughout the book. I choose the movements—women's, labor, LGBT, and disability—because of their contributions to current organizing sensibilities and the diversity of issues that they span. Also, one of the most important contemporary social movements is the global-justice movement, to which I devote an entire chapter at the end of this book.

In each of the following sections, I briefly present an overview of the movement, including a bit of its history, key moments, predominant leaders, the issues addressed, frames utilized, and the organizing tactics employed. I conclude by offering some overall analysis focusing on lessons learned for community organizing practice.

WOMEN'S MOVEMENTS

In 1848, the first Woman's Rights Convention, organized by Elizabeth Cady Stanton and Lucretia Mott, was held in Seneca Falls, New York. This early groundwork of suffragists would eventually lead to the passage of the Nineteenth Amendment, granting women the right to vote in 1920. Once this decisive victory was achieved, however, feminism arguably lost its unifying cause of suffrage (Berkeley, 1999). Nonetheless, new organizations would emerge, such as the League of Women Voters, and new issues would be raised by this powerful block of voters. These issues included maternal health care and the issue of equal pay for equal work.

The next wave of feminist organizing, which began in the late 1960s, was initiated by many women who had worked in the civil rights movement. Though inspired by the work of the New Left, these women also critiqued the ways in which civil rights organizing discriminated against them and operated on assumptions of male superiority. While black men and, to some extent, white men held positions of power within the civil rights movement, such as writing position papers, meeting with community leaders, and engaging in voter registration, white women often found themselves confined to the offices, where they did secretarial work such as typing and answering phones. In the communal homes where civil rights workers lived, "white women not only found themselves assigned to housekeeping tasks but also pressured to engage in sex (especially interracial sex) as a test of their 'commitment to black and white equality'" (Berkeley, 1999, p. 40). Though black women did work alongside black men within the movement, even black women still did not share power equally in the civil rights movement.

By 1964, white women civil rights activists began writing about and organizing themselves on these issues, arguing that the assumptions of male superiority are as pervasive and every bit as crippling to women as white supremacy is to black people (Berkeley, 1999). Feeling that their voices were still not being heard, as they were ignored and ridiculed by male civil rights activists, white women staged a walkout from a general meeting of Students for a Democratic Society (SDS) and organized a "Women's Caucus" to discuss sexism within the New Left (Berkeley, 1999). Black women would not follow suit, arguably a reflection of an ambiguity toward challenging the sexism of black men, which potentially could make them appear disloyal. This early rift between white and black women would continue in later women's liberation struggles, such as the struggle for reproductive justice (Silliman, Fried, Ross, & Gutierrez, 2004).

The women's movement historically has utilized a range of tactics, including broad-based community education about women's issues, small group consciousness-raising efforts, protest, and policy advocacy. According to Berkeley (1999): "Almost from the beginning, the women who joined liberation groups could not agree on either the root cause of their oppression—capitalism or male supremacy—or on a single strategy for achieving liberation—direct action or consciousness-raising" (p. 44). One of the defining characteristics of the women's movement has been its ability to raise consciousness among women (Ferree & Hess, 2000). Unlike the early women's movement in the 19th century, which never generated a feminist consciousness or addressed the collective inferior status of women, the contemporary movement fostered a "radical awakening" (Reinelt, 1994, p. 3), a "conversion" experience (Davis, 2001), a sense of "we-ness" or what *Ms. Magazine* called a "click" experience (Ferree & Hess, 2000, p. 28). Robin Morgan, author of the 1972 classic *Sisterhood Is Powerful*, tapped into a wellspring of "five-thousand-year-buried anger" (Berkeley, 1999, p. 45). Some of her writing at the time had been described as the "shot heard round the Left" for its radical, feminist zeal (Berkeley, 1999, p. 45). Consciousness-raising groups of women who discussed their personal experiences with intimate-partner violence, rape, and body-image issues elevated these seemingly isolated experiences to a level of real social significance. These groups would come to embody a message that the "personal is political." The virtue of this process of gaining a collective identity was that, rather than beginning from a theoretical construct imposed by men or others with power, women began with their lived experience and then developed a framework for organizing that made sense to them.

Issues such as equal pay for equal work and other problems related to equal access to the political and economic system were important rallying points for women. But, equally important has been the struggle for the liberation of women's bodies, which has included organizing around sexual assault, domestic violence, sexual harassment, the portrayal of women as objects in the media, and reproductive health. In 1977, feminist and lesbian poet Adrienne Rich wrote:

> I know of no woman—virgin, mother, lesbian, married, celibate—whether she earns her keep as a housewife, a cocktail waitress, or a scanner of brain waves—for whom the body is not a fundamental problem: its clouded meanings, its fertility, its desire, its so-called frigidity, its bloody speech, its silences, its changes and mutilations, its rapes and ripenings. There is for the first time today a possibility of converting our physicality into both knowledge and power.... We need to imagine a world in which every woman is the presiding genius of her own body. In such a world, women will truly create life, bring forth not only children (if we choose) but the visions, and the thinking necessary to sustain, console, and alter human existence—a new relationship to the universe. Sexuality, politics, intelligence, power, motherhood, work, community, intimacy, will develop new meanings; thinking itself will be transformed. This is where we have to begin. (Cited in Zinn & Arnove, 2004, p. 446)

Women of color and poor women's contributions to the women's movement in the third wave have been somewhat different from that of white women. The hallmark of such activism "has not been their *articulated* gender or race or class analyses, but rather their activities growing out of their immediate needs" (Gluck, 1998, p. 33). Johnnie Tillmon, who would become a leader of the National Welfare Rights Organization (NWRO) in the 1960s, worked hard all her life but found herself going on welfare in order to take care of her youngest daughter. After overhearing negative comments about welfare mothers, she convened a meeting of other women in her public housing project. This grassroots community-based group would be a link in a chain of a poor women's movement that would result in the formation of NWRO. According to Gluck:

> The main issue for these women was survival. For many, their jobs did not pay enough to support their children. For others, like Tillmon, their children were beginning to get into trouble and needed more supervision. The women ... demanded attention, respect, and the full share of benefits to which they were entitled under various federal programs. (p. 38)

The NWRO organizing work focused on the patriarchal social welfare policy establishment and challenged definitions of gender roles. Organizing by women of color, like that of poor women, emerged out of necessity, but with the added component of drawing from their own cultural roots (Gluck, 1998). This organizing coincided with post-colonialist writing that facilitated the reclaiming of cultural identities for marginalized women across the world. The Asian American Political Alliance drew from works such as Morgan (1970), but also drew from the women involved in the revolutionary struggles in Vietnam and China. A Chicana feminist discussion group, called Hijas de Cuauhtemoc that formed in the late 1960s, discovered an underground newspaper that had been published by Mexican women during the 1910 revolution. One participant recalled:

> It was like I had been in a cave and someone has just lit the candle. I [suddenly] realized how important it was to read about your own kind, the women of your own culture, or your own historical heritage, doing the things that you were doing. [It] reaffirmed and validated that you're not a strange, alien person, that what you're doing is not only normal but a part of your history.... So then they become our models, our heroes. (Cited in Gluck, 1998, p. 39)

The complexities of racial and class difference across the movement cannot be understated. Chapter 10 will further clarify these issues of identity politics and solidarity issues.

LABOR MOVEMENTS

The earliest labor unions were trade unions modeled after the craft guilds of the European Middle Ages, exclusive organizations of individuals composed of skilled craftspeople. When the American Federation of Labor (AFL) was established, following the European model, it also focused on organizing skilled workers. These workers were mostly male and white (Zinn, 2003). Today, the ramifications of this legacy and its concomitant tensions reverberate within the leadership and rank and file of union organizers, as the need to organize women, people of color, and unskilled workers is pressing.

During the 1870s and 1880s, Chicago was a principal hub of labor activism and radical ideas. Making a claim that an eight-hour workday was a reasonable request, industrial factory workers struck on May 1, 1886. Lucy and Albert Parsons and other organizers led 80,000 workers up Michigan Avenue. On May 3, companies had locked out the workers and called in replacements; when a skirmish broke out, police fired shots and four workers were left dead. On May 4, a meeting was called in Haymarket Square to address the issues; the police arrived and apparently a bomb was thrown by an unknown attacker. The police responded the next day by rounding up leaders in the anarchist labor struggle, including Lucy and Albert Parsons and many of their associates; many of them were not at the event. Eight anarchists including Albert Parsons were sentenced, though Lucy Parsons was released; four of them were hung, not for the bombing but for their views on anarchism. Following the execution, Lucy Parsons, a woman who was born a slave and was an important labor organizer, courageously and persistently brought attention to the Haymarket events through her speaking engagements (http://www.lucyparsonsproject.org; Zinn, 2003). The Haymarket events were a significant moment in the effort to establish the eight-hour workday. International appeals for clemency for the Haymarket activists led to the establishment of May 1 as International Workers' Day.

The Industrial Workers of the World (IWW), also know as the Wobblies, was formed in 1905, a more radical organization than the AFL. They focused on organizing unskilled workers, women, and people of color. The IWW was influenced by socialist and anarchist ideals and the radical climate of the early 20th century. Their literature at the time stated:

> The working class and the employing class have nothing in common. There can be no peace so long as hunger and want are found among millions of the working people and the few, who make up the employing class, have all the good things of life.... By organizing industrially we are forming the structure of the new society within the shell of the old. (Zinn & Arnove, 2004, p. 257)

One of the founding members of the IWW was Mary Harris, also known as Mother Jones, an organizer for the United Mine Workers.

Governmental attempts to control labor activism have waxed and waned historically, sometimes allowing concessions and other times becoming more restrictive. The Wagner Act of 1935 set up the National Labor Relations Board and has been viewed as a social contract between the U.S. government and labor, allowing for the right to engage in collective bargaining and other workers' rights. However, the passage of the Taft-Hartley Act of 1947 limited the abilities of workers to strike. Various states have different laws and climates for union organizing. Many labor organizers today argue for the repeal of the Taft-Hartley Act. From an international perspective, there are also a wide range of labor organizing climates; developing countries that may have signed deals with corporations or international trade organizations sometimes limit the ability of workers to organize legally.

Labor organizers traditionally have engaged in a variety of tactics, including direct actions such as work slowdowns, boycotts, and strikes (economic actions); these strategies have been used more often than political or judicial processes. Piven and Cloward (1979) have noted that the electoral influence of unions has been limited, and that union strike power has been limited by political opportunity structures. Organizing has given workers higher pay, shorter hours, and the right to organize themselves, as well as job security (Piven & Cloward, 1979).

The United Farm Workers (UFW) were often successful using boycotts of California grapes in grocery stores as an organizing strategy. Latino and Filipino workers (drawing from their organizing work that eventually brought down Marcos in the Philippines) were the central players in the farm workers' movements. Cesar Chavez, a leader of the UFW, was one of the great union organizers, known for his charisma and persistence, inspiring workers with the chant, *"Si, se puede!"* or "Yes, we can!"

Piven and Cloward (1979) identify several barriers to union solidarity. First, the market conditions themselves are a factor in union solidarity. A strike would not be effective during a significant economic downturn, such as during the Great Depression. The economic instability of the Depression facilitated the uprising of industrial workers, giving them power; under more stable economic conditions, they would not have had the power that they did (Piven & Cloward, 1979). Second, there are often divisions in occupational status as well as divisions between races and ethnicities. Workers sometimes tend to fail to recognize what they have in common. Third, the lack of opportunity for advancement or to acquire land is a barrier, which has been something that has helped sustain hope for those left behind. Fourth, oligarchic organizations may tend to emphasize organizing skilled labor rather than unskilled labor. Also, there is often collusion with employers.

As the welfare state began to wane in the late 1970s and early 1980s in the United States, so did the U.S. labor movement (Scanlon, 1999). A new surge of union organizing activity appears to be on the rise, however, with organizing of service-sector employees at the forefront. An unprecedented globalizing and service-oriented economy has revealed new needs and opened the door for the use of new tactics in the labor movement. In recent years, the AFL-CIO has launched "corporate campaigns," the goal of which is to go beyond confronting a company at home (such as picketing a shareholders' meeting or a board member's house) but exposing them elsewhere (Featherstone, 2002). Today, AFSCME (American Federation of State, County and Municipal Employees) is the largest union for workers in the public service arena with 1.4 million members nationwide, including nurses, emergency medical technicians, bus drivers, child care providers, custodians, and librarians.

A recent outgrowth of the labor movement has been the living-wage movement. Living-wage ordinances have passed in 130 cities around the United States, and there are campaigns in the United Kingdom, Canada, Australia, and New Zealand (Luce, 2005). The relationship between labor organizing and living-wage organizing is somewhat complex, i.e., if workers can get higher wages through legislation, why would they struggle for a union? (Luce, 2005). However, there are many examples of successful efforts to link living-wage campaigns to unionization. For example, after a living-wage ordinance in Los Angeles passed, the Los Angeles Alliance for a New Economy and the living-wage coalition worked closely with unions to get food concession contracts awarded to employers at Los Angeles International Airport (LAX) that agreed not to stand in the way of union organizing, using anti-retaliation language in the living-wage ordinance that protects workers' rights to organize around living-wage issues. The Service Employees International Union (SEIU) reported that, after this effort, they moved from representing one in ten workers at LAX to representing more than half (Luce, 2005). Luce reviewed 10 years of living-wage campaigns and has offered lessons to union organizers based on the successes achieved by living-wage campaigns:

- Labor needs allies and a long-term approach.
- Labor needs a moral vision.
- Labor needs to be willing to break from mainstream parties.
- Labor needs to work from the inside and the outside.
- Labor can't avoid conflict.
- Labor must do a better job of involving their rank-and-file members.

LESBIAN, GAY, BISEXUAL, AND TRANSGENDER (LGBT) MOVEMENTS[1]

The Stonewall uprising was one of the most important moments in the struggle for gay rights. On June 27, 1969, police stormed a Greenwich Village bar in New York City called the Stonewall Inn. Working on the premise that the bar was serving alcohol without a license, the police tried to shut down the bar and arrest the patrons, who were gay. The supposed reason for the shutdown was serving alcohol without a license. However, the group of patrons fought back and helped propel a new phase of the struggle for gay liberation.

The Stonewall riots were an important part of the contemporary movement for gay and lesbian rights and are considered "one of the most important moments of resistance from the 1960s" (Zinn, 2003, p. 456). This particular event was also marked by the nuances of tactics employed, which included the use of violence on the part of gay and lesbian activists. Additionally, however, the group also utilized humor and the absurd to make their point. Historian Martin Duberman tells the story of the Stonewall riots.

> [The police found themselves] face to face with their worst nightmare: a chorus line of mocking queens, their arms clasped around each other, kicking their heels in the air Rockettes-style and singing at the tops of their sardonic voices: "We are the Stonewall girls, We wear our hair in curls.... We wear our dungarees, Above our nelly knees." It was a deliciously witty, contemptuous counterpoint to the [police]'s brute force, a tactic that transformed an otherwise traditionally macho eye-for-an-eye combat and that provided at least the glimpse of a different and revelatory kind of consciousness. (Zinn, 2003, p. 460)

Like many other social movements, a key part of the gay liberation movement has focused on civil rights and equality, and the removal of social stigma. The Lambda Legal Defense and Education Fund was formed in 1973 as the first public law organization to be created and operated by lesbian and gay individuals (Rimmerman, 2002). Focusing on pursuing greater equity for gay and lesbian people, they worked through a mainstream legal-rights strategy focusing on a diversity of issues, including marriage rights, job discrimination, child custody, and inheritance rights.

By the late 1970s, the emphasis of the gay rights movement was more on the celebration of the unique differences of gay and lesbian people (Young, 1990). "Gay pride asserts that sexual identity is a matter of culture and politics, and not merely 'behavior' to be tolerated or forbidden" (Young, 1990, p. 161). Other thinkers framed the problem of homophobia as a kind of sexism or gender bias (Pharr, 1988). Queer theorists argued that identity is much more fluid than fixed; this perspective would challenge an organizing strategy that was based so solidly on a notion of gay identity. During

---

[1] Some activists and scholars utilize the term LGBTQ, where "Q" refers to Queer/Questioning.

the 1990s, gay, lesbian, and bisexual organizers began to ally themselves with transgendered individuals, identifying the common interests that they had as people with sexual identities that differed from the heterosexual society in which they live.

LGBT activists have used a range of tactics, including those within the electoral and legal processes as well as those outside the conventional political process. College students have played an important part in the movement for gay liberation, as they have the freedom not to worry about ruined careers with which older activists would be concerned. In addition, because college students were often far away from home and families, they did not have to deal with the fallout of the disclosure of their orientation (Marcus, 2002).

During the 1980s and 1990s, AIDS activism was at the forefront of the gay rights movement. These activists pursued four main strategies: (a) publicizing the message that AIDS is not a gay disease, (b) heightening the visibility of the lesbian and gay movements through cultural outlets, (c) separating AIDS-specific reform from structural reform of the overall health-care system, and (d) direct action (Rimmerman, 2002). This last tactic would be actualized in the founding of the AIDS Coalition to Unleash Power (ACT UP), which emerged in 1987 in response to the lack of attention by the Reagan administration to the growing AIDS epidemic in the United States (Shepard, 2005). The emergence of ACT UP "represented the rebirth of one form of unconventional politics—one rooted in participatory democratic principles and dedicated to nonviolent civil disobedience" (Rimmerman, 2002, p. 96). Early marches in the late 1980s focused on a variety of targets, such as politicians and corporations. In New York, ACT UP held a march on Wall Street; this target was identified because the group came to understand that the business community had responsibilities because businesses were profiting on AIDS drugs and insurance companies were refusing to cover people (Marcus, 2002). Identifying issues to address could also be an internal struggle for some local ACT UP chapters. One organizer reported:

> There are those within ACT UP who don't think it's appropriate to do anything under the aegis of ACT UP that isn't directly and intimately connected with AIDS, the illness. My definition of things that are AIDS related is virtually everything, including racism, homophobia, sexism, and class issues. We are not going to solve the AIDS epidemic unless we deal with these issues, and vice versa. I think they're all interrelated. (Marcus, 2002, p. 320)

Contemporary organizing has focused more on mainstream channels including politics, courts, media, and the Internet (Marcus, 2002).

As with the women's movement, backlash against the LGBT movement has been significant. The Christian Right has been incredibly successful in their organizing strategies to achieve their goals. They have focused on bans on military services, battles over school curriculums, same-sex marriage issues, and attempts to "cure" gay and lesbians with therapy. From the perspective of resource mobilization theory, the resources internal to the Christian Right have contributed to their effectiveness. These resources include leadership, organizational capacity, and wealth (Rimmerman, 2002). In addition, the perception of political opportunity on the part of the Christian Right has helped them advance their agenda over the LGBT movement. These opportunities include "changes in who occupies the White House, who controls Congress, and the political, cultural, and social milieu" (Rimmerman, 2002, p. 124). Drawing from the values of the Bible and traditional approaches to gender relations, the Christian Right employed the framing message in their actions that "Adam and Eve, not Adam and Steve" should be the norm (Rimmerman, 2002, p. 150).

DISABILITY RIGHTS MOVEMENTS

As recently as 1979, it was legal for some state governments to practice enforced sterilization of people with disabilities. Discrimination against people with disabilities occurred in employment, housing, and other public accommodations (DiCunio, 2004). These discriminatory practices also prevented children with disabilities from full engagement in public schools. In 1978, 45 people in wheelchairs surrounded city buses in Denver, Colorado, to protest the lack of accessible transportation in the city (Blank & Terkel, 1997). This action brought the traffic at a busy intersection to a halt; 19 people occupied the buses throughout the night. These activists, known as ADAPT (originally standing for American Disabled for Accessible Public Transportation), were pioneers in such organizing and have continued to be leaders in the disability rights movement. ADAPT eventually took on the American Public Transportation Authority, a lobbying group for public transit systems.

The tactical strategies of the disability rights movement have been to confront targets face to face, mobilizing the people who have the most stake in the issues to engage in nonviolent direct action. Justin Dart, one of the most prominent disability rights organizers in history, was influenced by writings on nonviolent direct action and has been labeled the Martin Luther King, Jr., of the disability rights movement (Barnartt & Scotch, 2001). In addition, the ability of disability activists to organize their own constituents, i.e., people with disabilities, and nurture their leadership capacities has been an innovative and sustainable practice that has inspired a wide range of organizers, both inside and outside the disability rights setting. The development of the idea of "self-advocacy" has been a defining feature of the disability rights movement. Because of the stigma and presumed lower competence of people with disabilities, self-advocacy is a radical concept that affirms the rights of people to speak on their own behalves and to make their needs known (Stroman, 2003).

Like other movements, the promotion of group identity and consciousness has been an important strategy for the disability rights movement. The growing belief in disability culture emphasizes that disability is not just a physical aspect of a person, but a cultural aspect as well. "Disability culture includes the rejection of some personality characteristics (passivity, dependence) in favor of others (assertiveness, control) as well as disability art and theater, which celebrate disability pride" (Barnartt & Scotch, 2001, p. 48). This idea of disability culture has served to unify people with disabilities and recruit new members into the movement (Barnartt & Scotch, 2001).

The disability rights movement also includes the mental health consumer movement, which began in 1970 growing out of the movements of the 1960s such as civil rights, gay, and feminist movements. The mental health consumer movement began as resistance to such issues as involuntary hospitalization, electroshock treatment, and forced medication (Cohen, 2004). It was and has been an attempt to reject the subjugated role of the mental patient (Foucault, 1973).

The mental health consumer movement has attended to various issues of tremendous relevance to community organizing, including the political nature of language used within the movement, consciousness-raising, accountability to constituencies, organizational administration, and cross-collaboration with other movements (Chamberlin, 1978; Cohen, 2004). Chamberlin, a former mental patient and author of the seminal book *On Our Own*, identifies the multiple ways that "mental patients" come to understand their common situation. She writes:

> Consciousness raising is an ongoing process. Negative stereotypes of the "mentally ill" are everywhere and are difficult not to internalize, no matter how sensitive one becomes.... Like sexism, mentalism is built into the language—*sick* and *crazy* are widely used.... The struggle against mentalism is one of the long-range activities of mental patients' liberation. (p. 66)

These constituents have recognized their rights and conceptualized alternatives to hospitalization and the oppression that they believe psychiatry perpetuates. Chamberlin (1978) continues by talking about the common problems experienced in institutions:

> Having experienced the dehumanizing effects of mental institutions, we saw that large facilities with rigid hierarchies could never be the kind of places we had in mind. It quickly became clear that there was no way to fix up the current mental hospital system. What was needed was an entirely new model. People who had been in places with carpets on the floors told the same stories of indifference and cruelty as those who had been in dingy, barren state hospitals. (p. 67)

Groups such as the Mental Patients' Liberation Front emerged in 1971 during this time of heightened consciousness among mental health consumers. One of the first projects of the Mental Patients' Liberation Front was to publish a 56-page pamphlet entitled "Your Rights as a Mental Patient" (Stroman, 2003). In addition, the group filed a landmark lawsuit against Boston State Hospital that would alter significantly the rights of mental patients. The case of *Rogers v. Okrin* resulted in a court ruling that the mental hospital could not continue its practice of secluding patients and drugging them against their will (Stroman, 2003).

Today, the Freedom Center in Northampton, Massachusetts, is run by and for psychiatric survivors and "people who experience extreme emotional states." Their vision is to: "Create voluntary mutual aid networks of caring support among equals, based on safety, listening to our experiences without judgment, and helping empower ourselves for change" (http://www.freedom-center.org). This group has implicated the pharmaceutical industry in their framing of the social issue, arguing that they push drugs on children, adolescents, and adults. In addition, they demand that the professional mental health community:

> Stop imposing degrading, scientifically-unsound diagnosis labels on people. Labeling people with "disorders" spreads lifelong hopelessness and removes attention from trauma, poverty, nutrition, and oppression. Allow us instead to define our experiences for ourselves in ways that work for us.

Arguing for the use of the term *diverse ability* rather than disability, the group operates from a strengths perspective (Saleebey, 1997). In addition, they make connections between mentalism and other "isms" such as racism, sexism, classism, and homophobia.

With an emphasis on strengthening communities, The Freedom Center works to promote low-income access to alternatives such as holistic health, peer-run services, safe houses, nutrition, exercise, housing, income, the natural world, and voluntary individual and family therapy. Their demands to the existing mental health system are to:

> Oppose all force and coercion in mental health: end restraints, seclusion, forced drugging and involuntary commitment. Care must do no harm: replace force with effective alternatives, and respond to crisis without further traumatizing people. Services and housing should never be tied to treatment compliance. (http://www.freedom-center.org)

The Freedom Center underscores the development of alliances across issues and works to educate the public, professionals, and family members about people coping with mental health issues.

For the entire disability rights movement—which encompasses physical and mental disabilities—deinstitutionalization, civil rights, and self-determination have been central frames or rallying points (Stroman, 2003). The movement to deinstitutionalize mental health treatment reached its height in the 1960s, when there were favorable political opportunity structures in place such as the leadership of President John F. Kennedy, which resulted in the passage of the Community Mental Health Centers Act in 1963. This act deinstitutionalized mental health treatment and emphasized social integration and community-based approaches to mental health care.

The passage of the Americans with Disabilities Act (ADA) in 1990 was a major victory for a diverse coalition of organizers, including Paralyzed Veterans of America, United Cerebral Palsy Associations, Disability Rights Education and Defense Fund, Association for Retarded Citizens, and others (Barnartt & Scotch, 2001). Extending the frame of civil rights to persons with disabilities, the ADA attempts to ensure access for persons with physical and mental impairments in the areas of employment, public accommodations, and transportation by mandating nondiscrimination in those sectors.

The idea of "independent living" extends the frame of self-determination and emerges from the context of institutionalized living, a situation whereby people are "told what to do and when, where, and with whom to do it" (Barnartt & Scotch, 2001, p. 42). Independent-living advocates argue that society should help make it possible for people with disabilities to be able to live independently in a community, in a residence, and with people of their own choosing (Barnartt & Scotch, 2001). Demands for independent living were met with the passage of the Rehabilitation Act of 1973, which provided funding for independent living centers.

REFLECTIONS ON SOCIAL MOVEMENTS

There are many lessons to be learned as progressive community organizers reflect on the historical and practical aspects of social movements. These movements have manifested the notion of empowerment through sophisticated and complex organizing campaigns of broad-based coalitions as well as acts of resistance by small groups of individuals. The actors in these movements have engaged in astute analyses that inform their framing of social issues. They deconstruct narratives that perpetuate oppression and further inquire into the circumstances of people's lives, uncovering the winners and losers of specific social arrangements. The movements have not been without strife, as they have had internal struggles about issue identification and public struggles around identity politics and coalition building. A hallmark of these movements has been their tactical diversity, where organizers have engaged in an array of settings, including political, cultural, legal, and corporate.

It should also be clear that these movements are not isolated from each other. Indeed, many civil rights organizers were inspired by organizers from the Progressive Era, feminist organizers surfaced from the civil rights movement, gay and lesbian activists often simultaneously operated in the women's movement, and disability rights activists had been part of the civil rights movement. This situation is not a coincidence, for it seems clear that many of these issues are interconnected. In addition, many social movements have always had global and transnational components to them—women's groups grappling with their diverse ethnic identities and a labor movement that attempts to build bridges across the boundaries of nations.

The modern civil rights movement in the United States began in the 1950s as a response to Jim Crow laws that were the legacy of the enslavement of Africans. Though the due process guarantees and the voting rights protections of the Fourteenth and Fifteenth Amendments existed on paper, the apartheid system of segregation was clearly still in place in the South and in some parts of the North (Markowitz, 2004). Building on the efforts and legacies of the previous 100 years of abolitionist and other civil rights struggles for African-Americans, the years between 1954 and 1970 arguably represent the greatest legacy of community organizing in the United States to this day. Thus, the decade of the '60s is often heralded as a kind of golden age of organizing. Katsiaficas (2004) offers some words of caution about such attributions:

> Glorification of decades (or of great events and individuals) diminishes the importance of continuity and everyday activism in the life of social movements. As a social construction, the myth of the sixties functions thereby to discourage people from having authentic movement experiences now, in the present. (p. 9)

To learn from and be inspired by past social movements are vital steps of an organizer's journey. While all organizers stand on the shoulders of giants, excessively fervent attachments to the past can leave organizers confused, disappointed, and/or paralyzed. It is more realistic and efficacious for organizers to attend to current social, cultural, political, and organizational conditions in any given moment. Recognizing that organizing practice can be "characterized by creative and spontaneous reflexivity, as well as moment-to-moment decision making in continuous relation to the social context" (Walter, 2003, p. 320), organizers are better prepared to act in the fluid, socially constructed environments in which they operate.

QUESTIONS FOR REFLECTION

1. What are some lessons learned from past and current social movements for the contemporary community organizer?
2. Discuss the synergies and intersections of various social movements. Why are such intersections important for social change?
3. Discuss some contemporary strategies for promoting workers' rights.
4. The consumer mental health movement is often at odds with traditional, professionalized mental health practices. What are some ways to bridge these differences and find common ground?
5. Discuss your understanding of the legacy of the 1960s in terms of organizing. In what ways is this legacy helpful or a barrier to contemporary organizers?

SUGGESTIONS FOR FURTHER INQUIRY

BOOKS

Chamberlin, J. (1978). *On our own: Patient-controlled alternatives to the mental health system*. New York: Hawthorn Books.
Green, J. (2000). *Taking history to heart: The power of the past in building social movements*. Amherst: University of Massachusetts Press.
Nash, J. (Ed.). (2005). *Social movements: An anthropological reader*. Malden, MA: Blackwell Publishing.
Payne, C. M. (1995). *I've got the light of freedom: The organizing tradition and the Mississippi freedom struggle*. Berkeley: University of California Press.
Zinn, H. (2003). *A people's history of the United States*. New York: Harper Collins.

WEB

Coalition of Immokalee Workers. http://www.ciw-online.org
Critical Resistance. http://www.criticalresistance.org
Disability Rights and Independent Living Movement. http://bancroft.berkeley.edu/collections/drilm/introduction.html
Modern Social Movements. http://www.fordham.edu/halsall/mod/modsbook56.html
UNITE HERE. http://www.unitehere.org

KEY TERMS

Collective action frames: Offer strategic interpretations of issues with the goal of organizing people to act. Such frames identify an aggrieved group ("we"), places blame ("them"), and encourages the "we" to effect change.

Independent living movement: Emphasizes the empowerment of people with disabilities in response to medical model approaches to disability. Because people with disabilities are the best experts on their needs, proponents argue that they must organize themselves for political power.

New Left: Sociologist C. Wright Mills used this term to describe progressive social movement actors in the 1960s who were going beyond the labor issue focus of the Old Left and focusing on countercultural movement activities. New Left groups such as Students for a Democratic Society emphasized antiwar and civil rights organizing.

Political opportunities: External structural factors that impact the outcomes of social movements, including channels of access to political decision making, the availability of political allies, stability of political institutions, and divisions among political elites.

Resource mobilization: Social movement approach that emphasizes the internal resources available to a social movement organization as the determinant of success.

5 Critical Organizing Frameworks

> The men who pile up the heaps of discussion and literature on the ethics of means and ends ... rarely write about their own experiences in the perpetual struggle of life and change. They are strangers, moreover, to the burdens and problems of operational responsibility and the unceasing pressure for immediate decisions.
>
> **Saul David Alinsky (1971, p. 25)**

APPROACHES TO COMMUNITY ORGANIZING

Before turning to a discussion of frameworks to guide community organizing practice, it is necessary to clarify further some ideas about what types of activities community organizing encompasses, a discussion that began in Chapter 1. Many scholars, particularly in the fields of social work, political science, and urban planning, have attempted to make sense of and typologize community organizing practices (Fisher, 1994; Mondros & Wilson, 1994; Ross, 1967; Rothman, Erlich, & Tropman, 2001). Such categorizing can be very useful for explaining the orientation, context, and activities of disparate approaches to community organizing practice. The categories have been referred to in the literature as community organizing "approaches," "modes," "styles," "models," and "methods" (Mondros & Wilson, 1994; Rothman, 2001). In this section, I will identify and discuss the three modes identified by Rothman (2001), the three models identified by Mondros and Wilson (1994), and the three approaches to neighborhood organizing articulated by Fisher (1994). Because these scholars are categorizing the same phenomena, it will be clear that these categories overlap with each other.

ROTHMAN'S MODES

One of the most commonly cited conceptualizations of organizing types was put forward (and later updated) by Jack Rothman (2001), who articulated three modes of intervention that are widespread in community settings: (a) locality development, (b) social planning/policy, and (c) social action. First, locality development, also referred to as community development, has the goal of enhancing community well-being. This activity places special emphasis on developing the capacities of communities to address problems, enhance local leadership, and promote social integration. An example of this would be a Puerto Rican neighborhood in Chicago that has worked to revitalize the Division Street corridor, Paseo Boricua. Led by groups such as the Division Street Business Development Corporation and the Puerto Rican Cultural Center, the neighborhood has focused on after-school cultural programs, the development of locally owned businesses, and progressive educational opportunities. Second, social policy/planning is a technical process for addressing social welfare issues through public policies and programs. This mode tends to utilize empirical social science methods to determine population needs and program efficacy. An example would be a child welfare advocacy organization (ideally, one that is parent driven) that seeks to effect change in the child welfare policy arena, such as foster care, family preservation, or adoption. Third, social action is concerned with the redistribution of power and gaining access to resources for marginalized groups. A gay and lesbian activist group that coordinates a campaign to pass a city human rights ordinance that would protect gay and lesbian citizens from discrimination in housing, employment, and other venues is an example of social action organizing. These modes, Rothman argues, are interwoven, and some organizations or coalitions engage in more than one mode. All of Rothman's modes of intervention are relevant to the project of progressive community organizing, as I articulate in this book.

MONDROS AND WILSON'S MODELS

Another way of thinking about community organizing practice has been highlighted by Mondros and Wilson (1994), who identified three models of social action organizations, i.e., groups that seek to accumulate and wield power. These models are (a) grassroots, (b) lobbying, and (c) mobilizing.

The grassroots or populist model emphasizes the differences between people with privilege and those who are marginalized. The goal of this model is for regular citizens to work together to organize themselves into a powerful group with the intention of targeting power holders, i.e., public or private figures with authority who tend to be resistant to change. The success of these groups depends on high levels of leadership and participation from constituencies. The community-based organizing of Saul Alinsky is a prime example of this approach, which will be discussed in more depth in this chapter.

The lobbying model is based on a pluralist pressure change orientation. The government and the legal system are the mechanisms for change; political actors are seen as open to change. These groups tend to have more staff and focus on instrumental objectives over empowerment and have less participation of the poor and marginalized. This group would be considered similar to Rothman's social policy/planning mode.

The mobilizing model is also referred to as the movement approach, an approach which was emphasized in the previous chapter on social movements. Here, the government is viewed as resistant to change, and participants tend to be political activists. Richard Cloward and Frances Fox Piven's work at Mobilization for Youth on New York City's Lower East Side in the 1960s utilized the tactic of disruptive protest, such as rent strikes and "flooding the rolls" for welfare transformation. They argued that low-income groups can win victories, not when they form organizations, but when they use disruptive protest. They disagreed with Alinsky's approach that victories come from building powerful organizations; they emphasized the power of disruptive tactics. These tactics included "incendiarism, riots, and strikes waves, sit-ins and other forms of civil disobedience, great surges in claims for relief benefits, rent strikes, sabotaging the workplace, such as disabling mining machinery or assembly lines" (Cloward & Piven, 1999, p. 171).

As with Rothman's types, the three models identified by Mondros and Wilson (1994) are all relevant to progressive community organizing practice.

FISHER'S NEIGHBORHOOD ORGANIZING APPROACHES

Fisher (1994) has distinguished three approaches to neighborhood organizing: (a) social welfare, (b) political activist, and (c) neighborhood maintenance. The social welfare (or social work) approach tends to focus on increasing access to social services through coalition building and lobbying. The organizer tends to function as an "advocate," and the overall practice generally maintains current social arrangements. This approach shares commonalities with Rothman's social policy/planning model and Mondros and Wilson's lobbying model. According to Fisher:

> At their best, social welfare projects coordinate and deliver needed social services to the poor and working class and complement services with social action. At their worst, they are elitist and manipulative, seeking to maintain existing class arrangements by palliating social problems and co-opting social disorder.... But in general the reformist vision, liberal objectives, consensus strategies, scanty resources and power, and professional orientation characteristic of the social welfare approach militate against developing democratic grassroots projects that, by altering class and power arrangements in their favor, could truly serve the interests and needs of neighborhood residents. (p. 211)

The political-activist approach focuses on obtaining and restructuring power. This may be achieved through empowering working-class and low-income citizens to confront power. The development of alternative institutions as a social change strategy can be a key component of the political activist approach.

Neighborhood maintenance tends to be carried out by middle- and upper-class individuals with the goal of maintaining the neighborhood status quo and property values. The residents of middle-class neighborhood associations in post-Katrina New Orleans, whose organizing activities have focused on returning their neighborhoods to pre-Katrina status, are a good example of this approach. These groups worked to restore historic homes and advocate for neighborhood infrastructure such as utilities and road repair. Though the neighborhood-maintenance approach is less relevant to this text's concern with marginalized communities, progressive community organizers draw from both social work and political activist approaches.

As one can see, there are many ways to characterize and categorize community organizing practice. In fact, the reader may be finding him- or herself more confused than ever! Some typologies may be more useful than others, in terms of helping people understand the range of activities in which organizers tend to engage. This book is less concerned with discriminating about how to typologize the activities of organizers. Instead, I focus on some influential organizing frameworks, all of which can be useful to a person's burgeoning organizing practice.

PROGRESSIVE ORGANIZING FRAMEWORKS: A SPECTRUM

The penetrating words of organizer Saul Alinsky at the beginning of this chapter express the long-standing dilemmas of community organizers. While organizers may hold strong values and be interested in attending to the means or processes of organizing, in reality they find themselves working in a practical world where achieving concrete, measurable outcomes in real time for communities is necessary. Alinsky, as will be discussed later in this chapter, preferred focusing on achieving practical victories in his work and concentrated less on clarifying values and engaging in consciousness-raising efforts, approaches that are favored by some organizers. He did not take lightly, however, the ubiquitous tension between the two. This conflict is just one dimension of the array of issues with which community organizing frameworks are concerned and is a mark of what differentiates various approaches to organizing.

In this chapter, I present progressive organizing frameworks in some detail. I believe that most organizing frameworks rest in the tension discussed here, namely, a tension between utilitarian approaches and transformative approaches (see Figure 5.1). Another way of thinking about this spectrum is to consider organizing as ends-oriented and means-oriented. Movements, organizations, and campaigns that seek to transform the conditions that perpetuate a problem lie on the means-oriented or transformative side of the spectrum. These groups attend to the way power negatively impacts people in their communities and seek to transform such power structures not just in the larger community and social systems, but within their own organizations, and even within themselves. Groups that focus on achieving victories or gaining incremental changes tend to fall into the utilitarian or ends-oriented category. The utilitarian groups are concerned with inequality and the differences between those with power and those without it in society; however, their work does not necessarily attempt to change the fundamental nature of society. Some organizations may engage work from both frameworks.

A sexual assault organization that actively seeks to address the interlocking oppressions that perpetuate sexual assault (transformative) may also focus on changing rape laws or getting public funding for better services for assault victims in their communities (utilitarian). The former activities may include educational programs about sexism, racism, and homophobia; a mandate that the board of directors consist of a majority of people of color, low-income, and sexual assault survivors; and staff/volunteer meetings that include time for personal reflection and group process. Of course, any critically minded organizer should actually be wary of the presentation of dichotomies that are

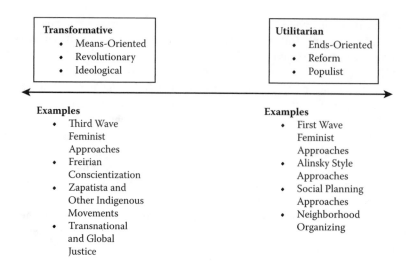

FIGURE 5.1   A Progressive Organizing Spectrum

presented as either–or. In logic, this is known as the fallacy of the false dilemma, and it would be appropriate to ask whether there might be a third choice or to question whether these practices are really so discrete. These are the right questions, and I merely submit that this is the most distinctive difference among frameworks. I propose this divide as a heuristic device for thinking about organizing frameworks on a spectrum.

Community organizers, just like therapists, urban planners, and other practitioners, may approach their work from multiple paradigms or frameworks. Though many organizers and organizations may have a primary method or framework that guides their work, many may also draw from multiple approaches, depending on the circumstances. While one may argue that this is problematic or is representative of a schizophrenic approach, it seems that a blended approach to organizing is that of an astute practitioner, one who privileges evidence in a particular context over a blanket ideology that is applied in all situations at all times. In the following sections, I present two major frameworks that I believe represent the most prominent approaches to doing community organizing work—the Alinsky tradition and the consciousness-raising tradition. These traditions are not intended to be exhaustive, nor are they completely discrete from each other. I think all of them have the potential to inform a critical progressive community organizing practice.

As one reflects on the frameworks highlighted in this chapter, it might be useful to consider the following questions as a guide to one's deliberations. One might want to ask which approaches:

- Facilitate sustained engagement over time?
- Engender empowerment among constituents?
- Result in real improvement in people's lives?
- Foster changes to oppressive cultural and institutional practices?
- Would be useful in cross-cultural and transnational settings?
- Would be personally gratifying in which to operate?

These questions reflect many of the principles and central concerns of this book, including issues of empowerment, sustainability, social change, liberation and oppression, globalization, and self-awareness.

THE ALINSKY TRADITION

Saul Alinsky (1909–1972) was born to immigrant Jewish parents in a Chicago ghetto. After studying archaeology and sociology at the University of Chicago, he began his graduate studies in criminology doing engaged field research on organized crime. For several years, he worked as a criminologist, studying poverty and crime; his field methods entailed working from the inside by building relationships and getting to know people in the neighborhood. One day his boss, the University of Chicago sociologist Clifford Shaw, sent him to a West Side neighborhood called the Back of the Yards. This neighborhood was "a foul-smelling, crime-ridden slum, downwind of Chicago's Union Stockyards" (Finks, 1984, p. 13). The Back of the Yards was an area of Chicago that had been the inspiration for Upton Sinclair's novel *The Jungle* (1906), where working conditions at the meatpacking plants were depicted in all their horror—long hours, dangerous working environment, and unhealthy living conditions. Shaw's instructions to Alinsky were to get to know the neighborhood by searching out the local leaders and, in partnership with them, to organize a community program to combat juvenile delinquency. Unlike Jane Addams's work at nearby Hull House, the virtue of this program in Alinsky's eyes was that it would be run by the people in the neighborhood rather than outsiders.

Fortunate timing for Alinsky, union organizer John L. Lewis, the president of the Council of Industrial Organizations (CIO), had sent a team to organize the workers in Chicago's meatpacking industry (Finks, 1984). These organizers:

> entered into the lives of the stockyard workers. For these professionals, organizing was a full time job. It involved agitation—convincing people that their problems were not unique, but connected with the problems of poor, exploited people everywhere. They preached unity, solidarity, action, and reform. (Finks, 1984, p. 15)

Alinsky was particularly impressed with the fact that these organizers were interested not just in studying poverty, but in organizing people to change the conditions which kept them in poverty. He also noticed that the union organizers were attuned to issues beyond the packinghouse union, making connections to other social and political issues of the time—blacks in the South, the Dust Bowl migrants, the Spanish Civil War, government relief programs, and rent strikes.

In 1938, Alinsky, rather than build a program to combat juvenile delinquency as he was instructed, organized the Back of the Yards Neighborhood Council (BYNC). BYNC brought together the entire community, including the United Packinghouse Workers Union as well as most of the Roman Catholic parishes in the Back of the Yards neighborhood. Building a powerful coalition that included unions, church leadership, and local citizens was a significant innovation of Alinsky's. Finks (1984) describes the role that Alinsky came to play in the BYNC:

> Behind the scenes Alinsky worked hard to keep the council moving ahead. Like a shrewd fight manager, he arranged ever tougher bouts for the organization. After every action Alinsky made the leaders take the time to talk about what had happened. They dissected, analyzed, and criticized each event until they understood the reasons why they won or lost. Each victory was celebrated with speeches and impromptu parties. People began to notice that after every successful battle, more residents joined the Back of the Yards Council. (p. 21)

The group would go on to win victories in the areas of child welfare, public school improvement, and neighborhood stabilization.

Alinsky's successes in the BYNC would eventually call him to other parts of the country as an itinerant organizer. This led to the founding of the Industrial Areas Foundation (IAF), which could financially support Alinsky's services to other communities, particularly ones where CIO unions were forming, drawing on his previous techniques of bringing the community, churches, and union together into a solid community voice. Because of the growing demand for his organizing services across the country, Alinsky would train other organizers, including Fred Ross and Ed Chambers, to carry on the techniques he had been developing.

In his books *Reveille for Radicals*, published in 1946, and *Rules for Radicals*, Alinsky (1971) called for people in urban areas to engage fully in the democratic process. An early adherent of what would now be called a civil society perspective, Alinsky's populist approach was that democracy implied the formation of voluntary organizations, neighborhood-led governing, as well as citizen protest when necessary. "Alinsky considered the political system, despite its corruption and bias toward the rich, to be open to change if people could organize to demand inclusion" (Warren, 2001, p. 45). A true believer in American democracy, his heroes were Thomas Jefferson, James Madison, and Alexis de Tocqueville (Finks, 1984).

Alinsky's approach to organizing emphasized conflict-oriented, direct action techniques. These confrontational tactics were based on his power analysis of social structures. Though not an adherent of Marxism nor an advocate for the overturning of democratic capitalism, Alinsky identified the "haves" and the "have nots" in society as being by their very nature in conflict. To achieve change, he argued, it is necessary for oppressed groups to pressure those with power by creating demands or engaging in other confrontational tactics. Alinsky engaged in boycotts of stores, strikes against meat packers, rent strikes against slumlords, picketing of business, and sit-downs at city hall. Many of these actions were rooted in the labor movement of the 1930s and the techniques of his mentor John L. Lewis. Alinsky believed in polarizing issues and personalizing the enemy. He sought to take back power, i.e., to "wrest power from elite groups and redistribute it to their constituency" (Betten & Austin, 1990, p. 152).

Alinsky believed that the purpose of organizing was to win a victory; this may entail the use of creative, irreverent, or dramatic tactics (Boyte, 1984). His approach to direct action was to catch the "enemy" by surprise, to "hit them outside the usual realm of experience" (Betten & Austin, 1990, p. 158). This could involve embarrassing public officials and engaging in public displays. His groups would also try and get public officials to attend their meetings and commit to promises such as funding for a new low-income housing development or other programs. In the early 1960s, things were changing in the United States regarding race relations. Woodlawn was an all-black South Side Chicago neighborhood and would be "the first attempt by Alinsky—or anyone—to organize an entire black urban community" (Finks, 1984, p. 136). In Woodlawn, they used creative tactics, such as confronting the board of education by holding a "death watch," where mothers dressed in black to mourn their "educationally dying children" (Finks, 1984, p. 151).

In 1966, Chambers and Alinsky had been working in Rochester, New York, to assist a local organizing group called FIGHT. In one of the most prominent struggles of Alinsky's career, FIGHT sought to hold the Eastman Kodak company accountable for providing jobs to low-income and African-American community members. The company made a promise that it would create new jobs; however, within a day of making the announcement, the company had reneged on this promise. Members of FIGHT, with the help of Alinsky, decided to confront the shareholders of Eastman Kodak on this issue. FIGHT cleverly bought a few shares in the company in order to be able to attend the shareholders meeting. They confronted the shareholders in their meeting and made their demand—they gave the shareholders one hour to decide whether or not they were going to honor their agreement. The group marched out of the facility and returned in one hour, and when the shareholders said that they would not honor the agreement, the group said, "Then, it's going to be a long, hot summer!" Not backing down or giving up, the organizers protested and pressured throughout the summer and eventually won their victory—much-needed jobs for community members.

Alinsky engaged in a wide range of organizing campaigns across the United States. He was hired by organizations to help strategize tactics. He believed in the idea that one should "organize himself out of a job," recognizing that indigenous leadership will always appreciate the community the most and that it is the best way to sustain organizing efforts over time. While the skills of trained, professional organizers are sometimes needed, it is the job of the organizer to pass on those skills and be a mentor to future organizers. Having a strong understanding of empowerment, Alinsky engaged in the practice of identifying leaders and nurturing organizing skills as the path to organize oneself out of a job. He criticized do-gooders and charities and believed that one should never do things for people that they can do for themselves.

THE ALINSKY LEGACY

The new populism of the 1970s, emerging out of an economic recession and the beginnings of government social welfare retrenchment, resulted in high levels of participation in neighborhood groups across the country. While the organizing of the 1960s tended to be more ideologically focused, the populist approach emphasized what Alinsky had been focusing on all along—practical, down-to-earth organizing rooted in the community traditions of working-class people (Fisher, 1994). This approach

> rejected the emphasis on anticapitalist political ideology, the focus on "consciousness raising," the sectarianism, the single-minded attention to a particular constituency—whether African-Americans or students—all of which, new populists contended, isolated late 1960s organizers from working people and prevented the development of effective grassroots neighborhood organizations. (Fisher, 1994, p. 140)

Alinsky's legacy of organizing methods was a perfect match for this new wave of populist neighborhood-based organizing. Successful organizing groups such as the Association of Community Organizations for Reform Now (ACORN) and the National Welfare Rights Organization (NWRO) had its roots in the organizing strategies of Alinsky (Fisher, 1994).

Communities Organized for Public Service (COPS) was also founded in the Alinsky tradition, specifically by Ernesto Cortes, Jr., who was trained under the IAF in the early '70s (Warren, 2001). COPS organized a potentially powerful group of Latino citizens in San Antonio, Texas, who represented a majority of the population in the city but had little political power. Drawing from Alinsky's strategy that entailed engaging local churches, Cortes would follow suit, but with some unique innovations. Cortes came to see leadership differently and believed that leaders were not necessarily people who held important positions or who had good public speaking skills; leaders were people who had social networks (Warren, 2001). These leaders tended to be women who were already engaged in parish councils, fundraising committees, and PTAs. Alinsky tended to emphasize a utilitarian approach to organizing people around an issue, but Cortes began to bring people together based on their common values, including religious values and the identification of community needs. Developing a practice that COPS and IAF would call "relational organizing," Cortes facilitated community leaders coming together to talk about community needs and then identify issues around which to act (Warren, 2001). Whereas Alinsky's approach emphasized organizing male position holders in the community who determined up front what issues to mobilize around, Cortes's plans "emerged out of conversations at the bottom, rather than issues identified by activists at the top" (Warren, 2001, p. 51).

COPS has achieved and continues to achieve many victories. One of their early victories was a critical intervention in the Community Development Block Grant (CDBG) program in San Antonio (Warren, 2001). They advocated for CDBG funds to go to long-neglected projects in their constituent neighborhoods. Engaging in planning, research, and mobilization at public hearings, they were able to have great influence over the council's allocations. From 1974 to 1993, 69.9% of CDBG went to council districts where COPS was instrumental in organizing (Warren, 2001).

Overall, COPS was building a vision of what community could be like. Boyte (1984, p. 133) points out that Alinsky had failed to offer a vision of what communities were really working for:

> Much of the organizing that claimed his legacy gained a reputation for the narrowest of concerns and vision. "Organizing for power" was often described as the end in itself with little or no reflection about how power was to be wielded, or for what purposes.

While Alinsky believed that people organized primarily out of self-interest, Cortes believed that a common love of family, faith, and culture could bring people together.

The heritage of Alinsky cannot be underestimated; many organizers today can trace their organizing lineage back to Alinsky. Training in the art of organizing has been a way to pass down his tactics and the innovations that have developed along the way. In this book, I identify his approach as utilitarian because it focuses on winning campaigns, generally embracing the idea that "the ends justify the means." Building community power and confronting power holders to achieve incremental gains in the community are the hallmarks of the original Alinsky tradition.

TRANSFORMATIVE APPROACHES

In this section, I turn now to some approaches to organizing that fit into the "transformative" end of the organizing framework spectrum. These approaches are grounded in the belief that societal change necessarily entails a change in individual consciousness. These consciousness-raising approaches—Myles Horton and the Highlander Center as well as Paulo Freire's problematizing educational methods—emphasize popular education methods of adult learners as the groundwork and necessary condition for effecting change.

MYLES HORTON AND THE HIGHLANDER CENTER

Myles Horton (1905–1990), an educator and organizer, founded the Highlander Folk School in eastern Tennessee in 1932. He developed and engaged in popular adult education techniques using ideas from Danish folk schools that he had visited. Highlander served as a support organization to many organizers over the years, providing a space to engage in critical thinking about important social change issues. Since those early days, the Highlander Folk School has trained labor organizers from the CIO, civil rights organizers such as Rosa Parks, and contemporary environmental organizers working against mountaintop removal.

Horton learned that traditional teaching methods influenced by the formal school systems did not work with rural workers and others living in poverty. The teaching at Highlander would be guided by the problems brought forth by the students and included learning experiences that utilized improvisational drama, songwriting, and singing (Peters & Bell, 1989). Horton and his cohorts came to believe in the axiom that the people themselves are the authorities on their experiences and thus on their own learning needs and educational agendas. Critical of top-down educational approaches and decision making about what is taught, Horton was interested in education for social change. A reflection of his commitment to democracy in all forms of human endeavors, he advocated that education be grounded in the learner's experiences and included the use of questions to stimulate self-examination as well as an examination of social systems. According to Peters and Bell (1989):

> Horton's belief in the imperative of control over their lives [adult learners] and the means of production parallels his belief in control over a learning activity by a circle of learners whose experiences and problems are being discussed. He argues equally convincingly that laborers need to develop confidence in their ability to direct change in their working conditions and to learn from their own experiences. Dependency on authority is believed by Horton to be antithetical to freedom of thought and expression, whether it is in labor–management relations or in the relationship between student and teacher. Horton's approach to education is a restructuring process that places more control and responsibility in the hands of the learner, not only for the purpose of democratizing the experience, but also as intended practice for learners who are interested in achieving the same ends in other arenas in their lives. (p. 50)

Accordingly, there are a few key features of Horton's approach to adult popular education:

- Leadership development
- Social analysis
- Experience, learning, and social meaning

Because Horton was interested in building a social movement for social change, the development of leaders to implement that change was imperative. Success in Highlander's teaching meant that former students would become key leaders in their community or enhance current leadership skills. If leaders were to change social systems, it was necessary to be able to critique social systems. This activity was not "neutral" in the way that traditional education purports to be; instead, the purpose of popular education is not to support the status quo, but it is to critique and alter it. Thus, social analysis included a long-range analysis of the overall social and economic structure of society and an analysis of a learner's local situation back at home (Peters & Bell, 1989). Though Horton did not hide his own analysis from students, he did not impose it and instead sought to engage in a dialogue between equals. By getting students to talk about their lived experiences in the world (such as working in a coal mine), his techniques entailed drawing information from them and supplying information to complete the analysis. The learners then decide what actions to engage in based on the analysis. Finally, Horton emphasized the importance of people's ability to learn from their own experiences. Learners can develop meaning from their lives and subsequently develop a social meaning that resonates with other learners' experiences (Peters & Bell, 1989). The learner has ownership of the social meaning that will form the basis for social change.

The Highlander Folk School (now called the Highlander Research and Education Center) would go through many changes over the years, educating many influential organizers including Martin Luther King, Jr., and Septima Clark. Set in the context of the beautiful, rolling foothills of the Smoky Mountains, Highlander conducts residential workshops for organizers. An additional feature of these workshops has been their emphasis on cultural expression because of its integral role in social experience. Culture serves the purpose of maintaining community, an antidote to an individualistic narrative in society. The cultural program at Highlander Center has its roots in the Southern traditions of the United States of organizing

> in the Appalachian strip mine country or at civil rights rallies in Black Belt churches; on picket lines outside piedmont textile mills on in the jails of Albany or Birmingham; in low country citizenship schools or Native American teaching circles; in rural Alabama Blues clubs or South Louisiana Zydeco halls; in the midst of struggle and in the midst of celebration. (Sapp, 1989, p. 307)

Today, the Highlander Center frames its work as part of a global justice movement, making connections between the conditions of laborers in the U.S. South and the global South. The organization is concerned with the liberation of all people, including LGBT (lesbian, gay, bisexual, and transgender) individuals, immigrants, women, and people of color. By continuing to engage in popular education, cultural programs, and consciousness-raising, the Highlander Research and Education Center is a social movement supportive organization that is carrying on a legacy of social change that focuses on the transformation and reformation of society.

THE EDUCATIONAL METHODS OF PAULO FREIRE

Paulo Freire (1921–1997), a Brazilian educator, was an important contributor to transformative and consciousness-raising approaches to social change. Indeed, he has become the patron saint of empowering approaches to social change for many organizers and activists worldwide. One of the things that is particularly interesting about the legacy of Freire's oeuvre has been the wide range of ways in which people enter into his work. Some are interested in his specific techniques of adult literacy, while others are moved by his educational philosophy for social change organizing, and still others are concerned with what he actually contributed to Latin American social movements.

Paulo Freire was born in Recife, Brazil; due to the global economic problems of 1929, his family moved to Jaboatão, Brazil, which is where he first began to be aware of extreme poverty. Eventually, he was able to return to Recife to go to a private upper-class high school. In time, he married a school teacher and attended law school but decided that being an educator was better for him. Between 1940 and 1950 he engaged in a scholarly study of education, focusing on the problems of education in a systematic way. In 1946 he became director of the Department of Education and Culture of SESI (Social Service of Industry), a government agency that used funds from a national confederation of factory owners to create programs for the betterment of the standard of living of their workers. In 1959 his thesis was accepted, and he was appointed as professor of the history and philosophy of education (Gadotti, 1994).

Concerned with the problem of illiteracy and poverty throughout Brazil, Freire came to believe that adult education of illiterate individuals had to have its foundation in the consciousness of the day-to-day situations lived by the learners. He believed that educational work toward democracy would only be achieved if the literacy process was not about or for people, but with people. He believed that a more progressive segment of Brazilian society was ready to break with the archaic, discriminatory, elitist traditions that had restricted the Brazilian poor for centuries (Gadotti, 1994).

He tried out his educational method with 300 sugarcane sharecroppers in a Brazilian village in 1963; when the experiment proved successful, he was invited by the president to implement a national literacy campaign. The program intended to make 5 million adults literate and politically progressive within the first year. (According to the national law at the time, adults could only vote if they were functionally literate to some degree; this limitation had worked in favor of the contemporary powers in Brazil.) The landowners became threatened by the possibility that the peasants would organize into leagues, become literate, and swell the ranks of voters. A coup in 1964 deposed the government and imposed military rule, which lasted over 20 years (Gadotti, 1994).

Because of Freire's participation in social movements for popular education, he was arrested twice and imprisoned; he eventually received political asylum and was exiled for 16 years. In Santiago, Chile, he worked as an adult educator for two organizations having to do with agricultural improvement and land reform. In Cambridge, Massachusetts, he taught for one year at Harvard, and in Geneva, Switzerland, he worked and traveled under the auspices of the World Council of Churches as a kind of roving ambassador of literacy in the Third World. Freire returned to Brazil in 1980 with the dream of "relearning it" and worked as a professor (Gadotti, 1994). His party (Workers Party) won the elections in 1988, and he was invited to take over the position of municipal secretary of education. At this time, he implemented a new educational model. He eventually went back to teaching and writing until he died.

Just like Myles Horton, Freire argued that traditional education occurs in a culture where the person being educated must listen and obey. Freire was highly critical of what he called *banking education*, which he argues assumes that knowledge is a possession that teachers give to students. According to Freire (1970):

> Education thus becomes an act of depositing, in which the students are the depositories and the teacher is the depositor. Instead of communicating, the teacher issues communiqués and makes deposits which the students patiently receive, memorize, and repeat.... In the banking concept of education, knowledge is a gift bestowed by those who consider themselves knowledgeable upon those whom they consider to know nothing. (p. 58)

This traditional "banking" education is a barrier to developing a critical consciousness about the world, a necessary condition for transforming the world. To be educated for critical consciousness, it is necessary to follow a long path, along which the person who is being educated will reject the oppressor who has been living inside him or her. According to Freire, oppressed individuals come to internalize the oppressor's characteristics and, thus, the oppressed desire to take on the role of the oppressor. For example, they may come to have some power in a lower management position and become tyrants themselves. In addition, they come to fear the possibilities of freedom and liberation. Because freedom is really the core of humanity, the oppressed suffer from a kind of dualism (fear of freedom and desire for freedom) and thus an inauthentic and incomplete existence.

Freire identified a "culture of silence," a term he employed to describe the illiterate inhabitants of Northeast Brazil (Freire, 1994). He believed it was necessary to "give them the word" so that they could "move" and could participate in the construction of a Brazil where they would be responsible for their own destiny and where colonialism would be overcome (Freire, 1970). He popularized the term *conscientization*, which is an ongoing process involved in colearning. It shows the relationship that should exist between thinking and acting; a group of people is able to discover the reasons why things are the way they are. Through this consciousness-raising process, a new vision of the world is learned, which contains a critique of present circumstances and an attempt to overcome these circumstances. The means for this quest are not imposed but are left to the creative capacity of the "free" conscience. A single isolated individual is never conscientized alone but as part of a community whereby solidarity is developed in relation to a common situation. Freire also embraces the idea of praxis, the unity that should exist between what one does (practice) and what one thinks about what one does (theory). This idea is based on the Marxist philosophy of praxis, which designates the reaction of people to their real conditions of existence.

Freire differentiates between banking education and *problematizing education* (Gadotti, 1994; Shor, 1993). Problematizing education is a critical dialogical reflection on knowledge that is usually taken for granted. To problematize something goes beyond mere critique and involves the use of critical questioning by a teacher encouraging students to "question answers rather than merely to answer questions" (Shor, 1993, p. 26). Freire believed that banking education was by its nature antidialogic and that problematizing education for critical consciousness embraced a dialogic theory. Antidialogic theory entails a conquest of people; it divides the oppressed, creating and deepening differences through a wide variety of methods in order to dominate them. Antidialogic theory is a way to manipulate that invades people culturally, imposing on the oppressed the invader's vision of the world. Dialogic theory, on the other hand, involves collaboration, union, organization, and cultural synthesis (Gadotti, 1994).

Community organizers have drawn from Freire's popular education methods, identifying the work of organizing people as a kind of dialogic educational process. This process of engagement becomes a political act and is always necessarily connected to the development of a plan for action. Shor (1993) has identified four qualities of critical consciousness, the goal of Freirean education: (a) power awareness, (b) critical literacy, (c) desocialization, and (d) self-organization/self-education. Power awareness involves an understanding of history and how marginalized groups have tapped into their own power to effect change. This sense of empowerment includes an understanding of how power works in society and how social action can transform it. Critical literacy is the development of analytic habits of thinking, writing, reading, and speaking that go beyond traditional myths and assumptions. Problematizing reality and knowledge is to uncover the deeper meaning of a policy or practice. Desocialization is to critically examine the "regressive values operating in society, which are internalized into consciousness" (Shor, 1993, p. 32). This includes questioning not just racism, classism, sexism, and homophobia, but also societal values such as consumerism and individualism. Self-organization/self-education is social change activity in the world, including transformative acts in communities, schools, organizations, and other contexts that may be authoritarian or undemocratic.

It should be clear that, from a popular education perspective, developing group work skills is a central component of transformative community organizing practice. These group work skills are not neutral, however; they are necessarily biased toward social change. Holding study groups is another way of raising consciousness among a group of individuals (Bookchin, 1999). Such study groups date back to the years before the French Revolution, and such groups "provided the indispensable intellectual ferment that fed into the French Revolution" (Bookchin, 1999, p. 337). Reading books as a group about progressive ideas can be a way of learning about new ideas and formulating a value-based outlook as a group. Such study groups could evolve into publishing a newsletter clarifying the ideas, or they could evolve into action.

FEMINIST CONTRIBUTIONS

Though women have historically played key leadership roles in community organizing campaigns, it has only been in the last 35 years or so that models of feminist-oriented ways of organizing have been advanced. To understand this emergence, it may be useful to consider the battered women's movement as a case study of feminist contributions to transformative organizing frameworks (Schechter, 1982). In the early 1970s, diverse groups of women began meeting in small groups to talk about their common personal experiences with a variety of conditions, including battering and sexual assault. As they came to talk about these issues, they realized that their experiences often shared many commonalities. What emerged was a kind of political consciousness that pinpoints patriarchy as a common oppressive force that condones violence against women. Here the practice of consciousness-raising developed into a framework that affirmed that the "personal is political." Though the idea of consciousness-raising first emerged in communist China in the 1950s, feminism would embrace it as an end in itself and a central mechanism for organizing.

Grounded in ideas of radical feminism, a key upshot of the process of consciousness-raising was the emergence of nonhierarchical and collectively structured organizations led by survivors of violence (Ferree & Hess, 2000; Pyles, 2003; Schechter, 1982). These structures reflected the radical feminist critiques of the patriarchal construction that supported violence against women (Walker, 2002). Audre Lorde once said: "The master's tools will never dismantle the master's house. They may allow us temporarily to beat him at his own game, but they will never enable us to bring about genuine change" (Lorde, 1981, p. 99). This insight implies that organizing strategies too often replicate injustice and thus inhibit real social change. Making decisions by consensus highlights the strengths and empowerment of women. Such practices also encouraged women, including battered and formerly battered women who had been silenced and conditioned to accept hierarchal authority, to trust themselves. This empowerment, in turn, can translate into a stronger sense of political self-efficacy and more successful outcomes in the community.

Service provision has been an essential part of the battered women's movement; the movement has been a prime example of social service practice with a social change orientation. With an emphasis on empowerment and self-determination, these advocacy and service approaches are grounded in the insights gleaned from consciousness-raising practices. Hotline services, emergency sheltering, counseling, and court advocacy were the major service provisions offered. As the movement evolved and gained more political maturity, legislative advocacy became a key tactical strategy (Schechter, 1982). In more recent years, the direction of the movement has certainly shifted from an organizing model to an advocacy approach in which professionals engage. This has been due to internal and external influences, including advanced legislation with more complex funding structures. While the growth of professionals within the movement has enhanced some of the services available to survivors of violence, as well as enabling politically astute legislative advocacy, movement away from a grassroots organizing approach has arguably negatively impacted the ability of the movement to effect transformative social change. In Chapter 11, I discuss in more detail some of the struggles of feminist organizing, including those in the battered women's movement.

Feminist organizing has been conceptualized by some as a form of mothering, a kind of community caretaking (Bookman & Morgen, 1988, p. 3). What has been central to the study of women's activism has been "recognition of the significance of women's social networks and their constructions of community for their political work" (Bookman & Morgen, 1988, p. 4). Gittell et al. (2000) conducted a study of female community development leaders and found common themes among the group. These themes included emphases on: (a) human needs, (b) the connectedness of issues, (c) a holistic approach to social and economic development, (d) a "process-oriented" approach, (e) emphasis on community participation, and (f) the importance of networking. Similarly, a group of social work women organizers developed a feminist conceptual organizing model (Joseph et al., 1991). This framework emphasizes the importance of feminist organizing to address issues that affect women while also empowering them. The framework affirms values that are traditionally ascribed to social work but also goes beyond these values to include the belief in the idea that the personal is political and an emphasis on cooperation over competition. The feminist approaches emphasized by the framework also stress "process" to be equally as important as the outcome. Such a process-oriented approach entails the creation of an emotionally safe environment that empowers people and develops leadership skills. In addition, the model emphasizes consciousness-raising, consensus building, and collective problem-solving.

Given the various contributions for feminist organizing, I offer what I take to be the most important insights from feminist organizing, articulating four defining features of a feminist organizing framework:

- Concern with power, oppression, and pathways to liberation
- Nonhierarchical and/or consensus-oriented decision making
- Valuing of group process
- Coalition building and concern beyond single-issue organizing

These features are dependent on each other for their meaningfulness. For example, group process is a method that helps organizers see how power relationships can affect women's everyday experiences (Weil, 1995). One of the primary features of feminist organizing is to inquire into the root causes of women's inequity and other forms of oppression. This practice of inquiry enables women to see how issues, such as battering and poverty, are clearly connected. Thus, in the last 10 years, engagement in coalition work that focused on poverty and welfare policies has been a natural step for organizers working on gender-based violence issues.

In a discussion of contemporary university antisexual assault organizing, Martell and Avitabile (1998) identify the tensions between feminist organizing and the realities of working to achieve utilitarian goals. In a study of campus organizers who were attempting to employ feminist organizing models, the organizers found some aspects of feminist organizing theory difficult to apply. Martell & Avitabile (1998) recount one particular example:

> They wanted to bring a gender lens to the analysis of sexual assault, but this perspective raised the question of whether sexism was the root cause of all forms of social oppression against women. Although the organizers and a number of group members supported this perspective, it became clear that the group was split on the causes of sexual assault. Deciding that this debate was counterproductive, the organizers decided to abandon it. Instead, they focused on reaching agreements on particular goals and tasks. This tactic allowed the group to accomplish goals that resulted in group solidarity and pride and progress in changing institutional policies. However, the lack of agreement on causality resulted in the disintegration of the group when this question came under fire as a result of the backlash movement. (p. 407)

The authors later identify that, in hindsight, it would have been better not to abandon the issue and further seek understanding among the group. At any rate, the case illustrates the point that feminist organizing, like other consciousness-raising approaches, is often in conflict with the realities of achieving particular goals. Feminist organizers, like many organizers, often must choose utilitarian tactics to achieve needed reforms for communities in crisis.

RECKONING WITH THE PAST

Author Naomi Klein (2007) has argued in her book, *The Shock Doctrine*, that one of the harmful practices of capitalism has been the tendency of corporations and government partners to take advantage of citizens during a crisis, such as war, terrorist attacks, or natural disasters. When people are in a state of shock, experiencing a kind of vertigo as a result of a crisis, people are particularly vulnerable to being taken advantage of. This may happen through the enactment of policies that restrict freedoms or that commandeer public and private property for the gain of the private sector. Examples might be the Patriot Act, which was implemented after 9/11, or the Davis-Bacon Act (an act that protects workers on publicly funded projects) in the Gulf Coast after Katrina (later repealed). The economist Milton Friedman was a proponent of this approach and argued that crisis is the time to push through painful policies all at once (Klein, 2007). Communities that are resistant to such practices, indeed what Klein calls "shock resistant," are ones, she says, that have "metabolized" histories of oppression. She argues for processes that entail a collective reckoning with the past that can help communities build resilience and strengthen their capacities to organize themselves.

In order to move forward and create positive social change in communities, it is often necessary to face painful issues that may be perpetuating social injustice. Such mechanisms might manifest as a truth commission, a tribunal, or any group process that promotes communities coming to terms with collective histories. These processes may entail a detailing of wrongdoings, an acknowledgment of injustice by perpetrators, forgiveness by victims, and other specific ways that perpetrators could be held accountable for their actions, such as by means of reparations. Through such mechanisms, communities are better able to be rooted in their own histories, building resistance to future oppressive events or policies that can surface. This kind of power in truth makes citizens more likely to recognize such practices in the future.

Many groups, in a variety of contexts and concerned with a wide range of issues, have attempted such reconciliation efforts. The Southern Truth and Reconciliation Group was convened in Atlanta, Georgia, to assist communities in the South who are struggling with the ongoing effects of racial violence. Other efforts have been carried out across the globe in South Africa, Australia, and Rwanda. In post-Katrina New Orleans, the Southern Institute for Education and Research, the Tulane Institute for the Study of Race and Poverty, and the People's Hurricane Relief Fund are examples of groups working to address the underlying issues of racism that have manifested themselves since Katrina and the flooding of the city. Some groups have also advocated that perpetrators and victims of domestic violence engage in community-based restorative justice models. The practices of these groups represent unique social change strategies that can enhance understanding of the effects of past policies on people's lives, enhance solidarity, and foster empowerment for future organizing endeavors.

The international tribunals on Hurricanes Katrina and Rita resulted from the work of a coalition of local and national organizations, including the People's Hurricane Relief Fund and Oversight Coalition, the U.S. Human Rights Network, Malcolm X Grassroots Movement, National Conference of Black Lawyers, and Common Ground Collective. One of the unique elements of this event was the transnational, or global justice, component, which sought to connect peoples of African descent who have been victims of colonization and slavery for hundreds of years, suffering the effects of the earliest stages of globalization in the world. Clear frames were articulated at this tribunal that connected the shared oppression of people of African descent across the globe. Jurists at the tribunal hailing from the United States, Brazil, France, Haiti, Venezuela, South Africa, and other countries listened to the stories/testimony of survivors of the disaster. The tribunal resulted in a petition demanding accountability to the U.S. government for levee failures, human rights violations, and the right to resettlement and return. The organization of the tribunal was enhanced because of the communication facility that the technology of globalization has offered.

One may argue that such efforts are not effective in that they are not working toward changing a particular policy or implementing a program. "It's just a bunch of people sitting around talking and not taking action," one might be inclined to say. However, reconciliation approaches are a form of consciousness-raising and serve the purpose of clarifying history, and they can foster a greater understanding of social systems and perpetrators of oppression. Structures such as the South African Truth and Reconciliation Commission (TRC) have been criticized for overemphasizing reconciliation and underemphasizing justice and accountability. The Centre for the Study of Violence and Reconciliation (Hamber, Maepa, Mofokeng, & van der Merwe, n.d.) studied the TRC in South Africa and has highlighted concerns and weaknesses. Conducting focus groups with survivors of apartheid, many people viewed the process of reconciliation and truth telling as a useful step in breaking the silence about the atrocities that happened over the course of over 40 years. Victims believed that the process was not effective for many reasons, such as the fact that there were not enough white people who showed up at the tribunals to make it effective and that perpetrators were offered amnesty and were not held accountable for reparations or other forms of justice.

It is imperative that any reconciliation practices with the goal of coming to terms with the past be thoughtfully planned. Such events can be very painful or retraumatizing to victims; some may still be at risk of being victimized. In addition, if perpetrators or other groups with privilege are involved, it is important that they be fully committed to the process. The short-term and long-term effects of such actions can be evaluated through formal and informal means. Reconciliation practices potentially offer many lessons learned for organizers doing coalition work (see Chapter 5), practitioners seeking out creative tactics (see Chapter 8), and those actively working to address interlocking oppressions through identity politics (see Chapter 11).

REFLECTIONS ON PROGRESSIVE ORGANIZING FRAMEWORKS

Transformative approaches to community organizing often begin with the premise that success has as much to do with internal processes, cultures, and values as it does with the external wins that define political victory. Organizers who are committed to a transformative approach to change tend to emphasize a complete transformation of society, as well as the individual. There is arguably a new generation interested in individual transformation and the idea that the successful organizations are the ones that can be led by the will of those below. They focus on challenging a set of practices that contribute to oppressions in society. Some indicators of groups committed to a transformative approach are:

- Dedication to race, class, and gender analyses
- Framing construction in the words of those most affected by the issues
- Preference for consensus-oriented decision making
- Engagement in cultural critique
- Commitment by organizers to personal transformation
- Identification with a social movement

Not all groups will exemplify all of these characteristics. For example, a group that regularly talks about race and class in its work may participate in a coalition of organizations that are not focused on addressing such issues; it might engage in such coalition work as a relationship of convenience that can further the passage of a particular law or implement a new program.

Utilitarian approaches to organizing also share several key features, including:

- Common ground based on self-interest on a specific issue
- Hierarchical organizations that emphasize efficiency and winning victories
- Passing legislation or gaining funding support for new programs
- Campaigns that may be short term
- Issue-oriented coalition work

As previously noted, these two approaches are not always so distinctive. For example, while some groups may set out to do their work from a transformative approach, practical realities may put them in a position of adapting their vision to something more practical. Minkler (2005) discusses how public health students who were organizing low-income elderly adults living in single-room occupancy hotels in San Francisco faced this dilemma. She points out that although the project was originally envisioned as a project based on Freire's techniques "with the idea that student facilitators would use this approach when leading hotel-based and discussion groups, regular applications of problems, for example, often proved impractical when residents were motivated to organize quickly around problems that demanded immediate action" (p. 274). In addition, it is not uncommon for practitioners to approach their work from multiple perspectives, utilizing a practical, praxis-oriented approach. Such eclectic approaches in community organizing are realistic ways to doing social change work. Minkler (2005) further elaborates on the work of student organizers:

> Student facilitators used a combination of organizing and educational approaches to help foster group solidarity and eventually community organizing. A Freirian problem-posing process was used as appropriate, for example, to help residents engage in dialogue about shared problems and their causes to generate potential action plans. Similarly, facilitators followed Alinsky's admonition to create dissatisfaction with the status quo, channel frustration into concrete action, and help people identify specific, winnable issues. (p. 275)

It seems apparent that to effect long-term social change in communities that can unlock the manifestations of the interlocking oppressions of racism, classism, and sexism, some kind of deep and ongoing consciousness-raising practice is necessary. It is necessary that such transformative practices be complemented by the utilitarian practices first developed by Alinsky, which seek to achieve concrete ends for people in their communities. Some might argue that the two approaches to community organizing are incompatible with each other, but both approaches are vital for advancing a progressive agenda. The next generation of organizers is in an opportune position to identify the strengths of both approaches, with the possibility of merging them into a new paradigm for organizing.

THE RIGHT TO RETURN CAMPAIGN, PART I: HISTORY AND BACKGROUND

Anne Dienethal and Loretta Pyles

The period between 1900 and 1950 marked a major increase of federal involvement in housing provision across the United States. During this time, civic leaders, urban planners, and social workers began investigating and unmasking slum housing conditions (Bauman, Biles, & Szylvian, 2000). Having glimpsed progressive European housing developments, these groups vocally protested substandard living conditions in the urban United States. These efforts led to the first U.S. legislation to support construction of housing developments across the country, as well as the creation of the United States Housing Authority. Drawing from the political opportunities that were offered by the passage of the New Deal, organizers pushed for the passage of the Housing Act of 1937, which supported a low-income public housing program that provided funds to state agencies to build low-rent public housing in an effort to eradicate extremely blighted housing conditions (U.S. Department of Housing and Urban Development [HUD], 2007). Later, the 1949 Housing Act paved the way for further urban redevelopment, transforming the design of public housing into the densely populated high-rise developments that can be seen in major cities around the country today (von Hoffman, 1996).

PUBLIC HOUSING IN NEW ORLEANS

Many of the problems that have plagued public housing nationally also can be witnessed at the local level in New Orleans. Poverty and crime have been a continuous problem for residents of New Orleans developments. However, these resilient residents have used a variety of community organizing tactics, from direct action to policy advocacy, in an effort to improve their living conditions.

In the wake of the Housing Act of 1937, a flood of new public housing developments was constructed in New Orleans to meet the needs of working families. Six newly constructed developments—Iberville and St. Thomas, both reserved for white residents, and Magnolia (later called C.J. Peete), Calliope (later called B.W. Cooper), Lafitte, and St. Bernard, reserved for black residents—were built within three years of its passage (Mahoney, 1990). The developments were constructed with the hope of boosting low-income families into upward mobility and allowed only 20% of the units to be set aside for families on public assistance. The remaining 80% of housing was reserved for workers in the shipping, automobile, and longshoremen industries. The truly financially destitute were ineligible for spaces in any of the developments (Mahoney, 1990).

The new developments offered promise to black families who had been residing in inadequate slum housing and who were largely excluded from the private housing sector. Due to limited availability of public housing spots, in-depth interviews, including controversial character evaluations, were conducted to determine eligibility. Through petitioning and protest, black residents successfully applied pressure on the Housing Authority of New Orleans (HANO), demanding that they employ black social workers to conduct the eligibility interviews, thereby ensuring a more culturally competent assessment (Mahoney, 1990). Following the construction of the first wave of developments, subsequent housing was built through the 1960s, resulting in the construction of the Florida, Fischer, Desire, and Melpomene (later called Guste) developments.

In contrast to the high-rises constructed in many cities, New Orleans public housing developments were at first seen to be comfortable and attractive, with many of the low-rise apartments constructed of quality brick with pitched roofs and wrought-iron balconies (Reichl, 1999). While residents initially saw developments as a step up from inadequate slum housing, it soon became clear that development living was not a panacea. A sharp increase in unemployment after World War II and the flight of industry from the city's central business district resulted in increased poverty and geographic isolation for residents of the inner city (Mahoney, 1990). New Orleans's resulting suburbanization and further exclusion of black residents from the private housing sector led to the overcrowding of developments available to the black population and an increase in crime among residents (Mahoney, 1990). When persistent activism nationwide resulted in passage of the Civil Rights Act of 1964, HANO modified its policies and desegregated New Orleans public housing developments, offering broader availability of public housing spaces to black residents (Reichl, 1999).

In addition to crime and overcrowding, throughout its history New Orleans public housing, which is situated atop desirable real estate, has been at risk for demolition to make way for redevelopment. Since the 1980s, the Iberville project, for example, has been scoped for real estate opportunities due to its proximity to the French Quarter, a move that has been successfully staved off by vocal resident protest of redevelopment. Redeveloping both private and public housing in efforts at urban renewal has been a recurring theme through modern U.S. urban development history. These urban renewal projects have arguably been very damaging to African-American families and the dense social networks that exist in housing projects. Though there has been a long history of resistance to these efforts on the part of residents and their allies, the effect of such displacement has resulted in a kind of "root shock" to many urban communities, an inevitable result of people being ripped away from their homes, extended families, and social networks (Fullilove, 2005). Unfortunately, this displacement and the trauma have created another chapter in *The Story of African American History in the U.S.* (Mann, 2006).

Another key illustration of the effort to redevelop New Orleans public housing is the St. Thomas public housing development. Constructed in the 1930s and expanded in the 1940s, the development comprised 161 buildings spanning 50 acres in New Orleans's Lower Garden District. St. Thomas had a rich history of grassroots resident activism, as well as the highest rate of violent crime in the city (Reichl, 1999). In 1982, residents dissatisfied with the role of local community service providers organized the St. Thomas Resident Council (STRC) and joined forces with the antiracism organization, the People's Institute for Survival and Beyond, focusing on educating residents on the role of structural racism and their ability to empower themselves through knowledge and civic participation. In 1982, the STRC organized a takeover of HANO headquarters to protest inadequate living conditions, shortly followed by a rent strike that resulted in the rehabilitation of St. Thomas apartments (Reichl, 1999). In 1989, community service providers surrounding the St. Thomas development were served with contracts by the STRC ordering agencies to have greater accountability to the St. Thomas community or to close their doors.

Empowered by its many successes, when in 1992 the St. Thomas development was targeted for redevelopment by the city, the STRC demanded transparency in the process and direct involvement in the redevelopment plans (Reichl, 1999). The plans, which called for demolishing the majority of apartments to create space for mixed-income housing, were part of the city administration's first attempts to de-concentrate poverty in the area. Despite residents' efforts to displace as few residents as possible, by August 30, 2001, when 1,393 of 1,429 units were leveled, many residents did not have a place to go (Greater New Orleans Community Data Center, 2002). River Garden, New Orleans's first mixed-income housing, was built in place of the development and offered 40% of its apartments to low-income residents and 60% at market rate (Libson, 2007b). In January 2002, the Housing Authority of New Orleans (HANO) was taken over by the U.S. Department of Housing and Urban Development (HUD) due to "extensive mismanagement" (HUD, 2003). By 2003, against widespread protest, Orleans Parish's first (and still only) Wal-Mart was built on the former site of the St. Thomas development.

POST-KATRINA NEW ORLEANS

When Hurricane Katrina made landfall on August 29, 2005, New Orleans was immediately immersed in a housing crisis when thousands of rented and owned properties were damaged or destroyed. HUD documents show a pre-Katrina waiting list of 18,000 people for Section 8, indicating that the need for affordable housing after the storm was stronger than ever (Quigley, 2006b). In spite of the community-wide need for affordable housing, citing extensive damage to the buildings, HANO and HUD declared the properties off-limits. Residents returning to claim their homes and belongings were greeted with gates, guards, and warnings not to trespass onto the properties. Many residents were served with eviction notices. One year after the storm, only three public housing developments—Iberville, Guste, and Fischer—had units, 1,000 in all, available for reoccupation (HUD, 2006).

The efforts of HUD and HANO to halt reopening of public housing in the city have made local and national headlines and have prompted the organization and action of residents and housing activists citywide and nationally. Determined not to repeat what many residents view as mistakes made working alongside the power structure during the St. Thomas redevelopment process, strategies in the current housing effort focus upon direct action through protest and political theater in combination with lawsuits and policy advocacy.

QUESTIONS FOR REFLECTION

1. Alinsky emphasized confrontational tactics, where groups of powerful citizens confront those in power with a unified voice of their concerns. What are the benefits and potential pitfalls of such an approach?

2. What are the barriers to doing transformative or consciousness-raising approaches to community organizing? Consider barriers at the personal, cultural, organizational, and policy levels.

3. Are feminist contributions to organizing relevant to issues beyond those that would be considered women's issues?

4. What are the advantages and disadvantages of attempting reconciliation activities within communities, such as tribunals to hold perpetrators accountable or racial reconciliation?

5. How might some of the philosophical and technical aspects of popular education approaches be used with youth today?

SUGGESTIONS FOR FURTHER INQUIRY

BOOKS

Alinsky, S. (1971). *Rules for radicals: A practical primer for realistic radicals.* New York: Random House.

Baumgardner, J., & Richards, A. (2005). *Grassroots: A field guide to feminist activism.* New York: Farrar, Straus and Giroux.

Fisher, R. (1994). *Let the people decide: Neighborhood organizing in America.* New York: Twayne Publishers.

Freire, P. (1994). *Pedagogy of hope: Reliving pedagogy of the oppressed.* New York: Continuum.

Rooney, J. (1995). *Organizing the South Bronx.* Albany, NY: SUNY Press.

WEB

Catalyst Centre. http://www.catalystcentre.ca

Comeuppance. http://comeuppance.blogspot.com

Framework for Feminist Organizing. http://www.hunter.cuny.edu/socwork/ecco/woc.pdf

Labor/Community Strategy Center. http://www.thestrategycenter.org

Pedagogy and Theatre of the Oppressed. http://www.ptoweb.org

KEY TERMS

Banking education: A term coined by Paulo Freire, a Brazilian educator, to describe traditional pedagogical methods that dichotomize teacher and student and thus perpetuate hierarchies of knowledge.

Consciousness-raising: A practice that originated in early Communist China, it was later adopted by 1970s feminists to describe practices that included raising political awareness through discussions about individual realities.

Popular education: An educational tool for political change that stresses pedagogical techniques that empower citizens to learn about the connections between individual experiences and social systems.

Sustainability: An ecological term that refers to maintaining states at certain levels indefinitely. The term can be applied to visions of social justice as well as the organizational practices of social change whereby, for example, work is organized to maintain sustainable organizational resources. An organizational practice focused on preventing staff burnout is an example.

Transformative organizing practice: Based on an analysis of the intersectionality of oppression, this is an organizing practice that works toward the holistic liberation of both individuals and institutions.

Section II

Tools for Community Organizing

Many people often want to know how to "do" community organizing, anxiously hoping for a practice blueprint that can serve as a step-by-step guidebook. Fortunately, such a blueprint does not exist, as it would only unnecessarily conceal the complexities involved in organizing. A guidebook may incline a practitioner to overlook political and historical factors and the changing realities of social policies, culture, and communities. Indeed, divorcing form from substance could be a dangerous thing. The problem with such a guidebook is that it may dispose someone to use it universally or generically without considering the unique context. In the case of community organizing, the map is not the road. New empirical evidence is constantly presenting itself, and practitioners must be willing to change the course when necessary. Rather than offer a blueprint for organizing, I present in these next several chapters some tools and ideas from which practitioners can draw.

The progressive community organizer is always asking questions and analyzing his or her situation. While a carpenter's most useful tool may be his or her hammer, the organizer's is his or her critical thinking skills, asking: What are the problems? Who is benefiting from the situation? What kinds of stories are being told by power holders that may be masking the problems? What strengths or assets exist within the constituency? Is the organization empowering the most marginalized members of the constituency? Was the organizing campaign effective in achieving its goals? Posing and answering such questions (in an ongoing way) are the central practices of community organizing.

Though the next section of the book is not a manual or guidebook, the reader will explore the time-honored workings of community organizing practice. In 1967, Ross defined community organizing as a practice in which a community

> identifies its needs or objectives, orders (or ranks) these needs or objectives, develops the confidence and will to work at these needs or objectives, finds the resources (internal and/or external) to deal with these needs or objectives, takes action in respect to them, and in so doing extends and develops cooperative and collaborative attitudes and practices in the community. (p. 40)

It seems that these elements are still very relevant today in terms of what community organizers are charged to do.

Similarly, Murphy and Cunningham (2003) have identified 12 fundamentals of community organizing when doing community development work:

1. Creating and spreading a vision
2. Recruiting
3. Developing leadership
4. Forming and maintaining a cadre
5. Launching the organization
6. Researching and planning
7. Evaluating process and product
8. Staffing
9. Communicating
10. Implementing plans
11. Tapping resources
12. Building and strengthening interorganizational relations

These and other issues will all be addressed in the following chapters. Though the tasks of community organizers have been universally identified by many organizers and researchers, the focus here will be on what is unique about progressive community organizing, with a critical approach in the context of a globalizing world. Thus, the tools presented in the following chapters build on the philosophical foundations set forth in the first section of the book.

6 Organizing People
Constituencies and Coalitions

The organizer must bring people together in such a way as to create mutual trust, interdependence, broadly based membership, and diversified leadership.

Kahn (1994, p. 31)

Mississippi civil rights activist Fannie Lou Hamer once said: "There is one thing you have got to learn about our movement. Three people are better than no people." This is an unambiguous response to the ubiquitous frustration of a community organizer, namely, there are not enough people to do the work that needs to be done. The organizer may feel that people are too busy or do not care, and if there were just more people who were willing to become active, then the overwhelming task of social change would be possible. However, Hamer's point is that three people are better than two, or one, or no people. Still, the central task of organizing is to enlist more and more people to participate in the struggle for social change, i.e., to "build the base" (Fisher, 1994). The base is important because it comprises the people who have the most investment and interest in the outcome of organizing work. Indeed, the base is who actually engages in the day-to-day efforts of effecting social change. In addition, the base is who carries the struggle on over time, builds organizational or movement capacity and sustainability, and passes on the critical knowledge of the values and practices of organizations.

When determining who the base is for a particular issue or campaign, i.e., the constituency, it is useful to think of all the people who are affected by an issue or who may be key players in facilitating change—regular citizens who live in a neighborhood, people receiving public or social services, workers, parents, youth, older adults, and people who work at grassroots or nonprofit organizations. Those people who are most affected by an issue are the ones it is most important to organize. Also, other individuals may have the ability to make change, usually people who are in power, such as elected officials or corporate executives. These power holders tend to be considered the "targets" of change efforts and not the constituency itself.

KEY ELEMENTS OF ORGANIZING CONSTITUENCIES AND COALITIONS

Whether one is talking about organizing individual citizens affected by an issue or building a formal coalition with other organizations, it is useful to consider some of the central elements of organizing. These elements—empowerment, accountability, relationship, and social change—are essentially values and useful practices that progressive community organizers may consider employing as they engage in organizing.

EMPOWERMENT

The more meaningfully engaged that the people—those who are most affected by the issues—are in social change processes, the greater is the degree of empowerment that they can attain and sustain. If an organizer does something *for* people or *on behalf of* people, then such a service or advocacy model may not empower or enfranchise the group over time, even though the immediate outcome may appear positive. Saul Alinsky (1971) advocated that professional organizers should actually strive toward organizing themselves out of a job. By standing in solidarity "with" constituents rather than "for" them, social change is closer at hand. For example, a state-level labor policy may get changed due to the efforts of advocates working on behalf of workers, but what if the workers who are most affected by it have not been mobilized? These workers are not prepared for the next time that a policy that affects them needs to be changed; they are, in fact, dependent on the possibility that the advocate will be there to help them in the future. The idea of being "a voice for the voiceless" may come from a legitimate desire to help disenfranchised people; but, if there is an opportunity to organize people who are marginalized or to work in solidarity with them, then sustainable social change becomes more possible. In addition, marginalized people most affected by issues always have a greater understanding of their own needs and ultimately what agenda to pursue and what tactics to use to meet those needs. According to one organizer working in post-Katrina New Orleans:

> They're upset about an issue, and we're going to do something, but it's not going to be [me] coming in like Captain America or something and saving the day. That's not what's going to happen here because that would disempower the person and that would disempower people in that community. Then I have the power to change and you just have the power to sit back and go, "She will fix it." That's nothing. (Pyles, 2006)

Organizing people is when the idea of empowerment begins to get actualized.

Consciousness-raising through popular education approaches is a central organizing strategy for organizers working from a transformative perspective. Creating circles or other spaces where people can talk about their lived experiences can be a way to leverage people's concerns and strengths into action, whether the action is becoming a member of an organization, attending a direct action, or volunteering one's time to create or distribute fliers to the community. Offering people the opportunity to tap into their own personal power, which can be unleashed through working with other people to create real change, is central to progressive community organizing. Popular education approaches that allow people to name the issues that affect them, make connections to their personal lives, and articulate agendas are clear paths to empowerment.

To be sure, empowerment is not a black-and-white concept; it exists on a nuanced continuum. On one side of the continuum is a strong and engaged rank and file, i.e., a base that is leading the way, and on the other end is a legion of paid staff members who create the agenda. Most organizing happens somewhere along the continuum. Understanding this continuum is critical to doing social change work; being honest and transparent about where an organizing effort stands on this continuum is essential. This kind of empowerment approach to organizing is clearly connected to the ideas discussed below—accountability, relationship, and social change.

ACCOUNTABILITY

One way to think about organizing people may be to consider Arnstein's (1969) ladder of participation, which was discussed in the first chapter of this book. The more actively involved that regular people are in interventions and social change work, the greater is the degree of accountability to the constituency. Accountability is especially important when organizers are working in coalition with a variety of groups and one has representation from a variety of constituencies. If one is working with a diverse group of constituents to influence mental health policy reform and the majority of group members attempting to work on the issue are mental health professionals and other advocates, the likelihood of accountability to the constituency is reduced. When the majority is current or former mental health consumers, accountability to the constituency seems more likely. Though it is not ever realistic that every single person affected by an issue will participate in organizing activities, engaging a strong sample of the larger constituent universe is a way to enhance accountability.

Sometimes organizers may find themselves in situations where they feel accountable to multiple parties, beyond just the marginalized communities they work in. For example, many people working in nonprofits find themselves in the situation where they feel more beholden to funders than to their constituency. Activist Paul Kivel (2007) offers several questions for social service agencies to consider when thinking about accountability to grassroots communities:

- Who supervises your work?
- Are you involved in community-based social justice struggles?
- Is political struggle part of the work you do?
- Are you in a contentious relationship with those in power?
- Are you sharing access to power and resources with those on the frontlines of the struggle?
- Do you help people come together?

A critical approach to organizing involves constantly asking such questions about accountability. Because situations are constantly changing, one can never be satisfied that the questions have been answered.

RELATIONSHIP

No matter what kind of organizing framework that an organization works from, establishing a relationship with a constituent involves developing a rapport and nurturing the relationship over time. According to activist Carlton Turner, a cultural organizer:

> Relationships. You have to have relationships with the people that you're trying to organize. If you don't, people always see you as a stranger. One of the big things that was going on during the Civil Rights years in Mississippi early on was that people initially looked at the SNCC [Student Nonviolent Coordinating Committee] organizers as outsiders. The White population definitely looked at them as outside agitators. But what the SNCC people did was they came in and became infused in the community. The Civil Rights movement didn't happen in a ballroom. This was the epitome of grassroots. You're talking about people who went in and lived in communities for six, seven months. They didn't have a per diem. They didn't have any housing. They lived with whoever was willing to put them up. They ate whatever someone was willing to cook for them. They didn't have any transportation. They rolled around with whoever was willing to drive them around. (Cited in Szakos & Szakos, 2007, p. 98.)

This quotation affirms the realities within social movement work and the lengths that people are often willing to go to develop relationships. Similarly, this was the purpose of residential living with poor families in the settlement houses. The purpose of these efforts is ultimately about building authentic, sustainable relationships. Though it may not always be necessary to go to such lengths, organizers often underestimate the time that it takes to build these relationships with people.

Meeting people where they are has always been a mantra for organizers. This can apply to any level of organizing—organizing neighborhood people, social service consumers, or organizing people in coalitions. In order to meet a person where he or she is, one obviously has to understand where he or she is. The first step certainly entails the development of the important skill of listening. This listening should be coupled with the activity of pushing people forward into action. One labor organizer put it this way:

> One of the things about organizers is that they have to meet people where they are. They don't necessarily want to leave them there, but they have to be able to accept people where they are, at least for the most part, and not be terribly judgmental. (Szakos & Szakos, 2007, p. 98)

Though listening is a challenging task, it is virtually an impossible task when the organizer thinks he or she has all the right answers. Unfortunately, some organizers have a modus operandi that involves pounding the "right" answers into people's heads.

Community practitioners such as social workers have written extensively on the nature of relationships and partnerships between practitioners and constituents. Drawing from this wisdom can be useful to organizers. Miley, O'Melia, and DuBois (1998) discuss several qualities of such relationships that are easily adaptable to the organizing context. These qualities include genuineness, acceptance and respect, trustworthiness, empathy, cultural sensitivity, and purposefulness. Genuineness is the quality of "being real," ethical, spontaneous, and not phony. Such behavior is important when having an organizing conversation with a vulnerable constituent whose issues are palpable and whose time is valuable. Acceptance and respect are qualities that are exemplified through the actions of organizers. These actions include engaging with "unconditional positive regard," listening, and identifying strengths. Though organizers, unlike counselors or therapists, are often charged with the task of agitating constituents to the point where they want to do something about the problems in their communities, this can still be done in a way that is respectful. Trustworthiness is another important quality between an organizer and a constituent. Trust can be built over time; though trust is a two-way street, organizers can exemplify qualities such as reliability and credibility that can enhance long-term trust-building. Empathy is also an important quality to embody when organizing vulnerable constituents. Listening to the stories of underpaid workers or the parents of children at a low-performing school and validating their perspectives is critical and efficacious. Rather than pity or sympathy, being *with* individuals can foster empowerment. Cultural sensitivity is especially an important practice when working in diverse, globalizing communities. When working with people of different races, ethnicities, religions, and countries of origin, it is important that organizers develop the skills that will allow them to remain attuned to cultural similarities and differences. Finally, purposefulness is the idea that the relationship has a conscious goal to it. The goal of the relationship is to seek common ground and to organize the person into a campaign, action, or organization, and the organizer should always remain purposeful in this regard. Though listening to and bearing witness to people's diverse realities is an important practice, it is not the end in itself.

Whether organizing an individual in a one-on-one situation or building the strength of a group of constituents, relationship is central. Building relationship entails finding the common ground between human beings. One way that this common ground can be established is through the human and cultural practice of sharing food. Whether it's sharing a cup of coffee or a meal that everyone contributes to, food is a way to bring organizers and constituents together. Providing food can be a particularly good way to engage low-income people, who may be struggling to make ends meet. When organizing homeless individuals, providing food in a space that they are comfortable with can be a good strategy for getting them engaged in issues that have relevance to their lives. It is particularly important to keep in mind that the food served be culturally appropriate.

SOCIAL CHANGE

Doing social change work means that one is highly concerned with the way that one does one's work, that one does not wish to replicate injustices in the course of trying to achieve justice. Though nobody wants to replicate oppression when he or she is organizing, it is actually not uncommon. Sexism in the civil rights movement, racism in the labor movement, homophobia in the women's movement—this has been an unfortunate part of the legacy of progressive community organizing. The reality is that organizers, even though they are a subculture of society, are all members of a larger society that tends to support such "isms." Thus, it is not surprising that organizers replicate these oppressions in their organizing strategies. What makes progressive organizers who are committed to social change unique, however, is the fact that they are interested in being accountable for such oppressions and transforming them into a more just reality.

One of the greatest pitfalls in organizing work is to think of those with power as "the enemy" or "the other." Many groups teach their organizers to think this way. I myself have often thought of politicians, corporate executives, or state-level administrators or other gatekeepers in this way. These divisions and dichotomies can have the consequence of creating hierarchies of good and bad or superior and less than, which is exactly what social change work seeks to redress. But, I think this approach may not be so helpful if we break it down both philosophically and practically. The continual job of organizing from a critical perspective is to cut through such social constructions that might essentialize people as good and bad.

ORGANIZING INDIVIDUAL CONSTITUENTS

Labor organizer Cesar Chavez once said, "You have to convert people one person at a time; time after time,... the concept is so simple that most of us miss it." For a short time, I worked as a canvasser for an environmental organization. This meant that I went door knocking, one of the most challenging tasks of community organizing work. Each day, our coordinator would give us a map of the neighborhood to canvass and drop us off for a few hours in the evenings or on the weekends. Our goal was to raise awareness about environmental issues and get people involved in the organization. More specifically, we hoped to get people to become members of the organization, which included signing up and committing money on the spot. It did not take long to realize that many people were not interested in talking about the environment to someone standing on their doorstep. They often said they were busy doing other things. My favorite excuse was that they were watching television and specifically that they had to watch "The Wheel" (i.e., the *Wheel of Fortune*). Others had firm beliefs that the rights of corporations outweighed those of the environment and basically were not interested in what I had to say. It could be incredibly frustrating work. I had to hold unyieldingly to my belief that talking about the nearest nuclear power plant and how it could affect their children was really important. I firmly believed that having these critical conversations in neighborhoods was a great way to do this. Some people invited me in and really wanted to talk about the issues in depth, offering me water on a hot day and engaging in deep conversations that would sustain me for weeks. It seemed to be the best way to really connect with people about issues—better than a flier or a newspaper editorial ever could. When people had the visceral experience of engaging with a person, they might even remember me as a person and the way they felt when having the conversation.

I had similar experiences when I was organizing for a teacher's union. The excuses always seemed to be the same—too busy to get involved, afraid they'll get in trouble and lose their job, and feeling like getting involved would not improve the situation anyway. I had to learn how to respond to all of these excuses. Oftentimes, the best way to respond was to reply with a question back to them. Organizers have long talked about the importance of getting a potential constituent "agitated." This Socratic way of engaging in dialogue was often effective because the answers came from within the constituent and thus he or she had ownership of the answers. For those who said they were too busy, I would ask them if they thought that they could find 30 minutes or an hour a week to make phone calls. Many people agreed that they could find such a small amount of time in their schedule. For those who thought they could lose their job, I asked them if they had ever known anyone who had lost his or her job for being in a union. Not many people did. I had to help them deconstruct some of their own stories about the situation and in some cases help them break down their own fears. Sociologist Floyd Hunter (1953) identified many years ago: "fear, pessimism, and silence are three elements in the behavior of individuals with which any community organizer or social analyst must deal" (p. 228).

It should also be noted though that, in some situations, it really may not be safe to join a union; many workers have had experiences where they have been retaliated against or lost their jobs or even worse for their organizing activities. People of color, undocumented immigrants, LGBT (lesbian, gay, bisexual, transgender) people, and other marginalized individuals tend to be at significant risk for such retaliation. Thus, it is important to honor people's perceptions and experiences and help them think through their own risks and benefits when determining if they want to be a part of an organization. Letting them know about victories that the organization has achieved as a group in solidarity or reminding them that there can be power and safety in numbers are good antidotes to these concerns. Ultimately, achieving justice—for example, securing a union contract and getting better pay and benefits—is always the best antidote.

THE RELATIONAL MEETING

According to Chambers (2003), a disciple of Alinsky and a long-time leader in the Industrial Areas Foundation (IAF), a central practice of organizing is the "relational meeting." A relational meeting is a one-on-one meeting that serves the purpose of bringing into the public sphere those issues that are often only talked about in private, if at all. The purpose of the meeting is to find out what a person is thinking and feeling about an issue. Posing questions such as "Why do you say that?" or "What does it mean to you?" can be an efficacious technique to heighten awareness and build relationships with people who are potential allies. Relational meetings are also important points in time when one can begin talking about an organization's framework for thinking about an issue. However, it is not a time for ideological ranting on the part of the organizer, nor is it a time to find people who share your views or will follow the party line. Rather than pressuring people, Chambers believes that the relational meeting must also communicate to the constituent that the "agenda has some fluidity, that its tone or strategy might be altered, that newcomers are expected to bring something to the group's agenda" (p. 52).

According to Chambers (2003), the relational meeting has some of the following components:

- Develops a public relationship
- Centers on the spirit and values of the other person
- Requires special focus beyond an ordinary conversation
- Entails stirring up the depths of the other
- Obliges a certain amount of vulnerability on both sides
- Bridges the barriers of race, religion, class, gender, and politics
- Is an art form that takes unique skills and time to develop

Relational meetings can take place inside people's homes, on their front porch, at the grocery store, or in any number of places. It is important to remember:

> When a good relational meeting occurs, two people connect in a way that transcends ordinary, everyday talk. Both have the opportunity to pause and reflect on their personal experience regarding the tension between the world as it is and the world as it should be. And in that moment, a new public relationship may be born, through which both will gain power to be truer to their best selves, to live more effectively and creatively in-between the two worlds. (Chambers, 2003, p. 53)

Finally, the organizer should take notes after every relational meeting; these notes should be guided by questions such as: Does this person have grief, anger, passion, or vision about the issues? What strengths would he or she bring to an organization? Who else is this person connected to? What is the best way to follow up with this person? (Chambers, 2003).

ORGANIZING AS LEADERSHIP DEVELOPMENT

Ernesto Cortes, Jr., a leader of the group Communities Organized for Public Service (COPS), believes that rather than viewing leaders as people who speak to large crowds or have some kind of institutional power, leaders could be seen as regular people who have networks and relationships. When he finds someone who has potential, he works hard to organize him or her. One person with this potential was Beatrice Cortez, an office worker who was active in her church, whom he first met at a parents meeting about the closing of a neighborhood school (Warren, 2001). Mrs. Cortez was angry when she learned that the school district was planning to close three schools in the community and use the money for a new administration building. Inexperienced and nervous about speaking out, Mrs. Cortez was trying to avoid Cortes, who was encouraging her to take some action. She said,

There was a man, Ernie, sitting next to me at the meeting. He encouraged me to push for us to take some action. So I was asked to speak with school officials. But I was afraid because I had never spoken in public before. Ernie met me outside the meeting and pinned me down to agree to speak. (Warren, 2001, p. 51)

Though the group was never able to stop the school closing, they were successful in stopping the new administration building and were able to ensure that the dollars were funneled back into existing schools. The taste of success was enough for Beatrice Cortez to want to continue her work; she eventually became president of COPS. After that first victory, she remembered: "I told Ernie to teach me everything. I stopped being a victim. Now you know what's going on because you're making it happen" (Warren, 2001, p. 51).

Mondros and Wilson (1994) have identified three aspects of the organizing process—recruiting and engaging new members, keeping current members inspired and engaged, and deepening member participation. This last idea, deepening member participation, is the essence of leadership development and is a cornerstone of organizing. According to Murphy and Cunningham (2003): "Opportunities to take on responsibilities and learn new skills should be freely offered to a newly committed member. The more the new member develops capacity, the stronger the organization becomes" (p. 83). Mark Trechock is staff director at Dakota Resource Council. When asked to share his proudest achievement in organizing, he said:

One of the things that makes me really proud is seeing someone that I've recruited, either into membership or into leadership in our organization, blossom and discover their true gifts as a leader, and put those into the service of the campaign.… Standing and watching them give testimony, or talk to the press, or lead a meeting, or come in with a fistful of memberships of people they've gone out and recruited—nothing could make me happier than that. And that's about building power. Because building power entails building leadership. (Szakos & Szakos, 2007, pp. 117–118)

Leadership development is an actualization of the philosophy of empowerment. According to an organizer who was working with neighborhood leaders in post-Katrina New Orleans:

I'm just saying that our base that we want to support is a base that is local and a base that is driven by people—people and neighborhoods. That's where the emphasis is. And not driven to take over and clear power or to take over their voice, but to empower them to speak for themselves. So consistently, when I'm asked to do interviews by media, I say "well, what's the subject? You ought to interview this person, that's what you're interested in, talk to them." Last night, for example, NPR was at our meeting interviewing us doing some stuff. And Steve Inskeep asked me to do an interview, and I said "I'd rather you talk to [this] pastor, he's a neighborhood leader in the [neighborhood name] Area who is helping that neighborhood come back and is struggling, but has real stories from the trenches. Amazing stories, brilliant, insightful, nuanced New Orleans stories. And he's the vice chairman of my board, and that's who I want to be interviewed." Because I want to get as far away and as in front of this thing as I can. I really share the power, but show that the power of the organization—and this organization exists only because—of these neighborhoods. I'd like to emphasize them. (Pyles, 2006)

As this organizer insightfully points out, developing leaders may require that organizers step out of the spotlight and share power with constituents, allowing their strengths and achievements to shine.

ORGANIZING IN SOCIAL SERVICE ORGANIZATIONS

For people who work in social service organizations or have connections with agencies that may serve clients or other consumers, attempting to organize them can be perceived as both an opportunity and a challenge. Individuals receiving public welfare benefits, community mental health care, or other social services have a tremendous amount of wisdom and investment in the outcomes of many organizing campaigns. The welfare rights movement of the late 1960s and early 1970s, led by poor African-American women receiving Aid to Families with Dependent Children (AFDC), challenged prevailing perceptions about social service recipients and organized themselves into a powerful movement. Social service clients represent a potentially formidable base of support.

An initial temptation when thinking about organizing clients may be to merely obtain their "input" on issues, as Arnstein (1969) noted, rather than organizing them into positions of power or leadership roles. Such an approach to garnering client input has been explained by Kretzmann and McKnight (1997), who view traditional social welfare provision as needs-based. This traditional, needs-based approach tends to segment social problems and render social service recipients dependent on services as people with a laundry list of problems and needs. The assets-based approach to community development, they argue, entails seeing people as a part of a community with tremendous assets and strengths, seeing them as people with power. A low-income social service recipient who is working two jobs, who is having trouble maintaining housing, and whose child is having encounters with the juvenile justice system inherently understands that social problems are not separate from each other and, in fact, that the causes of social problems are often interconnected. Though there may certainly be legitimate reasons to only obtain feedback from clients about their needs, the community, or the services they are receiving, by organizing social service recipients, one can actualize the principles of empowerment, accountability, and social change. Engaging in critical thinking that deconstructs traditional practices of social welfare provision can be a useful way to make the most of a potentially powerful constituency.

One of the barriers to organizing "clients" to engage in social change work is that there is a perception that the "client" may not be "over" the problem that they sought to address in the first place. A mental health consumer may still be struggling with symptoms; a survivor of domestic violence may still be having issues with her batterer; a person recovering from substance abuse problems may relapse; a person who has received Section 8 housing may experience intermittent homelessness. The reality is that many low-income and marginalized individuals may continue to struggle with such problems all their lives, or they may not. Of utmost importance when thinking about such issues concerns whether the individual feels like she or he is ready or interested in participating in social change work. In other words, organizers should operate on a principle of self-determination, particularly with social service consumers. An alternative perspective on this topic is that any given person, regardless of economic class or ethnicity, could be working as an organizer and then finds himself or herself in an abusive relationship or in need of medication for mental health problems. Such strict notions of the helper and the helped that may be prevalent in social service settings are quite slippery in reality and not necessarily relevant in the context of community organizing.

Unfortunately, in organizations that do both organizing and social service delivery, I have seen policies that are antithetical to principles of self-determination, empowerment, and social change. For example, policies at domestic violence programs may require that people who have received advocacy or other services cannot participate in organizing activities for one year or two years or some other arbitrary timeline. Such policies purport to exist for the best interest of the client, and yet, they seem to be more paternalistic than anything else. It may certainly be appropriate for an organization to set up some kind of boundaries or create a mechanism to have a thoughtful discussion with former clients about engaging in organizing activities. In the case of domestic violence, working on a safety plan with a woman interested in organizing would be appropriate. Such mechanisms could be beneficial for the individual, the organization, and the larger social change issue. The client or consumer ultimately knows best what his or her needs and limitations are. Furthermore, community organizing may be the most healing activity that they ever engage in. It is also worth noting that no organizer I have ever met has all his or her "stuff" together.

In many cases, the staff at social service organizations may not be directly involved in community organizing; they may, however, be part of a coalition or consider themselves allies to other organizing groups. Consider social service workers doing health outreach with low-income immigrant Latino communities. Such an intervention could be a way to link people not just into health-care services, but also into local organizing efforts. Trained staff at the health clinic could talk to the patients about their situation, connecting them with racial justice or other organizations that are organizing around issues that would be salient to a Latino person. There are certainly challenges a worker faces by walking the line between the two worlds of organizing and service. But, just to provide the services, the band-aid, and not to seize the chance to organize people, would be viewed by many progressive organizers as a wasted opportunity. To be able to walk such a line, workers certainly need the right kind of social change training that focuses on deconstructing social issues, empowerment theory, and boundaries.

COALITION BUILDING

Coalitions are created because organizers see that they have common interests with others that can be leveraged into power to effect change. A coalition is a group of organizations and individuals that work together on a common social issue to effect change, usually focused on a specific campaign. In order to recognize the mutual benefits of working together, one must see the interconnectedness of issues and realize that people are mutually affected by issues. People live in a web of interconnections, and their fates are linked. As Martin Luther King, Jr., (1997) said, "Whatever affects one directly, affects all indirectly"(p. 186). Affecting and changing systems is an enormous task, and it is virtually impossible to do so without coalitions. In recent years, college students and other young people organizing against global injustice have become conscious of the ways that globalization affects not only workers, but also themselves. They have become aware of how they have been manipulated by corporate advertising, which attempts to create unnecessary desires and hyper-consumerist behavior. Student groups have worked in coalition with unions and workers in the United States and abroad and achieved meaningful victories. AIDS activists are another example of a group that has done the important work of engaging in broad-based coalition work, i.e., working on issues that go beyond their own direct, immediate self-interest, but take a broader view of self-interest to include interconnected issues. AIDS activists have organized around immigrant rights, homelessness, and the rights of prisoners (http://www.nycahn.org).

The Coalition for Immokalee Workers (CIW), a Florida organization of farm workers from Mexico, Guatemala, and Haiti, tried to work for many years to engage in dialogue with growers to attempt to improve poor wages. Eventually, the group realized that it was the large corporations such as Taco Bell that demanded cheap produce from growers that were benefiting the most from the situation. After attempting to dialogue with Taco Bell directly about the farm labor conditions to no avail, CIW began a boycott against the company (Chavez, 2005). The ultimate success of this campaign, culminating in an agreement with the company to meet the demands for improving conditions, was attributed to coalition work, namely a coalition between farm workers and allies. According to Chavez:

> Through our organizing, one of the most important lessons we've learned is the necessity of building strong alliances.... Now we know that we are not alone and will never be alone again. Today, thousands of students and young people from all over the country know of our struggle, and they have come to understand that this is their struggle as well. As the multinational fast food corporation oppresses farm workers with the tyranny of extreme poverty, they oppress the youth of this country with their marketing based on the assumption that youth are hedonistic and apathetic. But we know differently. Young people across the country are taking the initiative to fight shoulder to shoulder with us for a world in which all of us may be heard—a world in which if one of us shouts for justice, there will always be thousands of voices echoing that shout. (p. 204)

When building coalitions or alliances, it may be useful to think of such efforts as resting on a spectrum. On one end of the spectrum is a *sustainable collaboration* over time, and on the other end is a short-term *relationship of convenience*. Sustainable collaborations may focus on consciousness-raising about issues, values clarification, and relationship-building across organizational differences.

Relationships of convenience are related to utilitarian organizing frameworks and emphasize short-term coalitions that focus on achieving a one-time goal such as changing a policy or implementing a program.

There are several considerations to keep in mind when engaging in any kind of coalition work (Sen, 2003)[1]:

1. Membership, values, and politics
2. Degree of formality
3. Resources and infrastructure
4. Power within the coalition

First, it is important that the groups working together have some kind of values and/or political beliefs in common. While there always will be differences between coalition members, which are indeed strengths, there should be some basic values in common. This is true whether the coalition is a relationship of convenience or whether it is a sustainable collaboration, where the latter group would tend to have a stronger values bond. The values discussion goes hand in hand with deciding who is to be included in the coalition. These discussions are important front-end tasks in setting up a coalition and also in ongoing ones. Membership can include large social welfare and advocacy organizations and small, grassroots organizations. But they can also include members of marginal-ized communities and other individual citizens.

Second, there are many kinds of collaborations—coalitions, councils, alliances, networks, and other even more informal types. Social movements can be considered a form of coalition work. The degree of formality of a coalition is an important consideration and is directly related to whether the group is focused on sustainable collaborations or relationships of convenience. Some coalitions and networks may choose to become more permanent by seeking legal nonprofit status, while others may prefer to stay informal. Informality may afford groups the capability of being more politically powerful and being less susceptible to co-optation by the internal and external pressures of a formal nonprofit organization.

Third, allocation of resources and the creation of infrastructure in the group should be consid-ered. Coalition members can contemplate whether everyone should contribute something to the group or not; decisions about the division of tasks can be based on the strengths of the people in the coalition. For example, who in the coalition is best suited to be the media spokesperson? This person must have the ability to communicate the message of the group to the outside. In addition, he or she has to be able to focus on the message of the larger coalition and not confuse it with the message of one's individual organization. Creating infrastructure in a coalition means establishing protocols for how meetings are conducted, how decisions are made, and how members communicate outside of meetings. Even if a coalition has been formed for the sake of convenience and is very ends-oriented, it will likely meet with more success if issues of resources and infrastructure are established from the outset.

Fourth, coalitions should be attuned to the ways in which power within the group is distributed. Transparency in decision making is probably one of the best ways to avoid negative power dynam-ics. Paying attention to power issues is an ongoing part of coalition work; it is especially important when the coalitions are diverse in terms of race, class, gender, sexual orientation, ability, etc. Are the men in the coalition the leaders and the women in the group the ones taking minutes? Is the organization that has the most resources making the majority of the decisions? Attending to these kinds of issues are what social change activists do; they do not want to replicate injustice in the way they do their work. Sometimes, there are varying levels of commitment in a coalition. Additionally, nonparticipating members may be reaping the rewards of membership in the coalition, but they may

---

[1] Besides Sen (2003), some of these ideas were inspired by a workshop called "Multi-Racial Coalition Building" at the Institute for the Study of Race and Poverty (ISRP) at Tulane University in July 2007.

not be committing time and resources. Such situations may be appropriate, but the coalition should be clear in how they get addressed in terms of decision-making practices and the distribution of rewards that may result from the coalition work.

OVERCOMING BARRIERS TO COALITION WORK

Uniting in coalition can increase the effectiveness of organizing practices and enhance the chances of victory; such organizing often involves overcoming divisions and barriers with which separate organizations are often confronted. In 1966, the National Farm Workers Association (NFWA) had been growing in strength and achieving victories for grape pickers in California under the leadership of Cesar Chavez (DiCanio, 1998). To thwart the effectiveness of the NFWA, the DiGiorgio company, a large corporation that owned vineyards in the region, devised a strategy that would permit the Teamsters Union (which had a reputation for illegal practices) to recruit workers in the field. This conquer-and-divide strategy resulted in a union election being held between three different unions: the NFWA, the Teamsters, and AWOC, a small union associated with the AFL-CIO. Chavez came to understand what was happening and saw that NFWA and AWOC had common ground to build on. So, he developed the strategy that the NFWA and AWOC could defeat the Teamsters. The two unions merged and became the United Farm Workers (UFW) and won the election by 530 votes to 331. Rather than succumbing to being pitted against each other, the groups worked in coalition and were able to be successful.

There are several reasons why groups may have trouble coming together to form coalitions. These reasons include substantive and philosophical differences, organizational and tactical differences, and cultural differences. Though these differences may be very real, it can also be the case that the dissimilarities are socially constructed by society. By engaging in critical reflection, groups can often overcome real and perceived barriers and come together as powerful forces in their organizing work. Here I discuss some barriers to coalition work and some remedies that can help organizers overcome them.

Substantive and Philosophical Differences

One of the biggest barriers to doing coalition work is that organizers often believe that they may not have much in common with other groups, both substantively and philosophically. For example, if one works for a group that advocates for people with disabilities, one may not consider a group that works to alleviate children's poverty to be an ally. Part of this barrier has to do with the segregated ways in which people are conditioned to think of social problems and social services, which is also a function of the segmented thinking that informs public policy funding mechanisms. If one is able to see social problems as interconnected and begins to understand the strengths of various sectors and community organizations, one can begin to get more clarity about who one's allies are. Maybe the statewide children's poverty group and the statewide disabilities group realize that they have both been victims of recent budget cuts—say less funding for children's health insurance programs and less funding for independent living centers. As the groups further discuss their issues, they come to understand that both children and people with disabilities have been historically groups without a "voice" and for whom policy decisions have been made without their input. Finally, the two groups may see themselves as in alliance with each other because of barriers such as discrimination in employment and low wages that both people with disabilities and low-income families with children face. Finding this common ground can be achieved through a variety of mechanisms such as workshops, popular education groups, and by continuing to invite new members to coalition meetings.

Some organizers may be hesitant to enter into coalition work because they believe that their frameworks for understanding social issues are vastly different from those of other groups. Schechter (1999) has studied and commented on how domestic violence activists sometimes isolate themselves from other groups, noting that they have been described by others as "suspicious and cynical" because they "refuse to acknowledge their limits ... they think they can do everything" (Schechter, 1999, p. 7).

Other community advocates have noted that "being with them is like trying to get into the most exclusive women's sorority" (Schechter, 1999, p. 7). Organizers can transcend ideological and other divides by learning the art of compromise and learning to frame their issues within a dominant discourse by softening or changing their language (Pyles, 2003). Organizers have often chosen to act in coalition to get work accomplished by concealing ideological differences (Arnold, 1995).

When I was working as an advocate for low-income battered women, I defined myself as a "feminist," specifically as an advocate for an oppressed population, namely women. In the mid and late 1990s, my group was focusing on the effects of welfare reform on survivors of sexual and domestic violence. One of the interesting things about these times was that welfare reform was so damaging that it was calling for a uniform response from community organizers and advocates. We could not work in isolation from other groups; we had to work with a variety of organizations and constituencies. Because the devolution of public welfare services was being placed in the hands of the states rather than the federal government, statewide advocacy was becoming more important than ever before. Thus, we participated in a state-level welfare reform advocacy group that included a children's poverty organization, a hunger organization, the Catholic archdiocese, and my group, the coalition representing domestic violence and sexual assault programs. I admittedly became somewhat wary of the possibility of working with a Catholic organization. In my mind, this organization likely did not have the same philosophy that I did regarding women's lives and, in particular, the rights of women to make choices for their own lives regarding reproductive health. In my naïveté, I thought that this meant that I could not work with this group. And then I met Sister Therese; Sister Therese was a well-respected organizer on poverty policy issues at the state legislature. The barriers I had erected in my mind became irrelevant, as I came to realize that we had common values when it came to families struggling to make ends meet. I was able to break through the attachment I had to my philosophy and pay attention to the new reality that was presenting itself. These common values were strong enough to not just develop a relationship of convenience on the particular issue of welfare reform, but they were strong enough for us to foster a sustainable collaboration over time. In the end, she would become a tremendous mentor for me, and we later recruited her to speak about legislative advocacy techniques with our constituency.

Organizational and Tactical Differences

Another reason why coalitions are difficult to form and coalesce is not only that the substantive issues with which organizations are engaged are so different, but also because the ways in which organizations operate can be so different. Organizations may have different philosophies in terms of decision making, staff–volunteer patterns, and funding streams. One group may be a locally based grassroots organization, while another group may be a large national organization with different chapters across the country. Finding common ground on other issues can be a way to overcome the barriers. Furthermore, these differences can also be leveraged, as the grassroots group may have stronger leadership from its base constituency and a stronger amount of accountability, while the national group may have more access to resources, which when combined could be formidable.

During the World Trade Organization (WTO) protests in Seattle in 1999, a wide range of activists came together to express their right to organize against a global economy that has been destructive to workers and the environment. The groups that came together were not only diverse in terms of the issues that they worked on and the ways that their organizations functioned, but they were also dissimilar in terms of the tactics that they utilized. A few groups broke the windows of businesses as a way to express their dissatisfaction with corporations. This resulted in the use of police violence against all of the participants in the protest. After the event, activists reflected that difficult discussions within the global justice movement were necessary, as some groups were using nonviolent tactics and were committed to them, while other groups were using more provocative tactics, which inadvertently put the peaceful protesters at risk. Though most organizers would never advocate the use of violent tactics, in general tactical differences should be viewed as strengths in coalition work, as the radical flank effect teaches that the activities of extreme groups can open doors for the more moderately situated groups. On the other hand, extreme tactics can have a negative effect on the entire movement or action.

Cultural Differences

There are a variety of differences among groups that come under the heading of cultural differences; such differences might be racial/ethnic, gender, age, sexual orientation, country of origin, ability, etc. In a recent study by Mizrahi and Lombe (2006), the authors found that women of color were less likely to engage in coalition work as an organizing strategy. This is a complex finding, but it can possibly be explained by a greater understanding of the historical realities faced by women of color. It is not uncommon for women of color to experience exclusion and silencing in women's organizing activities. As the dynamics of power and privilege are played out, the voices and agendas of the white women can easily come to dominate. It is not the case that the women in the study are noncooperative or do not see the potential of coalition work per se. However, based on past experiences, there is a belief that some coalition work may erase issues of difference, and the unique needs of women of color may get subsumed. These groups believe, and quite reasonably, that they need to focus on building their own base more strongly before attempting to build bridges.

Some recent sustainable coalition-building activities have focused on the need for intergenerational coalition building. Due to the rifts that have been identified between older and younger activists, some groups are actively working to bridge such rifts. In antiracism work, this has meant bridging the civil rights generation activists with the hip-hop generation activists. The community organizing leadership development institute, Southern Echo, operates on what they call an "intergenerational model." Such important coalition-building work focuses on helping the newer generation learn the historical and organizing lessons of the past. However, it is also important to remember that such intergenerational organizing is a two-way street, and more-advanced organizers have a lot to learn from the younger generation as well. Older activists may hold stereotypes about younger organizers, believing that the current generation does not care about issues or that they do not respect the older generation and their accomplishments. The younger generation of activists has different strengths, including their sense of self and community. They also face different issues than previous generations, including cultural, environmental, and technological issues.

The Zapatista model of *encuentro* can offer organizers good insights into overcoming barriers, as this model represents a unique approach to coalition building that emphasizes consciousness-raising while also allowing for differences to appear within and among actors. One such *encuentro* was held in 1996, bringing together 5,000 activists from all over the world to discuss how neoliberal globalization affects people politically, economically, culturally, and socially. Callahan (2004) describes *encuentro* as "a political space convened for dialogue, analysis, and direct action that deliberately and creatively acknowledges and respects difference, i.e., different political proposals and cultural practices that emerge from a variety of subject positions, histories, and political commitments" (p. 13).[1] It also serves as a mechanism for bridging local struggles with larger networks of global struggle.

Coalition work means finding common ground and bridging differences to effect change. Coalitions can be valuable at the local, city, state, national, and global levels. In the contemporary context, coalition work is vital at the global level, as transnational alliances offer excellent possibilities for achieving global justice victories. Overall, coalition building is really our best hope for achieving social change across constituencies and issues.

---

[1] One should be mindful when considering whether to borrow practices of indigenous people for use in their social change work. This could be considered a form of culture stealing that has negative associations with damaging colonialist practices. Nonetheless, relating to other human beings in the ways of *encuentro* and other similar practices is our birthright as human beings. Organizations can develop their own practices based on their own values and interests.

THE RIGHT TO RETURN CAMPAIGN, PART II: COALITION BUILDING

Anne Dienethal and Loretta Pyles

In the struggle to reopen public housing in New Orleans, multiple organizations have come together, realizing the value of joining forces, sharing resources, and building strength in numbers. The United Front for Affordable Housing (UFAH) was formed as a concentrated effort on the part of several organizations to address illegal evictions of public housing residents and the threat of demolition to public housing in the post-Katrina environment. Initially organized by activists from C3/Hands Off Iberville and Common Ground to form the New Orleans Housing Emergency Action Team (NO HEAT), the network of participants broadened when, in February 2006, public housing residents began to attend meetings to provide their input. It was these same residents who chose the UFAH name and who were instrumental in the growth of the movement, resulting in formation of a coalition of organizations with the mission to "call on local, state and federal officials to abide by international law, and honor the right of return of Internally Displaced Persons, citizens of New Orleans, citizens of public housing" (Survivors' Village, 2006). Functioning as an umbrella organization, the UFAH, using a human rights framework that identifies New Orleans residents as internally displaced people, began to reach out to anyone in New Orleans who cared about affordable housing and who wanted to work to mitigate cutbacks and to lobby for the return of displaced residents.

Very few of the activists working within organizations of the UFAH are paid; therefore, the success of the actions and demonstration organized by the coalition is the product of donations, as well as hard work on the part of its members and volunteers. The coalition's processes are informal and loosely structured, with resources and responsibilities shared democratically and in line with group consensus. In the absence of the need for emergency action, weekly meetings at a local community center use input from members to determine meeting agendas and the coalition's next course of action. Targeting issues that link all of the participating organizations together is an essential focus of the coalition. In addition, as within all groups, building and maintaining effective communication has been vital to the health of the partnership. The UFAH communicates regularly through e-mail and word of mouth, aided by a listserv in which members and the community at large can exchange information about upcoming demonstrations, provide feedback, and post possible meeting agenda items. Decisions are made by votes from attending members at weekly meetings before any action is taken.

STRENGTH IN NUMBERS

The strengths that result from having a broad-based organization such as UFAH include the sharing of tangible and intangible resources, from ideas to meeting space, and the wealth of knowledge and talent that comes from bringing a large group of people together. One of the key strengths cited by members of UFAH is the sheer number of members involved who can be deployed quickly when necessary to form a critical mass of people. The more organizations that participate under the UFAH umbrella, the easier it is to pull people into an action or demonstration within a short amount of time, meaning a more effective action and broader awareness of the targeted issue.

Not surprisingly, working within a coalition presents a number of challenges. As noted by one member and housing activist, one of the greatest challenges of working in a coalition is working together as individuals with various personalities in a large group of people brought together with a shared focus but different ideas about how to achieve goals. Being especially mindful of how and where ideas originate and giving credit where appropriate is essential in maintaining healthy relationships among the organizations, due to the threat of turf wars and organizational biases. One of building blocks of the success of UFAH is a great deal of patience and respect for the people involved.

Another challenge, inherent in working with disadvantaged populations, is the need for cultural competence. Similar to government tactics used throughout the civil rights movement, city officials have at times attempted to divide groups such as UFAH by perpetuating the belief that it is not in the best interests of the African-American community to work with white activists. Preserving the bond between activists and residents is essential and can be accomplished by having decisions come from residents as much as possible while also acknowledging the fact that what is at stake is a public resource, and that everyone has a right to his or her own viewpoints, ideas, and strategies.

One of the primary goals of UFAH has been not only to engage residents of public housing, but to build capacity citywide by engaging allies who may not immediately identify themselves as stakeholders. By reaching out to the entire community, members of UFAH seek to not only address those in need of public housing, but also to identify issues that draw all residents together. For example, by framing the lack of access to and planned demolition of public housing as a federal attack on public services, the group seeks to engage others affected by federal cutbacks, including those impacted most by lack of spending on education and health care. By reaching the community at large, the coalition broadens its parameters to increase support from not only community members, but also agencies and institutions within the community, thereby building capacity and sending the message that change is essential.

Embracing grassroots direct action, UFAH has sponsored and organized many events in support of public housing since its inception, including multiple rallies, press conferences, and marches staged in front of public housing developments. In June 2006, UFAH members and allies set up a tent city called Survivors' Village outside of the 1,300 empty apartments at St. Bernard housing development. Residents pledged to reoccupy housing without permission from the housing authority and to resist demolition of their homes "by any means necessary" (Quigley, 2006a). In addition, being strong supporters of the Gulf Coast Hurricane Housing Recovery Act of 2007, members of UFAH have staged multiple demonstrations and rallies on the issue, urging Senate support of the bill.

Martin Luther King Day, 2006

A successful example of the product of collaboration between organizations can be seen in the Martin Luther King Day March to Rebuild the Gulf Coast and the World, which took place less than five months after Hurricane Katrina on January 16, 2006. Taking place just prior to the official start of UFAH, the march was sponsored by multiple organizations, including C3/Hands Off Iberville, Forest Park Tenants Association, Coalition against War and Injustice (CAWI–Baton Rouge), New Orleans Housing Emergency Action Team (NO HEAT), Harlem Tenants Union, and the Workers Democracy Network. Sponsoring organizations around the country responded to the call of local organizations to support the demand for the immediate reopening of public housing and the rebuilding of the Gulf Coast.

The product of weeks of hard work consisting of phone calls, dispersal of press releases, and gathering donations, the resulting rally drew over 100 people five months after Hurricane Katrina. Using the slogan "Honor Martin Luther King—Bring all of New Orleans home," supporters marched from the Lower Ninth Ward to the Iberville Housing Development. Lower Ninth Ward community leaders and the city officials, including city council president, attended in support of public housing and gave speeches emphasizing the need to begin rebuilding rather than tearing down.

Three years after Hurricane Katrina, UFAH members have won some victories and suffered some setbacks. Nevertheless, many public housing units remain unopened and many residents remain displaced. Organizations of the UFAH continue to work together, using grassroots direct action to unite public housing residents and public housing supporters under the common goal of increased access to public housing. A recent setback occurred when city council members voted to proceed with the demolition of several public housing units. Future organizing activity will center on the need for one-to-one replacement of destroyed units and the passage of the Gulf Coast Hurricane Recovery Act.

QUESTIONS FOR REFLECTION

1. What are your concerns and fears about organizing people in their own neighborhoods or homes? What are the benefits of this type of organizing?
2. What are some strategies for maintaining and enhancing relationships with individuals who have been recently organized into a campaign?
3. If you ever worked in a social service organization, think about a client/consumer that you have worked with and discuss the strengths and barriers that they could have brought to a community organizing endeavor.
4. Discuss the benefits and limitations of coalition building to an organizing campaign or social movement.
5. What personal barriers to building coalitions do you identify in yourself? How can you go about addressing them?

SUGGESTIONS FOR FURTHER INQUIRY

BOOKS

Albrecht, L., & Brewer, R. (1990). *Bridges of power: Women's multicultural alliances*. Philadelphia: New Society Publishers.
Bandy, J., & Smith, J. (2005). *Coalitions across borders*. Lanham, MD: Rowman & Littlefield.
Chambers, E. (2003). *Roots for radicals: Organizing for power, action and justice*. New York: Continuum.
Murphy, P. W., & Cunningham, J. V. (2003). *Organizing for community-controlled development: Renewing civil society*. Thousand Oaks, CA: Sage Publications.
Warren, M. R. (2001). *Dry bones rattling: Community building to revitalize American democracy*. Princeton, NJ: Princeton University Press.

WEB

Catalyst Project: A Center for Political Education and Movement Building. http://www.collectiveliberation.org
Citizen Works: Tools for Democracy. http://www.citizenworks.org
Community Organizing Toolkit. http://organizinggame.org
Midwest Academy. http://www.midwestacademy.com
Wellstone Action. http://www.wellstone.org

KEY TERMS

Accountability: In community organizing, this term is employed to emphasize the importance of being able to answer to constituent communities and represent the needs of the most vulnerable members of society in organizing work. By focusing on constituency leadership development and empowerment practices, organizational practice can be most closely aligned with a community's desires.

Asset-based community development (ABCD): Strength-based sustainable community development that focuses on local assets of the environment, individuals, associations, and institutions. This approach is significant because it rejects traditional ideas of community development that focus on deficits and problems in communities.

Coalition building: Diverse organizers and advocates working together across organizations and issues to impact change.

Constituencies: The people for whom an issue is most relevant, such as residents of a neighborhood, citizens of a state, consumers of a social service, members of a racial/ethnic group.

Relational meeting: This organizing technique is used to engage potential organizers through engagement in dialogue that seeks common ground between the organizer and constituent.

7 Toward Empowering Organizations

> I happen to believe that what makes an organizer good is what organization they're with. You're not going to be a good organizer in an ineffective organization.
>
> **Scott Douglas, executive director, Greater Birmingham Ministries**
> *(Cited in Szakos & Szakos, 2007, p. 148)*

Resource mobilization theory posits that the amount of resources available to a movement is the strongest determinate of its success. Gamson (1990), in particular, has argued that the most critical kinds of resources are strong organizations. Moreover, in studies of social movement groups, researchers have found that successful groups tend to be more bureaucratized and centralized and do not have as many problems with factionalism (Gamson, 1990; Giugni, 2004). Alinsky and many of his followers have been strong advocates of the importance of building organizations as the pathway to achieving organizing victories. Others have argued just the opposite: movements are more likely to succeed when they avoid building strong organizations because they are better able to utilize the tactic of disruption (Giugni, 2004; Piven & Cloward, 1979). While mobilization may allow for more flexibility, spontaneity, and creativity, institutionalization may allow for more stability, development of resources, and sustainability (Tait, 2005). Rubin and Rubin (2001) have offered that organizations are able to focus power, offer continuity, develop expertise, and react quickly to changing conditions. In the context of a globalizing economy and neoliberal social welfare policies that have resulted in the abandonment of state interventions, the roles of nonprofit organizations and nongovernmental organizations (NGOs) are particularly salient in communities across the globe (Reisch, 2005). It is clear that organizations play an important though contested role in community organizing work.

Ferree and Martin (1995) have pointed out that "a movement organization is not a contradiction in terms, but it is, by definition, in tension" (p. 8). In other words, organizations that come into being to address social oppressions, a result of critiques of societal power structures, are also creating new power structures as an organization. Unfortunately, sometimes the survival of organizations misguidedly becomes the end of organizing efforts rather than the means (Ferree & Martin, 1995). One of the potential pitfalls for any organization trying to do social change work, particularly nonprofit organizations with 501(c)3 status, is that the organization can become more focused on keeping the organization financially afloat or preserving its status as a 501(c)3. This objective slowly and subtly can become the end in itself of the organization rather than that of its original mission, such as empowering a particular group or impacting a social issue. The dissonance between progressive agendas and organizational maintenance seems to be an enduring problem in organizing (Padgett, 2002).

Many books on community organizing explain "how to build an organization." The reality is that most organizers do not start their own organizations; they usually do their work in the context of an existing organization. Thus, it makes sense to begin a chapter about organizations with the premise that organizers enter into a variety of organizational milieus that offer opportunities to learn about and impact organizations. Building strong and accountable organizations whereby people practice and learn democratic processes is a vital part of empowering, social change efforts. The Highlander Research and Education Center calls this practice "constructing democracy," advocating that grassroots organizations be experiments in democracy and training grounds to prepare people for participation and leadership in a more democratic society (http://www.highlandercenter.org). In this chapter, after discussing some of the complexities of organizing in the nonprofit world, I focus on organizational capacity building in a few important areas: multilingual capacity building, fundraising, leadership and decision-making practices, and the role of research and evaluation.

ORGANIZING IN THE NONPROFIT WORLD

A recent publication by South End Press—*The Revolution Will Not Be Funded* (Incite, 2007)—contemplates the question of whether social change is possible through the mechanisms of the nonprofit sector. A play on the title of the 1974 Gil Scott Heron song "The Revolution Will Not Be Televised," the authors problematize organizing in the context of nonprofit organizations, including the limitations that social service provision poses to social change organizing. The institutionalization of a movement, campaign, or social change endeavor can easily lead to bureaucratization that can entail a silencing of the marginalized voices it was intending to amplify in the first place (Tait, 2005). Rodriguez (2007) argues that nonprofit organizations can manifest as mechanisms of control by the state to maintain current conditions and the existing social structures. Modeled on corporations and state bureaucracies, organizations originally intended for social change can easily succumb to the pressures of funding streams, the professional culture of the nonprofit world, and organizational maintenance. As Reisch (2005) notes, in an era of a globalizing economy, "Market ideas have influenced these organizations' vocabulary, program emphases, staffing patterns, funding sources, and their relationship with constituents" (p. 540).

For social workers, human service professionals, advocates, and others working in nonprofit organizations, especially organizations that are providing services, community organizing can sometimes seem at odds with the realities of a social service organization. This dilemma dates back to the time of Jane Addams during the Settlement House movement. Addams (1910) defends engaging in labor organizing in the context of a service organization:

> That a Settlement is drawn into labor issues of its city can seem remote to its purpose only to those who fail to realize that so far as the present industrial system thwarts our ethical demands, not only for social righteousness but for social order, a Settlement is committed to an effort to understand and, as far as possible, to alleviate it. (p. 150)

In contemporary history, social workers and others in nonprofit settings only rarely engage in community organizing activities. Several reasons for this exist, including perceived conflicts of interest with grant funds, a shortage of staff and skills, and a lack of social change climate in agencies. Specht and Courtney (1994) remind us that when many activists were engaged in protests against the Vietnam War, social workers were conspicuously absent. Fisher and Shragge (2000) argue that there has been a shift in emphasis away from social change in community organizing efforts through the 1980s and 1990s. The shift was already becoming clear in the 1970s, citing the relationship between the growth of professionalization and the reduction of grassroots power. Some have argued that it is the possibility of well-paying jobs in the nonprofit sector that has derailed many activists from community organizing, focusing instead on social service delivery (Smith, 2007).

Nonprofit organizations are often hesitant to engage in various types of advocacy and organizing work because they believe "lobbying" legislators could jeopardize their 501(c)3 statuses. The reality is that nonprofits can indeed educate their legislators about the issues that are important to them and their constituency; the only thing that they cannot do is endorse particular political candidates. Some grants and other funding sources may prohibit lobbying activities, but there is nothing in the 501(c)3 statute that prohibits it. Support organizations such as the Alliance for Justice can help organizations with legal issues related to such questions about nonprofit status.

Some organizations, noting that the 501(c)3 tax code was created not by grassroots activists but by wealthy philanthropists who were seeking a tax shelter, choose not to seek such legal status for their organizations. Such organizations may struggle to maintain funding. Foundations have the burden of exerting expenditure responsibility, and thus they tend to fund only 501(c)3 organizations because there is a higher burden on the foundation if there is no 501 status. Nonetheless, it is still possible to get donations from people in the community without legal, nonprofit status.

Amara Perez (2007) of Sisters in Action for Power has discussed the difficulties of doing social change and community organizing work in the traditional nonprofit model. Through many difficult lessons, her organization has focused its efforts on creating an organizational practice context that is compatible with social change values. Such mechanisms are built into the organization as a way to preserve the integrity of social change work. While not advocating that these practices are appropriate for all organizations, Sisters in Action for Power have identified important activities that can help maintain an empowering, social change organizational climate:

- Create a work plan that outlines the larger issues the organization seeks to address, including organizational strategies and annual goals
- Collectively evaluate and reflect on annual goals using the organization's political framework
- Meet every week as staff and/or volunteers to make decisions as a group, inform each other about work, and assess workload and organizational capacities
- Include journal writing and other methods for staff to communicate their personal work as part of collective movement building
- Schedule dedicated days for staff political education, including taking turns facilitating discussions
- Every three months, take time for team building and bonding
- Take care of personal selves by monitoring pace of work, hours worked, and time off

Due to the ongoing pressures of organizing activities, decision-making responsibilities, and accountability to funders, nonprofit organizations can build mechanisms into their policies, structures, and practices such as these. Such practices do not erase the innate tensions that exist in progressive organizations; they can, however, facilitate transparency, sustainability, and empowerment.

ORGANIZATIONAL CAPACITY BUILDING

Building the internal capacities of organizations is a way to enhance the abilities of organizations to achieve their goals. Capacity building may entail a variety of activities, including upgrading technological facility, developing fund-raising competence, enhancing financial management systems, and improving the multilingual abilities of an organization, to name a few. Capacity-building endeavors are not ends in themselves but, rather, are means to the ends of enhancing organizing capabilities and effecting social change. The following sections will extend the discussion on capacity building, focusing on key elements of working in organizations engaged in progressive community organizing: multilingual capacity building, fund-raising, leadership and decision making, and research/evaluation. Though these elements are certainly not exhaustive when it comes to organizational practice, they are particularly salient for progressive organizers interested in attending to social change organizing in a globalized world.

MULTILINGUAL CAPACITY BUILDING

Social issues cut across a variety of human differences, including culture, race/ethnicity, country of origin, and language. The lack of ability of organizers and constituents to communicate with one another due to language barriers is a common problem in community organizing practice. This problem manifests in a world where many people have been displaced from their homelands or have been forced to migrate in search of better work opportunities. Global and local communities are intersecting economically, socially, culturally, politically, and linguistically. As will be discussed in Chapter 12, one of the goals of the contemporary global justice movement is to bridge real and socially constructed differences, seeking common ground in the name of human rights. In a world reeling from the ongoing effects of colonialism, where articulating social identities and the needs and desires that accompany them is an important task, the ability to engage in discourse across language barriers is important for a postcolonial and postmodern world. The ability to communicate across language differences is particularly relevant in multiethnic areas, in communities with significant immigrant populations, in regions with indigenous populations whose languages are at risk of disappearing, and in transnational organizing contexts.

Creating multilingual spaces in organizations is a strategic way to build social movement and organizational power. It is a means to attend to the democratization of organizations whereby people who speak dominant and nondominant languages are better equipped to share power. This can necessitate creating environments where primarily English-speaking people learn the languages of fellow organizers and constituents. For some organizations, building in the costs of interpreters and language classes for organizers and constituents is a way to honor this value in practice.

For organizations that are led and driven by speakers of the nondominant language, multilingual capacity building would seem to be an obvious need. However, for organizations that are led by English speakers and do not have non-English speakers in leadership positions, the need for such resources may seem less pressing. It should be clear that empowerment of and accountability to constituents in certain contexts necessitates investment in interpreters and other resources for multilingual capacity building. Organizers and constituents should be able to contribute to organizing efforts in a way that allows them to share their deepest wisdom; this deep wisdom is best expressed in one's native language.

I have heard many organizations talk about how they want to organize more Spanish-speaking Latino/Latina people into their organization, but fail to prioritize the language capacity building that is necessary. This is a difficult issue, as organizations have many needs that are difficult to prioritize. However, progressive community organizing in a globalized world would surely entail such prioritization. Prioritizing may mean budgeting for interpretation costs as well as factoring in the extra time and logistics that interpretation can entail in meetings and events. At the first-ever U.S. Social Forum in Atlanta held in the summer of 2007, the planners of this broad-based organizing event were transparent about their aspirations and limitations when it came to multilingual capacity building. According to their Web site:

> To achieve a truly multilingual movement for social justice, we must transform the power of language so that it can no longer divide us but rather will unite us and make us stronger. While we are committed to continue to strengthen our multilingual capacity over time, we also want to acknowledge the limitations of our current capacity. The National Planning Committee has committed to support three languages at the US Social Forum: Spanish, American Sign Language (ASL) and English. This does not mean, however, that the entire Social Forum will be interpreted into all three languages. The opening march, the opening and closing ceremonies, the morning openings, the plenaries, and the People's Movement Assembly—conducted primarily in English—will be interpreted into Spanish and ASL. The Language Access Team of the USSF will provide Spanish interpretation for approximately 10% of the self-organized workshops. In addition, a number of workshops are being held in Spanish or interpreted into Spanish by the workshop organizers themselves. (https://www.ussf2007.org/en/multilingual_access, ¶ 3)

An organizational model for multilingual capacity building entails an organizational value statement, the commitment of resources, implementation of resources, and the acknowledgment of organizational limitations.

Fund-Raising

All organizing work requires a certain degree of financial resources; building power in organizations means building financial power. Though many organizations receive donations of time, services, and materials, it is virtually impossible for an organization to have an impact without some money. Securing money has typically been achieved through grant writing and fund-raising.

While many service organizations obtain grants from national and local governments as well as the private sector, obtaining grants to do social change work can be challenging. It is not likely that the government is going to give your organization money to stage protests in front of the U.S. Capitol. That being said, tapping into grant funds can be beneficial to organizations in spite of the challenges and drawbacks. The current grants and fund-raising climate in the nonprofit world encourages organizations to compete against each other for funding. In addition, philanthropists tend to make their decisions about what to fund behind closed doors, without the input of communities, organizations, and citizens. Such funders may not fund projects for very long, and the sustainability of social agendas can be compromised. However, there are alternative solutions to these practices. Such solutions empower the community to be a part of the decision-making process and enable them to be at the table when deciding who gets funding, how much, and for how long.

The Colorado Community Organizing Collaborative represents an alternative approach to philanthropy. A cooperative project of the Ford Foundation and the Piton Foundation, this collaborative of local community organizations works in conjunction with the philanthropies to make joint decisions about how the money is spent. The criteria for participation of these local community organizations are that they use grassroots community organizing as a primary strategy, with a strong emphasis on membership-driven self-governance. The purpose of the initiative is to foster collaboration among community organizing groups and support activities that build the field of organizing in the region. Other groups across the country, such as the Women's Fightback Network, Chahara, and the Immigrant Worker Center Collaborative, are trying similar alternative models.

Activists have noted that funding community organizing can be more difficult than funding social service provision. Engaged in organizing with low-income elderly individuals who were living in single-room occupancy hotel rooms, Minkler (2005) notes that when their group

> shifted to a pure community organizing project, it also discovered that its goals (for example, community empowerment and leadership development) were less attractive to most traditional foundation and corporate sponsors than were tangible deliverables such as hotel-based minimarkets and health promotion resource centers. Moreover, even progressive foundations that understood and applauded [the group's] new directions tended to avoid refunding the same project, so new sources of income continually had to be located. With an overworked board and no staff or volunteers specifically devoted to raising money, [the group's] two full-time organizers found themselves unable to respond to many requests to help organize in new buildings because they were too busy raising funds. (p. 279)

Despite the barriers, there are grants available to NGOs and nonprofits doing organizing work. Resources such as the *Grassroots Fundraising Journal* (http://www.grassrootsfundraising.org/) can provide useful information and ideas regarding the challenges of staying afloat in community organizations. The Third Wave Foundation funds new and emerging organizations and works with them to help them tap into other foundations.

Here I offer some questions and guidelines for group and organizational decision making about engaging in grant-funded activities:

- Carefully determine the campaigns and projects that your organization wants to engage in, making sure that such decisions are accountable to the constituency. Once this has been determined, then look for funding to do the work. Do not do it the other way around and have the funder determine your priorities.
- If the funder is a private foundation, research who the financier is. Is the foundation an arm of a corporation that is engaging in oppressive social or economic practices? What does the funder stand for? Are their values commensurate with your organization's values?

- If the funder is a governmental agency, consider the political climate and agenda that the state may be trying to promote. Is the agenda commensurate with the values of your organization?
- What kind of evaluation and reporting requirements does the funder have? Are there resources available to build the capacity of the organization to engage in such activities?

Many people in social change organizations consider fund-raising to be an unpalatable activity that only detracts from the time that could better be spent organizing. However, some organizations have reframed this complaint and consider fund-raising to be a central part of their organizing strategy. Project South: Institute for the Elimination of Poverty and Genocide is a grassroots organization in Atlanta, Georgia, focused on racial and economic justice. For this group, fund-raising itself has become a strategy for maintaining a connection to its base constituency. "We define *organizing* as building relationships and institutions to sustain community power, and it follows that fundraising *is* organizing" (Guilloud & Cordery, 2007, p. 108). Rather than hiring fund-raisers to do fund-raising, they hire organizers to do fund-raising. Their experience has been that dependency on foundations limits their effectiveness. The funders are often defining the programming trends, and then non-profits must "bend to these requests rather than assess real needs and realistic goals" (Guilloud & Cordery, 2007, p. 108). Thus, Project South's fund-raising strategy is based on the notion of a "community-based economy," where resources flow from and return to the same community. Though not all of their fund-raising comes from the grassroots community, their goal is to increase that amount each year. Many activists tend to hold an overly simplified view of philanthropists as a monolithic group of rich people running foundations, but in reality working and poor people can be considered philanthropists, as they are generous and give proportionally a significant amount of their income. Getting $20 from a constituent and getting her or him involved in the organization may be more valuable and sustainable in the long run than $100 from a wealthy donor.

LEADERSHIP AND DECISION MAKING

Most nonprofit organizations have historically modeled their decision making after for-profit organizations. The executive director position is modeled after a chief executive officer (CEO) position. Front-line workers report to department directors and coordinators, i.e., middle management. Leaders may be open to input from those working on the front lines regarding decisions to be made, but ultimately final decisions usually rest with agency directors. This kind of hierarchical decision making can be very effective when lines of communication are clear. In an environment where public policies and funding opportunities are in flux, it is often necessary to be able to make decisions quickly. When such decisions are in the hands of a single person, it can be very efficient.

But, how compatible are these traditional approaches with an organizational practice premised on empowerment and social change? Does the manner in which an organization operates, as long as it is engaging in successful campaigns and creating new opportunities in partnership with its constituents, matter? For progressive community organizers, particularly those working from a transformative approach, it does matter, for such an orientation necessarily entails a commitment on the part of community organizations to attend to its own processes and mechanisms, particularly when it comes to issues of leadership and decision making.

Much has been written about organizational development and leadership in progressive organizations and social movements (Barnett, 1997; Gordon, 2000; Padgett, 2002). Leadership has been defined as a "process of performing multiple roles and functions for the purpose of achieving some set of goals reflecting the needs, concerns, or desires of a group, including a social movement" (Barnett, 1997, p. 303). Leadership in the context of community organizing can take a variety of shapes. Leaders in organizations and movements may be the people who hold the vision and/or play an important role in making decisions. Martin Luther King, Jr., was a vision holder and hence leader of the civil rights movement. But, leaders may also take the form of rank-and-file activists who engage in significant actions that are inspiring to others; Rosa Parks was one such example.

Leadership and organizational structure in progressive community organizations can manifest in various ways, from centralized, hierarchical models to decentralized and nonhierarchical approaches in the form of collectives or other consensus-oriented structures. Often, organizational structures and leadership philosophies lie somewhere in between these extremes. Traditional notions of leadership focus on one or a few people who have power and lead others, the followers. Progressive community organizers recognize that such practices have oppressed many people in organizations and, more generally, in society. These approaches to leadership may tend to marginalize women, people of color, LGBT (lesbian, gay, bisexual, transgender) individuals, individuals who are not fluent in the dominant language, and people with disabilities (SPAN, 2005). Progressive community organizing rests on the idea that organizing greater numbers of constituents is a desirable goal, and for many this implies that each person has the capacity to be a leader. By teaching leadership skills and organizing constituents and organizational members into positions of increasingly greater responsibility, community organizers directly confront traditional models of leadership. Though the idea that no single person should make decisions on behalf of a constituency is a valuable one, it is also the case that some people must necessarily be in leadership positions to facilitate meetings, coordinate and implement visions, and engage in various other sundry leadership tasks.

Leadership, like many other phenomena viewed through a critical lens, can be problematized, i.e., broken down into its assumptions, determining who wins and who loses in various organizational structures in particular contexts. In a study of campus LGBT organizing, Meyer (2004) notes that those who are considered "leaders" and those who are considered "members" of organizations tend to view leadership differently.

> Leaders were perceived as "committed to the cause," often associated with their visibility in the community and their level of being "out" by both leaders and members of the community. As a result, participants in leadership roles tended to frame "leaders" as committed and "members" as apathetic. Participants in membership roles, however, expressed their frustration at the perceived apathy of leaders, observing that leadership styles in the community were sometimes "overbearing" and "silencing." (p. 505)

While hierarchical, bureaucratic decision-making structures can lead to silencing, egalitarian structures can lead to "unspoken hierarchies" (A. Smith, 2006, p. 69). The difference, though, between the types of leadership in progressive community organizations versus traditional organizations is that leaders are not afforded any more privilege than any other person in the organization. Of course, this can be complicated in practice. Leaders in organizations who have a considerable amount of longevity doing the work or who happen to have a lot of charisma may have a kind of unspoken privilege in the organization. Their voice may be more likely to be heeded during discussions about certain decisions.

Traditional hierarchical administrative models are not incompatible with progressive social change organizing. It is, however, necessary to consider the implications and complexities of such scenarios. Safehouse Progressive Alliance for Nonviolence (SPAN) has offered several qualities of leaders, such as CEOs and executive directors, who are committed to building multiethnic, inclusive, and antiracist organizations. These qualities include someone who:

- Is willing to acknowledge his or her own power and privilege,
- Utilizes a transparent decision-making process,
- Is not removed from everyday struggles, and
- Is committed to and models conflict-resolution processes when injuries and damages occur within the organization (SPAN, 2005).

Because power and privilege can easily and quite subtly be used to marginalize and silence people in organizations, such leadership qualities and actions can be effective in bringing about an empowered organization.

The Annie E. Casey Foundation partnered with the Leadership Learning Community (LLC) to learn about how to expand leadership opportunities for people of color (Perry, n.d.). In the study, LLC interviewed organizational leaders and learned about barriers to expanding such opportunities as well as what strategies can be useful to facilitate leadership opportunities. Based on focus groups and interviews with a variety of nonprofit stakeholders, Perry found that there are many barriers within organizations and among other key stakeholders that hinder more collectively oriented and people-of-color-driven organizational practices. The findings of this study included several possible solutions to these hindrances, including focusing on individual leadership development among people of color, with a particular focus on mentoring and skills development. Developing constituency, organizational, and interorganizational capacities appears to be just as critical to expanding such leadership opportunities. Recommendations included reviewing personnel policies, job descriptions, and decision-making standards for alignment with organizational values. In addition, funders can make diversity and inclusiveness in leadership and organizational management as part of their criteria for funding.

Consensus Decision Making

Consensus decision making offers an alternative model for making decisions in an organization (Avery, Stribel, Auvine & Weiss, 1981). Consensus is defined as agreement among a substantial number of members that is reached after group study and discussion. It is the sense of what the group supports. It is not a vote, not a majority, and not necessarily unanimity. Emerging from feminist and environmental organizing, this kind of decision making requires a group of individuals who are committed to the values and principles of nonhierarchical organizing. Searching for common ground through dialogue is the main practice of consensus decision making.

Before engaging in consensus decision making in an organization, it is necessary that the group has a clear sense of its mission and has a unity of principles, as without a common set of values, it would make little sense to engage in a value-driven activity such as consensus (Gelderloos, 2006). According to Gelderloos:

> Adopting a conscious consensus process is significant in a number of ways. Commitment to the ideal of consensus signifies a bold rejection of society's dominant values of order, hierarchy, competition, and formalized leadership.... The process also recognizes that the oppressive systems of our society deeply affect our own behaviors, and that people who are typically silenced by our society can also be marginalized within ostensibly anti-authoritarian groups unless there is an intentional structure that helps expose and overcome these power dynamics. (pp. 14–15)

Emerging from work in the antiviolence movement, Creighton and Kivel (1993) identify basic agreements that build trust and respect in a group, which one may consider central for achieving liberation and justice. Groups such as the Texas Council on Family Violence do trainings with domestic violence and sexual assault organizations to help them with this kind of work. Communication becomes the central mechanism for achieving consensus and is the basis of organizational empowerment. Grounded in principles of feminism, some group conditions that support consensus are:

- Principles of unity
- Equal access to power
- Autonomy of the group from external hierarchical structures
- A willingness in the group to spend time to attend to process
- A willingness in the group to attend to attitudes
- A willingness in the group to learn and practice skills

Dialogue is truly crucial for any social change organization with a transformative or conscious-ness-raising approach to organizing. Freire (1970) reminds us of the importance of dialogue as a way to hear the voices of people who can often get marginalized in group process.

By building mechanisms for communication about issues and regular organizational decision making into organizational decision-making processes, a supportive and empowering environment can be created. In this case, the process becomes as important as the ends. Besides the values and intention, each meeting or session can include assigning positions such as a facilitator, a note taker, a timekeeper, and a process watcher. The facilitator position is often rotated, but this is the person who keeps the process going, making sure that everyone in the group has a chance to participate. The process watcher pays attention to the emotions of the group, including people's body language. The timekeeper makes sure that the process is staying within the allotted time for each agenda item, while the note taker keeps track of what is happening.

The following are a few further guidelines for communication in a consensus process:

Confidentiality: Everything said in the group is confidential, allowing people to feel safe to express their perspectives.

Amnesty: People are not blamed for their beliefs, and an atmosphere of grace for human foibles is created.

Put-ups, not put-downs: Operating from a strengths perspective, the group seeks common ground.

Right to pass: Nobody is forced to speak when she or he does not want to. Some people contrib-ute to the process through means other than talking.

No cross talk, no piggybacking: Side conversations are not productive to group consensus. Piggybacking is a way to build an argument and position and is more conducive to a debate atmosphere rather than a consensus atmosphere.

Feelings: Feelings are often invalidated in traditional organizational settings. Being as aware and transparent about one's own feelings as possible is advantageous to group process.

Respect/listening: Listening is a vital skill in organizational decision making.

"I" statements: Speaking in "I" statements, such as "I believe this action would be beneficial because…," encourages personal accountability for statements. Speaking on behalf of oth-ers by using "we" statements can be marginalizing.

Try on the process: It is difficult to critique the process unless you actually try it with an open mind.

Utilizing these guidelines can make group discussions more productive. There are ways that group members who are not able to find common ground with the group can express this. By choos-ing to "stand-aside" from a decision, a member of the group agrees not to block the decision from happening. Finally, one person can block a decision that is the will of the group if he or she cannot find common ground.

One of the critiques of consensus work is that it takes too much time. To alleviate this concern, successful consensus-oriented organizations establish time parameters before every meeting and for every agenda item; they can agree to extend time for more complex issues. In the long run, it may actually take less time to utilize consensus decision making than traditional approaches. This is because consensus allows for reflection on decisions from multiple perspectives, giving everyone the opportunity to think through unintended consequences as well as to buy in to the decision. When groups do not have complete group buy-in on decisions, they often have to go back and undo those decisions anyway, which can ultimately be more time consuming.

Consensus decision making has been perceived as antidemocratic because a person who blocks a proposal can be viewed as having too much power. Essayist Murray Bookchin critiques the use of consensus, particularly as it played out in the Clamshell Alliance, a consensus-based movement formed to oppose the Seabrook nuclear reactor in the mid-1970s in New Hampshire:

On a more theoretical level, consensus silenced that most vital aspect of all dialogue, *dissensus*. The ongoing dissent, the passionate dialogue that still persists even after a minority accedes temporarily to a majority decision, was replaced in the Clamshell by dull monologues—and the uncontroverted and deadening tone of consensus. In majority decision-making, the defeated minority can resolve to overturn a decision on which they have been defeated—they are free to openly and persistently articulate reasoned and potentially persuasive disagreements. Consensus, for its part, honors no minorities, but mutes them in favor of the metaphysical "one" of the "consensus" group. (Bookchin, 2001, section 2, ¶ 9)

Consensus decision making may not be the right approach for all organizations at all times. Some organizations may choose to utilize consensus for a particular committee, for example, but do not use it for their daily decision-making process. Other groups may choose to employ consensus for all organizational decisions. I worked at an organization where every decision was made based on consensus. Even daily decisions could be made by a "Committee of 3" or what we called a "C of 3." Any three organizational members could make decisions, since we did not have an executive director or other supervisor whom we deferred to. I also worked for a different organization that attempted to utilize consensus decision making, but we quickly learned that the value commitment just was not there to make it successful. Each group has to determine what its own values are before deciding what kind of decision-making processes are most appropriate for the organization.

EVALUATING COMMUNITY ORGANIZING

Organizer Ed Chambers (2003) wrote: "Research, action, reflection … action is the middle term … sandwiched between moments of hard reflection" (p. 15). The evaluation of an organization's actions is a vital part of a feedback loop that informs future organizing endeavors. Demonstrating success is critical to organizational vitality from the perspective of members, the public, and funders (Mondros & Wilson, 1994). Women's, labor, and other types of grassroots organizations have historically valued an atmosphere that embraces a dialectic between active engagement and honest reflection. One of the primary ways of evaluating the work that organizations or movements engage in is through informal group process and reflection. These moments of reflection may include a diversity of members of an organization, including constituents, volunteers, staff, administrators, board members, and allies. An organization that has implemented the most sophisticated monitoring and evaluation system and yet does not take the time for reflection on the work that they do could be missing the boat.

Most practitioners doing community-based social change work agree that it can be very difficult to evaluate their efforts in a more formal way. Andrew Mott (2003) of the Community Learning Project has discussed how organizations can strengthen their social change endeavors through organizational learning and evaluation. According to Mott, social change "requires overcoming the status quo, making innovations and taking risks, often against great odds. It therefore involves trial and error, and messy, uncertain processes which are difficult to track and evaluate" (p. 3). Determining the effectiveness of organizing can be a problem because cause and effect are not always apparent. A logic model that evaluates the effectiveness of internal organizational strategies may mask the external variables that tend to have significant impacts on organizing. In fact, some have argued that the success of some endeavors is more dependent on external political factors than it is on internal organizational structures (Kriesi, Koopmans, Duyvendak, & Giugni, 1992; Piven & Cloward, 1979). This may include the formal arrangements that govern the decision-making process in any given country as well as the relationships that activists have to political authorities (Giugni, 2004). Thus, electoral factors, political will, and political alliances are as important as internal factors, such as the number of people participating in actions or the communication methods used. A politician may be unwilling to ally with an organization during an election year because of a belief that the alliance could negatively impact his or her ability to get reelected. It is difficult, then, to measure the efficacy of a group's efforts when so much seems to be out of one's control (Ohmer & Korr, 2006).

One of the predicaments of the contemporary climate of evidence-based and outcomes report-ing is that there is pressure on organizations to present their work as a "success." This burden can prevent organizers from having honest discussions about failures and the realities of the sometimes slow rhythms of social change (Incite! 2007). Grounded in an expanded notion of what counts as success, there are several types of outcomes that are legitimate when thinking about community organizing. Mondros and Wilson (1994) have identified four types of achievement, which I explicate through the use of post-Katrina New Orleans examples.

Instrumental changes in the environment are what organizations set out to do, such as securing funding for public schools or getting a union contract. Neighborhood associations in post-Katrina New Orleans have identified a variety of such successes – securing a FEMA trailer park, stopping new detrimental developments in neighborhoods, getting street lights working again, and obtaining funding for homeowners to rebuild.

Success in the area of *leadership development* is marked by an increase in current members tak-ing on leadership responsibilities. One organizer tells his story about getting more involved in his neighborhood association:

> I answered somebody's thing that said "we need volunteers," would you please volunteer? And, I did, I volunteered, and I was working in this community office where we give information out to people, and they asked me to take that over, and I did. Then we started with the Block Captains, and so ... I became the coordinator for all of the block captains.... So, that's how I became involved. I answered a call for volunteers, and I just—with being retired, I have a lot of time, I ended up taking the minutes at the infrastructure meetings and writing them up and sending them to everybody. (Pyles, 2006)

Development of an organization's resources and capabilities is another outcome measure of success. One neighborhood association defined success in the following way:

> The biggest way we can measure success at this point is by membership because it's very difficult to get people to join. We've been able to build this up very slowly.... We formed the association and one way we could measure success at least for us is the number of dues-paying members, and we have 100 dues-paying members. There are only 500 households in [our neighborhood] so 20% impact we feel is very good for neighborhoods because it is very hard to recruit people to join and pay dues. Dues are nominal—they're $15 for individuals and $25 for family. (Pyles, 2006)

Increasing membership and financial resources are key successes in organizations. *Increasing public awareness* is achieved when organizations get their message heard. One public housing orga-nizer in post-Katrina New Orleans identified the fact that there is a public debate about public hous-ing as one of his organization's successes. The group worked to bring the issue to the table, reframe the issue as a human rights issue, and encouraged the community to engage in discourse about the role of public housing in the community. All of these successes tend to influence the other; for example, increasing public awareness may be a direct result of an organization's enhancement of resources and capabilities.

Many organizations engaged in organizing endeavors may resent the fact that their funders require them to evaluate their work, often because it appears to be a time-consuming activity or just busy work. The feeling may be that it takes away from the real work of the organization. When a group of social change leaders and evaluators came together to discuss some of these important issues, they identified several principles on which evaluation should be based that could help allevi-ate many concerns:

- Social change organizations should be involved in developing, interpreting, and communicating the results of the evaluation and receive adequate support to carry out those responsibilities.
- Evaluation should be designed to be useful in improving the work of grantees, the field, and others.

- Evaluation should build the group's internal capacity for self-evaluation and/or build on existing mechanisms for reflection and self-assessment.
- Evaluation should respect and acknowledge the context in which the organization is operating.
- All the costs of conducting the evaluation should be fully funded.
- Candor should not be punished, inside an organization or by funders (Mott, 2003).

Recent movements in social work research and practice have focused on developing an "evidence base" for social work practice (Gibbs & Gambrill, 2002). The philosophy behind evidence-based practice (EBP) is that practice is driven by guidelines and protocols that come from research findings. One of the problems with this approach, particularly from a social constructionist perspective, concerns the possibility of replicating distorted discourses. Concepts, variables, and methodologies are all a function of a meta-narrative about social work and social change. Parton (2007) has written on the subject:

> While I am not, in principle, against the notion of EBP, my concern is that it has been used in a quite specific way that has the impact of reinforcing the political instrumentalism and aspirations for greater central control than that being implemented by the modernization agenda. It is consistent with attempts to manufacture a sense of certainty in an increasingly uncertain world. (p. 155)

The EBP movement is reflective of the marriage of human service practices to science and, arguably, a divorce from history, politics, and other social complexities. Scheyett (2006) has written about the role of EBP in relationship to mental health consumers, believing that EBP has a silencing effect on consumers. The EBP hierarchy of knowledge includes randomized trials at the top and qualitative studies, particularly first-person accounts, at the bottom. Consumer voices can thus be marginalized in this process. Oftentimes the research question and outcomes are determined by people who are not consumers. In mental health evaluation studies, researchers have pointed out that outcomes such as hope, meaning, and purpose are underemphasized.

Participatory Action Research

One way to alleviate some of the concerns with evaluation efforts that may marginalize constituents is through a research method known as participatory action research (PAR). Though this method can be used for other types of activities in the organizing process, such as assessment and issue development, PAR can also be used to evaluate organizational practices. Research and evaluation practices that are able to unearth subjugated and situated knowledge can be empowering for constituents as well as informative for organizational development. Participatory research can be contrasted to some research approaches that may be exploitative or colonizing. Many scholars, particularly postmodern scholars, have identified that power dynamics may be inherent to the production of knowledge (Stringer, 1999). PAR attempts to remedy power dynamics by engaging participants in research design, data collection, and analysis.

Traditional approaches to evaluation in community organizations are often premised on a kind of service model—a university, organization, or individual conducts an evaluation as a service to the organization, either as a hired consultant or as an in-kind donation. Sometimes, such approaches represent the best option available to busy organizations that prioritize organizing over evaluation. PAR offers an alternative that is possibly more empowering, participatory, and sustainable for the organization itself. Proponents of participatory action research believe that the development of research skills should be in the hands of organizers themselves. There are differing perspectives on PAR, but many argue that the overall goal is to create community researchers and to advance the self-determination of communities to do research. Traditionally, researchers in the academy and the private sector have been thought of as those with research skills, and thus there is a tendency to believe that only those with such skills are able to provide accurate information. PAR counters this social construction by advocating for putting the development and implementation of the research agenda into the hands of regular people.

According to research activists at the Data Center, a group that focuses on impact research for social justice, powerful change for social justice stems from the intersection of different types of knowledge (http://www.datacenter.org). This knowledge includes knowledge from experience, community knowledge, and mainstream knowledge. Practitioners at the Data Center attempt to democratize research by making data and data analysis tools available to community groups. This support organization works with community organizations, facilitating their learning about social science tools as a way to share "expert status" with academics and policy makers. They emphasize the synergy that can take place between different sites of knowledge production.

Traditional approaches to research, grounded in the philosophy of positivism, attempt to apply the principles of the physical sciences to the social world. Within this approach, the researcher/expert observes, queries, or otherwise studies the subject. The oftentimes linear questions can lead to answers that can mask the real issues. With its roots in popular education, PAR utilizes interview-based and qualitative research methodologies where individuals most affected by issues are at the center of the research process. Indeed, the processes of participatory research may be as important as the outcomes of the research. According to Stringer (1999), the purpose of this type of research is "to change the social and personal dynamics of the research situation so that it is noncompetitive and nonexploitative and enhances the lives of all those who participate" (p. 21).

THE RIGHT TO RETURN CAMPAIGN, PART III: A TWO-YEAR TIMELINE OF EVENTS

Anne Dienethal and Loretta Pyles

This two-year timeline of the Post-Katrina Right to Return to Public Housing Campaign offers a glimpse into a variety of public components of a long-term organizing campaign. These components include a wide range of targets both local and national, a diversity of tactics employed by organizers, and the mixture of constituents involved in the struggle. The most striking element of this section of the case study is the duration of the struggle, which still continues today.

August 29, 2005: Hurricane Katrina hits Louisiana. Breaches in canal levees result in massive flooding of New Orleans and surrounding areas.

October 2005: Iberville residents begin reoccupying apartments against the will of the Housing Authority.

November 3, 2005: Federal Department of Housing and Urban Development (HUD) Secretary Alphonso Jackson makes public promises to build $1.8 billion worth of public housing along the Gulf Coast, stating that it will not be "traditional public housing."

December 3, 2005: Housing rights advocates gather at the Iberville development on Basin St. in support of New Orleans residents' right to return to their homes and the reopening of the city's public schools.

January 16, 2006: Martin Luther King Day March to Rebuild the Gulf Coast and the World demanding restoration and reopening of public housing. Coordinating the march was a collaboration among multiple organizations, including C3/Hands Off Iberville, the Forest Park Tenants Association, CAWI (Baton Rouge), NO HEAT, Harlem Tenants Union, Workers Democracy Network, Campus Antiwar Network, and endorsed by the NAACP.

February 14, 2006: Rally to open St. Bernard housing development sponsored by NO HEAT, C3/Hands Off Iberville, St. Bernard Public Housing Network, and tenant council leader Malva McFadden.

April 18, 2006: Rally and march to stop eviction threats to Iberville residents and to reopen Iberville and compensate residents for losses from looting.

May 13, 2006: Protest of Housing Authority of New Orleans (HANO) to stop contracting out HANO jobs; recall all employees; reopen Iberville development in its entirety; remove metal doors from Lafitte development; reopen St. Thomas, Guste, and Fischer developments; and remove fences from around the St. Bernard, Cooper, and C.J. Peete developments.

June 14, 2006: HUD announces its intention to demolish over 5,000 of the city's 7,100 public housing units without a support plan for displaced residents.

June 17, 2006: Organized march of public housing residents, residents of New Orleans, and community supporters demanding the reopening of public housing.

June 24, 2006: Organized march and rally in front of Iberville development in support of public housing.

June 27, 2006: Attorneys from the Advancement Project, Loyola University School of Law, and the NAACP Gulf Coast Advocacy Center file a class action lawsuit against HUD and the Housing Authority of New Orleans (HANO) on behalf of New Orleans public housing residents displaced by Hurricane Katrina, citing violations of various sections of the Fair Housing Act, the Fifth and Fourteenth Amendments granting the right to due process and equal protection, as well as international law concerning internally displaced persons' right to return.

July 1, 2006: Survivor's Village march through the French Quarter.

July 4, 2006: Public housing residents and community supporters from all over the country gather at the Survivor's Village for a "Day of Unity" protest and rally.

August 28, 2006: Nine arrests are made in an attempt to assist residents in reoccupation of Lafitte development.

August 29, 2006: One-year anniversary of Hurricane Katrina. St. Bernard, Lafitte, Cooper, Desire, Florida, and C.J. Peete housing developments remain closed.

September 12, 2006: Former C.J. Peete residents reoccupy housing without housing authority assistance or permission.

January 14, 2007: Housing advocacy group begins 10-day reoccupation of St. Bernard housing project in protest of government plans to raze and then rebuild public housing developments.

January 15, 2007: St. Bernard residents and supporters march around the development. Residents take advantage of an opening in the fence to open up their apartments for cleaning and salvaging.

January 22, 2007: Lawyers representing HUD file a retaliatory trespassing and property damage suit against 10 residents and activists for reoccupying St. Bernard without HUD permission.

January 22, 2007: Lawyers representing HUD file retaliatory suit against 10 residents and allied activists waging a campaign to reopen public housing in the city of New Orleans. The suit seeks to bar residents from entering and cleaning their apartments. The suit is in response to residents and activists illegally entering into St. Bernard public housing development, trespassing, and doing property damage.

January 31, 2007: New Orleans Police Department (NOPD) SWAT team members raid St. Bernard housing complex in an effort to flush out individuals occupying the community center as part of an ongoing campaign to reopen public housing in New Orleans. Two individuals are arrested.

February 8, 2007: Federal Judge Ivan Lemelle refuses to dismiss class action lawsuit filed against HUD and HANO. The decision does not prevent HANO from moving forward with the demolition of the complexes.

February 10, 2007: Former residents of C.J. Peete Public Housing Complex reclaim their apartments without permission or assistance from the Housing Authority of New Orleans (HANO).

February 28, 2007: H.R. 1227, the Gulf Coast Hurricane Housing Recover Act of 2007, a bill sponsored by Rep. Maxine Waters (D-CA) and cosponsored by Rep. Barney Frank (D-MA), is introduced. The bill promises to assist in the provision of affordable housing to low-income families affected by Hurricane Katrina.

March 3, 2007: Displaced residents and supporters rally outside city council member Stacy Head's home to demand the reopening of New Orleans public housing and to protest Head's vocal support of mixed-income housing.

March 15, 2007: Members, supporters, and coalition partners of the People's Hurricane Relief Fund (PHRF) and Tenants Rights Working Group (TRW) through direct action win an agreement when city council's Housing and Human Development Committee agrees to develop policies to address rent control in New Orleans and to craft policy to address issues, as well as challenge the state legislature and state constitution to address crisis of price gouging and lack of tenant rights protections.

March 21, 2007: H.R. 1227 is passed in the House of Representatives by roll call vote with 302 ayes, 125 nays, 6 present/not voting. It passed the House, with 100% of Democrats supporting and 64% of Republicans opposing.

March 23, 2007: H.R. 1227 is referred to Senate committee.

March 24, 2007: Construction of Resurrection City, a strategy drawn from the concept of Dr. Martin Luther King, Jr., and the Poor People's Campaign of 1968, commences. Survivor's Village builds a "city" or living encampment along the fence line of the St. Bernard projects to draw attention to human rights violations by HANO and HUD.

April 2, 2007: Resurrection City is demolished under the leadership of Mayor Ray Nagin and the authority of the Housing Authority of New Orleans (HANO).

June 4, 2007: Supporters of H.R. 1227 rally outside the home of Lt. Gov. Mitch Landrieu's home to call on his sister, U.S. Senator Mary Landrieu, to sponsor the bill.

June 6, 2007: Protesters at the reopening of the Desire Housing Project rally to seek support for H.R. 1227 and to demand immediate action for displaced public housing residents.

July 4, 2007: Members of the Survivor's Village, People's Hurricane Relief Fund (PHRF), Common Ground, C3/Hands Off Iberville, Pax Christi members, visiting survivors of the 2004 Indian Ocean Tsunami, and other supporters of public and affordable housing gather across from city hall for a rally and press conference support and enact policy that will truly bring the working class home to New Orleans. "Homeless Pride" is formed by homeless individuals, beginning a 5-month-long encampment at Duncan Plaza in front of city hall.

July 24, 2007: Protesters meet in front of city hall to address Mayor Nagin and demand reopening of public housing and enforcing citywide rent control.

QUESTIONS FOR REFLECTION

1. Why is it difficult to do social change work in social service organizations?
2. Assess an organization that you are working with in terms of its ability to do social change work. Consider organizational funding, administrative structure, and communication and decision-making processes.
3. Imagine that you are working as a youth organizer with a focus on empowering teenagers to live healthy lifestyles. You are approached by a tobacco company that wants to fund your work. What do you do and how do you decide?
4. Assess your personal interest and ability to participate in consensus-oriented decision making. What could you offer such a process and what would you struggle with?
5. What are the benefits and limitations of engaging in participatory action research for community organizers?

SUGGESTIONS FOR FURTHER INQUIRY

BOOKS

Avery, M., Stribel, B., Auvine, B., & Weiss, L. (Center for Conflict Resolution, Ed.). (1981). *Building united judgment: A handbook for consensus decision-making*. Louisa, VA: Fellowship for International Community.

Chetkovich, C., and Kunreuther, F. (2006). *From the ground up: Grassroots organizations making social change*. Ithaca, NY: Cornell University Press.

Fetterman, D. M. (2001). *The foundations of empowerment evaluation*. Thousand Oaks, CA: Sage Publications.

Ostrander, S. A. (1995). *Money for change: Social movement philanthropy at Haymarket People's Fund*. Philadelphia: Temple University Press.

Stoecker, R. (2005). *Research methods for community change: A project-based approach*. Thousand Oaks, CA: Sage Publications.

WEB

Building Movement Project. http://www.buildingmovement.org

Center for Community Change. http://www.communitychange.org

Center for Integrating Research Action. http://www.cira-unc.org

Grassroots Institute for Fundraising Training. http://www.grassrootsinstitute.org

The Praxis Project. http://thepraxisproject.org

KEY TERMS

Capacity building: Endeavors conducted by internal and external actors to an organization that has the goal of enhancing an organization's abilities to do its work, both programmatically and administratively.

Consensus: A sense of agreement by all members of a small group that is charged with making decisions.

Empowering organization: A social change organization that emphasizes leadership development, equality, transparency, and consensus-building.

Learning organization: A term developed by Peter Senge to describe an organization that achieves the results it intends by understanding the processes of change in an organization through collective practices of feedback and reflection.

Transparency: A democratic value of governments and organizations that affirms open and accessible decision making and honest communication about decisions.

8 Language Matters
Issue Framing and Communication

Make Levees, Not War

T-shirt and bumper sticker slogan in post-Katrina New Orleans

When the United States government's levee system failed after Hurricane Katrina and tens of thousands of homes were devastated across the New Orleans area because of flooding, citizens were obviously devastated and outraged. As community activists analyzed the issues, they recognized that the government was spending more of its resources on the "war on terror" and wars against other nations than on important, life-saving infrastructure in its own country. These activists had broken through the mainstream frame, which affirms that the dangers to citizens lie outside of the country's borders and that solutions mean putting resources into the military and other institutions that are designed to protect people from external threats. The new framework, which came to be exemplified in the above quotation, has been an important rallying cry as citizens go about advocating for their community's needs. Arguing that the safety and well-being of citizens should be ensured through investment in public infrastructure from roads and levees to schools and housing, these activists reframed what they perceived to be a damaging social construction. While crafting catchy phrases is not an end in itself, reframing social issues is a fundamental element of any kind of social change activity.

Developing critical thinking skills that can facilitate a person's capacities to deconstruct narratives and rhetoric about social issues, as well as analyze organizing practices themselves, is a necessary condition of social change work. Because social policies and practices are grounded in ideologies, paradigms, values, and other social constructions, organizers seek clarity about assumptions and implications. This practice requires special attention to language that contains the assumptions, values, etc. Consider the language of "free trade," "trade rights," and "open markets" in relation to the global economy. These terms attempt to give the positive impression that unfettered economic growth is congruent with the ideals of freedom and rights. And yet, if one investigates the realities of fair trade policies in action, one will find that such policies have resulted in the exact opposite for many people—low wages; unsafe working environments; lack of access to clean water; poor health care; and, indeed, a lack of freedom and rights. One might argue that the "free" part appears to apply only to the wealthy and powerful. And thus, the exposure of contradictions in policies and language becomes fundamental to formulating issues around which to organize. This kind of dialectical engagement with social issues through a power analysis requires a relentless commitment to critical thinking.

Another example that can illustrate the linguistically based deconstructive practices of organizers emerges from U.S. labor laws. Some states have passed what are called "right to work" laws. This means that workers are not required to join unions at companies and organizations located in states where such laws are in place (even though they often reap the rewards of the union's presence). By utilizing the language of rights, the law conveys the idea or image that joining a union is an act that is in direct opposition to rights, an oppressive situation. Thus, this language and the sentiment behind it pose significant barriers to union organizing in such states. Organizers must then work to reframe this language so that it better coincides with the values that they are trying to promote. They must focus on such frames as worker safety, worker solidarity, benefits for working families, as well as redefining what worker's rights really means to them. Thus, deconstructing language, values, and other rhetoric is a critical aspect of framing the issues around which people organize.

Part of what may guide a person's understanding of social policies and social problems is the way one learns about history as well as current events. Historian and activist Howard Zinn (2003) has argued for a reframing of history that amplifies the voices of populations who have resisted oppressive social policies and practices, bringing much-needed magnification to the political activities of regular people. History itself is a social construction, and so history books that only tell the stories of politicians, army generals, and inventors who become rich deny the complexity of the scope of human experience. These stories often serve to perpetuate the status quo and may have the effect of marginalizing and silencing women, gay and lesbian individuals, immigrants, people of color, and individuals with disabilities. Unfortunately, such approaches to history have dominated educational sectors and media outlets, thereby skewing the average person's understanding of social issues. By learning about the resistance of citizens across the globe, one is reminded that not only are people resilient, but they are active subjects who have the potential to determine their own destiny.

SOCIAL CONSTRUCTIONISM, LANGUAGE, AND FRAMING

If the social constructionist position is right, i.e., that language constructs reality, then the language that one utilizes in organizing work may be the most critical component of community organizing practice (Gergen, 1999). Language frames issues and communicates messages to constituents, targets, and the general public. The mental health consumer movement can serve as a good example of the complex connotations of language. Many terms have been utilized to describe the movement itself and specifically its constituents (Cohen, 2004). The term *consumer* has been employed by organizers to signify the fact that such individuals are customers of mental health services, emphasizing the subjectivity and individual power that mentally ill people have but that have too often been silenced in professional mental health settings. However, the word *consumer* has been criticized because it implies a freedom of choice that does not necessarily exist and because of its connection with capitalist terminology. Alternatively, the term *survivor* has been used to emphasize a person's resiliency and innate capacity for recovery in the face of a devastating condition. *Ex-inmate* is used to depict the element of incarceration in prisonlike institutionalized hospital environments. Thus, this range of terms communicates diverse political messages, and a variety of factors influence what terms are chosen for particular organizations and coalitions. The mental health consumer movement is not alone in its ongoing struggle with language. Such framing processes are always enduring and evolving (Noakes & Johnston, 2005).

According to social movement theorists, "*collective action frames* are ways of presenting issues that identify injustices, attribute blame, suggest solutions, and inspire collective action" (Staggenborg, 2005, p. 755). Noakes and Johnston (2005) explain how the idea of the framing perspective in social movement studies came to be. They point out that scholars began to examine:

> the social-psychological processes by which people in controlled settings rejected authoritative explanations of events and constructed alternative understandings of what was occurring. Subjects had to "break the frame" that was officially provided as part of a contrived market research project that was shown to misrepresent its intentions. Once the old frame was broken, participants constructed new frames to explain events … these "reframing acts" as the first steps in calling attention to injustice and as a prelude to collective action. (p. 3)

There are many factors that influence the framing process, including the media, organizational capacities, and the individual tendencies of the constituencies. Clearly, a person's or group's social standpoint influences how issues are framed. One's social standpoint includes one's race, ethnicity, income, gender, sexual orientation, age, and other social factors. That is to say, labor organizers whose primary constituency is immigrant African women in New York City working in the service industry may frame issues differently than a group of primarily male Appalachian coal miners. These groups bring different experiences, needs, strengths, and cultural perspectives to labor issues. This epistemological matter is an important part of analyzing and identifying issues around which to organize.

Scholars suggest that framing can be considered from three perspectives—the frame makers' (organizing leaders), the frame receivers' (potential constituents), and the frame itself. Social movement scholars have added that movement leaders are often the ones who construct the frames (Noakes & Johnston, 2005). This is extremely important for organizers to understand, particularly if organization leaders are people with more social privilege.

Prior to the 1970s, domestic violence was considered to be a "private matter" that occurred in the seclusion of one's home, a dispute between a husband and wife that was not a matter of concern to the public. Through the course of the women's movement, as critical consciousness was raised among battered women, they were able to "break the frame" that defines what happens in the home as a personal or private matter. These women came to recognize that domestic abuse was happening to many women and that the dynamics looked strikingly similar across their experiences (Schechter, 1982). In addition, they came to identify that patriarchal culture, as exemplified in families and social institutions such as the criminal justice system, maintained and perpetuated this violence. Upon coming to the conclusion that personal experiences were political ones as well, they rejected the framework that had previously been asserted by law enforcement officials. Their framework had manifested in the common practice of driving husbands and boyfriends around the block to give them some time to "cool down," believing that it ultimately was not the business of the law to intervene in any meaningful way. In response to this indifference, the battered women's movement would frame their agenda and organize around the idea that domestic violence is not the fault of the victim but the responsibility of society as a whole. They would subsequently engage in widespread community education and systems change within police, courts, hospitals, and welfare systems. The initial act of breaking the frame was a necessary condition to engage in the social change efforts of the battered women's movement.

Another framing example concerns a group working on prisoner justice who broke the traditional frame that tends to segment crime as a unique social problem disconnected from other social problems1. They recognized that a poor educational system was directly responsible for the high rates of incarceration; they rejected the discourse that asserted that crime was a function of people who are inherently violent or lazy or otherwise. Thus, a recent campaign focuses on "Ending the School to Prison Pipeline," which particularly affects African-American young people. This frame affirms that poorly funded school systems set up poor African-American youth, especially males, to go to prison by denying them the educational opportunities that children in well-funded school districts have.

Linguistics Professor George Lakoff (2004) has pointed out that since 1970 conservative policy analysts have developed 43 think tanks spending some $2 to $3 billion to figure out how to work together to develop and implement their agenda. He notes that conservative think tanks frame phenomena in terms of values, especially family values. Frank Luntz, a conservative political strategist and linguist, noticed that while it appears that progressives are winning on an issue such as the environment because science is on their side, he proposed that conservatives can instead win with words and political frames (Lakoff, 2004). He suggested that they take words that people like, such as *healthy*, *clean*, and *safe*, and use them strategically. Thus, the Clear Skies Act of 2003 was proposed, even though it would actually increase pollution. He warns that people should be particularly wary of Orwellian language that means the opposite of what it says.

Lakoff (2004) has pointed out that progressives often talk in terms of programs, but he believes that programs bore people. He discusses the idea of a frame and notes that language always evokes an image, a frame. He gives the example of the word *elephant* and asks people to try not to think of

---

1   See Families and Friends of Louisiana's Incarcerated Children (http://www.fflic.org).

an elephant when the word is uttered, and of course, it is impossible to do. This exercise reveals just how powerful language can be in connoting images and ideas. The phrase *tax relief* is an example of an evocative phrase that has been utilized strategically. It conjures the idea that there is an affliction to be ended, i.e., taxes are a burden from which citizens need relief. The person doing the relieving is, of course, a hero, or a doctor who is curing this affliction. What follows from this kind of frame is that if one is against "tax relief," that person is a villain. The even greater problem stems from the fact that even if one says one is against tax relief, the frame has still been evoked. If one accepts a particular frame, it cannot be negated by putting a "no" in front of it. Lakoff argues that progressive activists should not agree to such unacceptable terms. Instead, one should frame facts from a different perspective, maintaining that one should shift arguments to one's own grounds. For example, environmental issues can be framed as a "commons" or an "inheritance"; gay marriage can be framed around the universal values of "love" and "commitment."

Overall, framing acts should be strategic, with an eye toward a larger social change agenda and with attention to potential coalition-building opportunities. This can be facilitated by developing an understanding of social problems as interconnected rather than separate, isolated problems. Identifying Katrina evacuees as internally displaced people (a human rights designation) who are endowed with the right to return to their homes has been a good example of a framing act. This framing act rejects many disempowering terms of Hurricane Katrina survivors and also places them in direct solidarity with people in many regions of the world, such as in the Middle East and parts of Africa, where many people are also displaced internally.

ISSUE IDENTIFICATION AND ASSESSMENT

Intimately related to the social construction of issues and the framing processes of organizers is the practice of issue identification. While framing is a practice that organizers engage in with the goal of broadly orienting their work, issue identification is a more specific practice that organizers carry out when looking at a particular situation or context. Issue identification is often a component of a campaign development strategy or other specific plan of action engaged in by organizations and coalitions. Issue identification entails making critical choices and setting priorities balancing what is most salient with what is most feasible (Kahn, 1994). For example, if an antipoverty organization needs to decide the focus of its next campaign, it must explore the needs and strengths of the community, assess the resources available to the organization, and evaluate the political opportunity structures that exist. This process may result in choosing from several possible campaign strategies focusing on securing a job development program, increasing childcare subsidies for low-income mothers, or a embarking on a local living wage campaign.

From an empowerment perspective, determining what issues are most worthy of pursuit for a group, organization, or coalition should be grounded in the needs and desires of relevant constituencies. For paid organizers or other professionals to make such decisions in isolation of constituencies is contrary to principles of self-determination. Such isolated decision making perpetuates power imbalances in the community and tends to isolate the most vulnerable members of society from the organizing process. In addition, pursuing issues that do not stem from the community's desire is not likely to be sustainable and can produce questionable results. Ideally, constituencies are the driving force behind any organizing campaign, and this includes the practice of issue identification. The Zapatismo philosophy of *mandar obedeciendo*, which translates to "leading by obeying," reflects a belief in direct accountability to the people, a kind of horizontal representation. It would be absurd for an organizer to presume to know what issues represent someone else's best interests. As an organizer in post-Katrina New Orleans recently told me:

> You organize people around their own issues. Let me just give you a quick story. It was during the hurricane in an area and it had just rained and I had to slosh through mud and water to get to this man's house. I get to this man's door and I'm thinking I know when I go in there when I ask him what his

issue is, I know what his issue is—he's going to be talking about that water out there and the fact that he had no drains or sidewalk out there. I knock on the man's door and [introduce myself], "I want to know what your issues are." The first thing he says is, "Damn people, loitering at the grocery store and I'm trying to go to the grocery store." His issue was not what my issue was, and that one thing taught me something very valuable. You don't tell people what their issues are. You don't descend into somebody's community and say, "I know what the issues are and this is what I'm going to do." You cannot get people mobilized around something they're not passionate about. He wouldn't have been passionate about getting that fixed. I would have because I'm thinking, "This is ridiculous. How can you go home every day like this?..." His issue was "I need to go to the grocery store in peace and I don't like to be harassed every time I go." His issue was important to him and that's the bottom line.

Approaches to issue development can extend across the spectrum of utilitarian approaches and transformative approaches to organizing. Utilizing popular education techniques, as exemplified by Freire's notion of dialogic inquiry, offers a mechanism for identifying issues grounded in a transformative approach. By working with constituents to problematize situations and identify these issues using their own language, an empowering, social change approach to issue identification is possible. To determine what issues should be addressed and focused on, one needs to have not only a frame about the issue, but also some basic facts on the ground, so to speak. This may also be achieved by gathering stories through individual conversations or focus groups.

Determining who the best people are to lead and participate in the issue identification process is a crucial consideration. Possible people may include constituencies such as citizens/neighbors and social service users, i.e., the people most affected by or who have the most stake in the issues at hand. Community leaders, social service providers, and organizers are also appropriate people to include. Sometimes organizers mistakenly believe that bringing service providers to the table is enough to represent the community. But, clearly, this activity is not necessarily a direct representation of constituent interests. Service providers may definitely have important and relevant things to say about their perceived understanding of needs, but ultimately only constituents can speak for themselves. Addressing barriers such as transportation and childcare that low-income or other vulnerable community members may face can enhance constituent participation in the issue identification process.

Sometimes the process of issue development may be highly dependent on the networks and coalitions to which an organization may be connected. It may be important to consider how "cutting an issue" might be effective for an organization, particularly if it is trying to gain a broad base of support. Though a group working on low-income housing may be primarily concerned with housing for poor people, they may find that talking about "affordable" housing would be a better way to cut the issue, as it would draw in support from low-wage working people rather than just the poor (Bobo, Kendall, & Max, 2001).

The Midwest Academy is a leading progressive training institute based in Chicago. This influential capacity-building support organization offers a checklist for organizers to consider when choosing an issue. The list includes 16 factors that a group might consider (Bobo et al., 2001), the top three of which are considered by them to be most central.

1. Result in a real improvement in people's lives
2. Give people a sense of their own power
3. Alter the relations of power
4. Be worthwhile
5. Be winnable
6. Be widely felt
7. Be deeply felt
8. Be easy to understand
9. Have a clear target—decision maker

10. Have a clear time frame that works for you
11. Be nondivisive
12. Build leadership
13. Set up your organization for the next campaign
14. Have a pocketbook angle
15. Raise money
16. Be consistent with your values and vision

It is important that all of these factors be weighed by the organization or coalition. A potential campaign may be deeply felt and appear to have the potential to alter power relations, but it may divide members of the coalition in a way that would be too damaging to the group's solidarity. Though it may not be possible for all of these considerations to be met, it is important for organizations to vet each of them and to be clear about which ones are being met and which ones are not.

COMMUNITY DEVELOPMENT ASSESSMENT TECHNIQUES

Exploring community development assessment techniques can help communities and organizations identify issues that are most important to organize around. Community development assessment techniques that are participatory and strengths-oriented can unleash local wisdom and passion that can be leveraged into action for change (Kretzmann & McKnight, 1997). Here I discuss one of those techniques known as the participatory rural appraisal (PRA). Such community development approaches have the potential to facilitate organizer and citizen understanding of the context they are living and working in and can thus influence their choices of issues and campaigns.

The PRA is a tool that can be used to simultaneously assess a situation and to help develop the capacities of individuals to organize based on the findings of the appraisal. Having its origins in international humanitarian relief and social development contexts, the purpose of the PRA is to learn about what is of most value to individuals in a community. Local community members have the opportunity to map and diagram their communities through participatory, visual techniques. Chambers (1994), in his critique of the status quo of international development, pointed out the professional tendency to base decisions on abstract, decontextualized information. This information often comes from secondary data or survey questionnaires. In response to such top-down approaches, the PRA is a method that is grounded in the voices, wisdom, and experiences of people (rural or urban) living in low-income and/or marginalized communities. With a questionnaire or survey, information is appropriated by and then owned by the interviewer. Such approaches arguably perpetuate hegemonic and colonialist practices with the effect of further marginalizing people in the community. However, the PRA seeks to resist such practices through genuine dialogue led by people in the community.

The PRA technique values visual sharing of a map or diagram or units such as stones or seeds, which are used for ranking or quantifying. According to Chambers (1994):

> All who are present can see, point to, discuss, manipulate and alter physical objects or representations. Triangulation takes place with people crosschecking and correcting each other. The learning is progressive. The information is visible, semi-permanent, and public, and is checked, verified, amended, added to, and owned by the participants. (p. 1257)

The PRA can be viewed as a "set of attitudes and behaviors" based on the values of trust and relevance. Community members must trust the facilitator and the process as well as believe that the efforts and results are relevant and useful to the situation. This work should come from a perspective of sharing and partnership with an open and nonpossessive spirit.

One of the greatest shortcomings of the PRA is that, while it attempts to hand over power to local people, the activities are primarily initiated by outsiders. This may not be an inherent flaw in PRA itself, but because progressive organizers strive for indigenous leadership, it is an element of the current practices that can be modified. Some authors have criticized PRA for its overemphasis on localism and lack of recognition of the power imbalances that exist locally (Mohan & Stokke, 2000).

Using similar participatory techniques in a social development context after Hurricane Katrina, community organizers at the New Orleans Food and Farm Network were faced with the task of needing to assess the strengths and needs of particular neighborhoods. Many of these neighborhoods were flooded and had few grocery stores, restaurants, or community gardens available to access healthy food. In addition, public transportation to access food sources was extremely limited. Because there were so many issues to address, only an assessment process could help them determine what the most pressing issues were. Two methods that they utilized to assess the neighborhood contexts were community food mapping and youth-led neighborhood story projects. The food maps engaged community members to map their neighborhood to determine strengths and gaps; this included locations of grocery stores, emergency food banks, operational community garden space, and potential community garden space. The other method—the Food Talk Project—engaged high school health students to interview community members, particularly older adults who were contributing something positive to the local food system. The students sought to learn how food had been traditionally grown and prepared before an era of fast food and soft-drink machines. These folks were local growers, cooks, and food-buying-club leaders. Learning about the local assets and wisdom has facilitated new programs as well as served to inform a community organizing campaign to adopt a food charter at the citywide level.

COMMUNICATING MESSAGES

Many organizers have noted that the mainstream media tend to perpetuate social injustice, a phenomenon influenced by the interests of elite corporations who own the majority of media outlets (Bobo et al., 2001). While the media is often controlled by the state in undemocratic countries, in capitalistic societies, the messages portrayed by the media are clearly constrained by the corporations' social agenda. Though corporations may not have an explicit, proactive agenda, their messages are not neutral and always have underlying assumptions and unintended consequences. In recent years, mega corporations have been buying smaller newspapers and radio and television stations in regional markets. The news is arguably filtered to suit the agenda of the corporations. Currently, seven media conglomerates own 90% of the U.S. media market. Many activists have argued that advertising and the bottom line (rather than the public's need to know) drive the choices editors make in terms of what the public sees, reads, and hears. Activist Noam Chomsky has argued that the governmental agenda has become equivalent to that of the corporate agenda, identifying this phenomenon as "manufacturing consent."

There are many potential antidotes to this situation with the media, ones that can also proactively contribute to organizing campaigns. According to Bobo et al. (2001), "Too often groups use 'corporate control of the media' as an excuse for not doing good media work" (p. 157). Communication strategies are an important part of any campaign or organizing endeavor and should be integrated from the outset of a campaign. Communication is relevant to not only internal framing, but also the message that a group wants to send to the public or targets. The use of media has been an important strategy not only for mobilizing people, but for getting a message out. The way a group frames its issue is related to the way in which a group communicates its issue. However, it should be noted that the internal communications about an issue may differ somewhat from the way a message is communicated to an external audience.

There are many components involved in using media, particularly in the context of an organizing campaign. This includes not only the message development process discussed already, but building relationships with media outlets and preparing spokespeople. There are several issues to be considered when developing a media strategy (MacEachern, 1994):

- Whether the media campaign reinforces the group's overall agenda
- The organizational resources that can be committed
- Time constraints
- Target audiences

Some options for using the media include getting the media to show up at events and direct actions, writing letters to the editor, holding press conferences, and participating in interviews or talk shows. Of course, communicating messages can also be done without media; organizers can simply get out into the street, which may be the best way to do outreach and get one's message across.

In recent years the Internet has been highly influential in terms of strengthening the potential of organizers to frame its declarations (Micheletti & Stolle, 2007). The antisweatshop movement has been a recent example of such activity. The advocacy group Global Exchange used the media and Internet to focus attention on celebrities and corporate leaders such as Nike CEO Phil Knight and U.S. talk show host Kathie Lee Gifford, who has her own brand-name clothing line. According to Micheletti and Stolle:

> Validation of the movement's hook into popular culture came and comes in a variety of forms, two of which are the Doonesbury comic strips in 1997 on outsourced Nike manufacturing in Vietnam that triggered a wave of university student activism and a joke by Jay Leno about Nike sweatshops on the Tonight Show in 1998. Within a few years, culture jamming with the encouragement of Adbusters Media Foundation, a global network of artists, activists, writers, pranksters, students, educators, and entrepreneurs wanting to advance what it calls the "uncooling of consumption," would exploit corporate vulnerabilities more fully by expressing antisweatshop sentiments in more humorous and radical ways. (p. 163)

Organizers working on post-Katrina social justice issues have utilized a variety of mechanisms to convey their messages. There have been multiple purposes of their messaging, including reframing the social issues, recruiting new members, publicly confronting power holders, and impacting specific policies. Public-access television would become an important mechanism for local individuals and groups to communicate their messages in post-Katrina New Orleans. For example, young African-American groups with Katrina-related messages made their own hip-hop videos and created their own talk shows that challenged mainstream frames about their post-Katrina world. These shows included video-recorded footage of devastated neighborhoods and conversations with local activists that highlighted their work.

During the early days after the flood, one of the most common ways to communicate was through basic signage in neighborhoods. Though this method was somewhat primitive in terms of technology, it was extremely effective. Having simple cardboard signs printed and posted around town was the most common way that citizens were communicating with each other. Because so few people had televisions and computer access due to flooding and damaged cable and phone lines, these simple ways of communicating became very powerful. The group levees.org mass-produced signs that said "Hold the Corps Accountable." This was one of the first social justice messages that citizens saw and was a way to begin to galvanize constituents. The group has continued to emphasize the significance of levee protection throughout their campaign, including having people showing up at actions and media events wearing life preservers.

As the organization came to realize that they were in it for the long haul, and as they were able to raise more money, levees.org was able to recruit celebrities with local New Orleans roots to do public service announcements (PSAs) that were aired on television. The text of one PSA delivered by actor, writer, and director Harry Shearer is as follows:

> You know there are levees in every state in the nation that we rely on to protect our homes, our businesses, our lives,… our land. Recently the Army Corps of Engineers admitted that over 120 of these levees may be vul-

nerable. Are you as safe as you think you are? What happened here in New Orleans could happen anywhere, to you. Go to levees.org and join us. Don't we all deserve levees that work? (http://www.levees.org/press)

This PSA reframed a local issue into a larger national social justice issue. Levees.org makes all their media materials, including this PSA, available to the public on their Web site. This additional media strategy is a useful way for both activists and media professionals to have access to their messages.

Another consideration when thinking about the use of the media to communicate a message is the use of alternatives to the dominant paradigm of media practices. Community-rooted media production not only is an antidote to dominant approaches to media construction, but it becomes an actor in community organizing. Grassroots media activists attempt to deconstruct the traditional and sometimes voyeuristic paradigm of media coverage and work toward the democratization of media. Consider that the usual approach of the media involves a reporter following a story (e.g., "spotlight on the homeless") and then moves on to the next story. An alternative approach involves not only the homeless themselves as doing the story, but the reporting itself becomes an integral part of the solution, e.g., embarrassing a landlord to cease an illegal eviction. Grassroots media producers can be active participants in community organizing campaigns and allies to other social movement actors. This represents a radical reframing of issues as well as the corporate paradigm of media praxis itself. This practice also directly confronts the profession of journalism itself, affirming the belief that one does not need a degree to report what is happening. Reporting requires honesty and good communication skills. Democratizing media practices may entail writing an article about something important and then imagining and implementing ways that are less costly to create and distribute news stories. Alternative media exist in a variety of formats, including local cable access and Web sites like Free Speech TV, Our Media, and Indy Media, which host grassroots video, audio, and public-domain works. Community radio stations are also appearing, including Internet radio stations, which can run through any number of media services like SHOUTcast or Live365. Also, alternative and low-power FM stations such as the Prometheus Radio Project and Pacifica Radio can get the message out. These range of media outlets offer news and analysis that is driven and funded not by corporations, but by individual donations of citizens, thereby democratizing the agenda.

Support organizations can provide capacity building to community organizations interested in enhancing skills related to media activities. Recently, at the U.S. Social Forum in Atlanta, the Ida B. Wells Media Justice Center (MJC), a consortium of media professionals and community media groups such as Pacifica Radio, Third World Majority, Poor Magazine, Yes! Magazine, the National Radio Project, and many others joined forces and held trainings in video, radio, Web, and print journalism and other media skills to progressive community organizers and activists. The Media Action Grassroots Network, or MAG-Net, is a national initiative recently launched by some of the country's most dynamic regional organizations to provide just such infrastructure. The membership and leadership team includes a variety of organizational constituents. MAG-Net works to strengthen the capacity and coordination of regional media activist hub organizations, develop the skills and leadership of organizers from underrepresented communities, and increase strategic effectiveness within and across regions, among media and social justice groups, and with Washington, D.C.-based allies. MAG-Net recently released its 10-point platform for media justice:

1. *Representative and accountable content*: Free speech is eroded when one powerful group of voices dominates the media. Racist, sexist, and homophobic diatribes broadcast over the public airwaves are hate crimes perpetrated against entire communities. Media must provide fair representation and offer opportunities for all people to participate.
2. *True universal media access: Full, fast, and free for all*: In today's modern technology environment, access to high-quality communications should not be dependent upon geography or demographics. Public-supported infrastructure should be expanded, and private networks must be held to broad and strong public-interest standards.

3. *Public airwaves—Public ownership*: It is time to bust the corporate monopoly over our broadcast and cable networks. We need more public-supported media that are authentically accountable to local communities and independent from both commercial and government editorial pressures.

4. *Community-centered media policy*: Media regulations should promote universal media access in the public interest, rather than protect the economic interests of entrenched corporate media. License and franchise terms should be limited and held accountable to effective local community oversight. New media-diversity rules are needed to increase media ownership and participation among historically underrepresented communities, including people of color and women.

5. *Corporate media accountability and just enforcement of media rules*: Federal government regulators must have the resources and the will to effectively sanction media outlets and networks that violate the public interest and the public trust.

6. *Redefine and redistribute First Amendment rights*: The Universal Declaration of Human Rights makes clear that the right to communicate and gather diverse opinions through all media is fundamental and universal to all people. We should reframe our understanding of the First Amendment in this light and hold all media and telecommunications policies to this high standard.

7. *Cultural sovereignty and self-determination*: Copyright and intellectual property regulations should protect the rights of artists without enclosing new and collaborative forms of independent creative expression. Private media owners must not be allowed to abuse their power as cultural gatekeepers through payola or other schemes that hinder independent cultural development.

8. *Full and fair digital inclusion*: Beyond Internet freedom and Net Neutrality, we need a digital communications policy framework that closes forever the digital divide, provides students with full access to new media technologies, and holds private telecommunications providers accountable to the evolving needs of diverse local communities.

9. *Another medium is possible—if we fund it*: We need more public funding to support alternative media infrastructure and independent media production and distribution. Philanthropic funding should prioritize regional and statewide organizing around media issues.

10. *Full and fair representation in the movement for media reform*: Media reform, properly contextualized, is a strategy for achieving social and economic justice. Media justice values must obtain at the center of this movement, and activist leaders from traditionally underrepresented communities must be at its forefront (http://mediagrassroots.net/ten_point_platform.html).

SPOTLIGHT ON THE ART OF THE MARCH

Like any form of direct action, having both a clear goal or demand and target is essential when conducting a march. Sometimes organizers strategically hold a march in a location where a target is sure to be affected, e.g., a state administrative building, outside the headquarters of a corporation, or at the home of a negligent landlord. The goals of such strategic marches are often very explicit, with painted signs and other media explicitly communicating a demand: "Support Bill X" or "Boycott Company Y."

Organizers may also wish to hold marches that have a more general claim. The purpose may be to hold the march in the public commons as an expression of solidarity and a show of the strength of the organizers. Such shows of power express to the public and target, "Hey, look at how many people we have here today. We are a strong movement, so be careful what policies you make, etc." Not only do such marches have an external effect on the larger community as witnesses, including the media attention it engenders, but they can also be a powerful force in terms of building the internal strength of an organization or coalition.

Participating in a march can be exhilarating and exciting. Because more people tend to participate in marches than they do in some of the other day-to-day activities of organizing, it can be a huge morale boost to be around so many people committed to the same cause. Feelings of anger, apathy, or burnout can be transformed by a march, leading to an increase in participation rates of activists.

When organizing a march, there are many logistical matters to keep in mind. Such matters include obtaining the appropriate city or municipal permits; utilizing local police escorts; establishing the march route; creating signage; and, of course, getting people to participate. March advertising and communications are critical for getting a big turnout. Capacity-building groups such as the Ruckus Society offer training and support to organizations interested in carrying out a march or other direct action to facilitate achieving a victory in a particular campaign.

Below are some sample chants that can be adapted for a variety of issues and occasions. Planning ahead and creating new chants relevant to the group's message is a good approach; sometimes new and creative chants can spontaneously appear in the passionate moment. It may be helpful to provide a handbill to marchers with the chants written out ahead of time so everyone can follow along or feel free to start a chant. Drums, horns, and other musical instrument can be an inspiring and fun addition to a march. Here are some samples:

"Ain't no power like the power of the people because the power of the people don't stop!"
***
"What do we want?"
"Justice!"
"When do we want it?"
"Now!"
***
"This is what democracy looks like!"
***
"Exploitation ain't the way, give your workers better pay!"

QUESTIONS FOR REFLECTION

1. What personal resources and barriers do you bring to the table when it comes to reframing social issues?
2. Discuss some recent social welfare policies that pose barriers for marginalized communities. What language is used to describe the policy? Attempt to "break the frame" and come up with some alternative language that describes what the policy really does and offers a new solution.
3. Why is the process of issue identification so important in community organizing?
4. Discuss the ways in which the mainstream media is a barrier to achieving the goals of social change work.
5. How might the mainstream media (such as television, radio, newspaper, Internet) be utilized by progressive community organizers to achieve their goals? Discuss the opportunities and challenges.

SUGGESTIONS FOR FURTHER INQUIRY

BOOKS

Condit, C. (1994). *Decoding abortion rhetoric: Communicating social change*. Champaign-Urbana: University of Illinois Press.

Johnston, H., & Noakes, J. A. (Eds.). (2005). *Frames of protest: Social movements and the framing perspective.* Oxford: Rowman & Littlefield.

Kretzmann, J. P., & McKnight, J. L. (1997). *Building communities from the inside out.* Chicago: ACTA Publications.

Ryan, C. (1991). *Prime time activism: Media strategies for grassroots organizing.* Boston: South End Press.

Wallack, L., Woodruff, K., Dorfman, L., & Diaz, I. (1999). *News for change: An advocate's guide to working with the media.* Thousand Oaks, CA: Sage Publications.

WEB

Asset-Based Community Development Institute. http://www.sesp.northwestern.edu/abcd/

Community Tool Box. http://ctb.ku.edu/

Everything Postmodern. http://www.ebbflux.com/postmodern/

Poor News Network. http://www.poormagazine.org

Training for Change. http://trainingforchange.org

KEY TERMS

Breaking the frame: A collective act engaged in by organizers and social movement actors that influences the values and actions of organizing work.

Epistemology: Refers to the study of what and how people know things, including the social production of knowledge. Some understanding of these processes is necessary for organizers who are analyzing social constructions and breaking through mainstream frames.

Manufacturing consent: Noam Chomsky's phrase to describe how the profit-driven, corporate media tend to serve the interests of dominant, elite groups in the society.

Media justice: An alternative to corporate-controlled media that seeks to ground social narratives in the perspectives of regular citizens.

Power analysis: A continuing reframing practice engaged in by critical progressive organizers, the purpose of which is to determine the winners and losers of social policies and practices, identifying how social and economic power operates in order to work to undo such retrenched power.

9 Tactics for Change

Diversity of tactics, organizations, and beliefs is one of the great strengths of autonomous social movements.

George Katsiaficas (2004, p. 8)

During the Progressive Era, future Nobel Prize winner Jane Addams was an activist and social worker who sought to address numerous issues, including war, poverty, public education, and labor (Addams, 1910). Not only did she take on many issues, but she embraced multiple tactics to alleviate the injustices. Many of her organizing activities were based out of Hull House, the settlement house in Chicago that she helped found in 1889. Her work on labor issues serves as an example of the variety of ways in which she advocated to change public policy and improve the lives of immigrants. Her first encounter with labor issues came through anecdotal experiences with the children of Hull House. These children of immigrants worked in sweatshops and told her stories of long hours and unsafe conditions. She also came to understand how the families of these children depended on the wages they earned. Hearing more and more stories, she approached the Illinois State Bureau of Labor and suggested they investigate the issue of child labor in a more systematic way.

The report produced by the bureau was presented to the legislature, which then appointed a special committee to investigate the matter further. Upon investigation, the special committee would recommend to the legislature provisions for significant factory legislation. Before its passage, Addams (1910) educated groups and mobilized people to ensure its passage. She recalled: "It was necessary to appeal to all elements of the community, and a little group of us addressed the open meetings of trades-union and of benefit societies, church organizations, and social clubs literally every evening for three months" (p. 135). Residents of Hull House were mobilized, and she worked in coalition with the Trades and Labor Assembly as well as the General Federation of Women's Clubs. She attempted to make clear to her allies and constituents the exact purpose of the law as well as the benefit to themselves and their children. The biggest opposition to this came from the large glass manufacturing companies who depended on child labor for their production. Eventually the bill passed and it became the first factory law in Illinois; it would regulate sanitary conditions and fix 14 years as the minimum age for factory laborers.

Besides such policy advocacy, Addams engaged in classic labor organizing, focusing on organizing women garment workers. At the time, the only women's union in Chicago was that of the bookbinders. Inviting the head of this union to Hull House, the union leader was at first skeptical of whether Addams and her cohort could be allies of working-class women. Eventually this union leader was won over by their sincerity. Through Hull House, the women shirtmakers and the women cloak makers were organized. One of the women workers who was living at Hull House also organized the Dorcas Federal Labor Union, which was composed of women members of all the unions in the city.

Strikes are a traditional form of direct action in labor struggles, and Jane Addams was involved in many of them. She struggled morally with the immediate effects of strikes, such as what the lack of transportation for a day during the Pullman strike would mean for people who needed transportation or the fact that the strikes could potentially incite violence. She was aware of how difficult strikes were to sustain as a tactic for union leaders as well as workers. In addition, she understood that their success was dependent on the changing flavor of public opinion and the ever-changing personal will of the employer.

Addams had a good understanding of politics, capitalism, community organizations, networks, and relationship building. She seemed to be comfortable employing a variety of organizing tactics geared toward social change. Though she had some awareness of her own privilege as a leader and definitely encouraged working-class people to get involved, some of the complex issues around class and power in community organizing were likely not at the forefront of her mind. Nonetheless, her work at Hull House showed that she did have an understanding of empowerment of poor and marginalized people and made attempts to promote the empowerment of workers as an organizing strategy. In this chapter, I discuss the importance of being able to employ a diversity of organizing strategies and discuss various organizing strategies to consider.

THINKING ABOUT TACTICAL DIVERSITY

During the Russian Revolution, a common question asked by the proletariat organizers was *Shto delyat*? which translates to "What is to be done?" While the political, economic, and social problems were clear to these revolutionaries, the solutions were not always so clear. The question itself, however, was always important and was to be continually posed. As a group comes to understand its frame, mobilizes its constituency, and identifies its issues, it must then ask the question of what specific tactics will be utilized to achieve needed reforms.

An organization's thinking about organizing tactics, i.e., the specific actions implemented to achieve reform or create social change, should not be separate from other aspects of organizing practice, including framing, and organizational considerations. Whether a group is more utilitarian or more transformative in its approach, it is critical that it has engaged in this front-end work before beginning to strategize about tactics. Tactics should never be decontextualized from an organization's context, including the resources available to them. Indeed, frames and particular situations should directly inform tactical choices. For example, a youth-led environmental justice organization concerned with hazardous waste disposal in a local playground may clearly frame a company's illegal dumping as a public health problem or a violation of the United Nations Convention on the Rights of the Child. But, what are the best tactics for this group to begin addressing the issues? Odds are, it will not be appropriate for the group to file a lawsuit against the company, as they probably would not have the capacities (money, attorneys, etc.) for such an action. This group of youth environmental organizers may be better situated, for example, to protest against the company by performing street theater. Such a production could bring media attention to the issue as young people expressed through their creative abilities the physical, emotional, and spiritual impact that the dumping was having on their development and overall quality of life.

Tactics can be measured in the context of a strategic organizing campaign. An organizing campaign is a thoughtful, proactive effort of a group of people over time with specific goals, strategies, and tactics. Successful organizing campaigns are often dependent on what are known as "political opportunity structures" (Noakes & Johnston, 2005). Such political opportunities may include some conflict between elites, a suddenly vulnerable incumbent politician, or a major crisis such as a natural disaster or economic recession. It is necessary to have good organization and tactics to take advantage of political opportunities that open up because they often are open only briefly.

One way to think about choosing tactics is to first think about the various types of power that exist and to vet strategies in terms of confronting such power. Bobo, Kendall, and Max (2001) identify four types of power available to achieve reforms: political/legislative power, consumer power, legal/regulatory power, and strike/disruptive power. Political/legislative power is basically getting legislation passed and programs funded by an elected body. Consumer power is the ability to conduct a boycott of a product or service. Legal or regulatory power is the ability to win in court or in a regulatory process. Finally, strike/disruptive power is cutting profits or income by stopping a company or agency from functioning. By engaging in critical thinking and group dialogue, organizers can identify the types of power for change that may lie behind their issue and then consider the power mechanisms that are feasible to pursue.

As an example, consider a coalition of organizations that is concerned about the health of low-income, inner-city residents. In this case, there are obviously many people and systems that have an influence on the health of low-income communities. This includes those that contribute to the problem of poor health as well as the strengths of people and systems to maintain good health. Such actors include the government, which has the ability to offer publicly subsidized health insurance; employers; insurance companies; hospitals; doctors; nurses; clinics; and corporations that market unhealthy food to poor people. It is a complex issue, and it can be challenging to nail down how in fact to get to the bottom of it. Sometimes issues present themselves explicitly; other times a group must go through a thoughtful process of discussion to develop or cut their issue.

Once the coalition has assessed what the issue is that they wish to address, they can begin to break down the power mechanisms that perpetuate the problem. This process is not exactly linear, as it is often useful and practical to develop an issue as one is assessing power mechanisms. That is why framing, issue identification, and tactical development are necessarily so interconnected. If the presenting issue is that residents are getting sick because of unsafe emissions of a local factory, there are still a variety of ways to conceptualize power mechanisms and thus choose tactics. For example, igniting consumer power against the company that owns the factory may be effective. In addition, working with the U.S. Environmental Protection Agency (EPA) as a way to leverage legal/regulatory power might also be employed. If the issue is a lack of access to health care for low-income people, then tapping into political/legislative power to secure funding to expand free clinics in the neighborhood for those who cannot afford health insurance would be a reasonable solution. Strike/disruptive power may be ignited against particular companies that refuse to offer low-paid workers health insurance.

Organizers work to unravel broad and entrenched social inequities and oppression. Such oppressions exist at the economic, political, social, and cultural levels. Thus, it would only make sense that strategies and tactics would be as diverse as the many types of oppressive institutions, policies, and practices. For example, addressing cultural oppressions may require the use of cultural tactics. Katsiaficas (2004), in a discussion about the global justice movement, reminds activists not to underestimate the efficacy of "tactical diversity" (p. 3). Some tactical strategies may be proactive, such as a grassroots mobilization to pass a local human rights ordinance that would allow gay and lesbian individuals in a community to be protected from discrimination. Other efforts may be reactive, such as those that are responding to a current policy or practice of a corporation or governmental entity. In the remainder of this chapter, I address a variety of tactics that organizers utilize to address the issues they have identified with their constituencies. These tactics are policy advocacy, legal and regulatory suits, asset-based community development, direct action, and alternative community and cultural development.

Policy Advocacy

One possible tactic for organizations and coalitions to address the issues they have identified is by means of policy advocacy, a tactic that taps into what Bobo et al. (2001) refer to as political/legislative power. Here I consider policy advocacy as an activity within the context of a larger organizing campaign of which policy advocacy may be one of several tactics utilized by a group, organization, or coalition. Human service and social work scholars have written extensively on the practice of policy advocacy and social planning (Avner, 2002; Ezell, 2000; Jansson, 2008). Because policy advocacy can take many forms, it is helpful to conceptualize the various types: ballot-based advocacy, legislative advocacy, analytic-based advocacy, and implementation advocacy (Jansson, Dempsey, McCroskey, & Schneider, 2005). Ballot-based advocacy seeks to change the composition of governmental positions through the electoral process. Legislative advocacy is the practice of securing, enacting, or blocking specific legislative proposals. Analytic-based advocacy is the data-driven critical study of social issues and reform. Implementation advocacy works in the context of the administrative implementation and evaluation of social policies and programs.

As one considers policy advocacy from a progressive community-organizing framework, one should be cognizant of the ways in which constituencies are included in the process. In particular, an organization or coalition should clarify the degree of empowerment that the policy campaign can engender. If one is working for a social service agency and the task is to monitor mental health policies within the state legislature, one must think about to what degree one's group is planning to engage people living with mental health problems in the process. The spectrum of constituent engagement is an infinite one and may include not engaging them at all, bringing them together once per legislative session to talk about policies and get their feedback, and being solely driven by the constituents.

Dealing with various levels of government is a reality faced by organizers. This may include city councils as well as state, national, and international institutions. Because organizing in the United States has been heavily focused on the local and neighborhood level, it has been challenging for organizers to be effective at the statewide level. State-level policy advocacy has been a particularly important venue in the era of the devolution of federal responsibility to the state level. Building the capacities of organizations and coalitions to impact state-level politics has been a challenge to community organizers. This has been a key achievement of the modern Industrial Areas Foundation (IAF), particularly in Texas under the leadership of Ernie Cortes. One of their key successes has been a statewide campaign to increase funding to school districts with low student achievement scores, emphasizing a need for funds for dealing with immigrant students and bilingual education (Boyte, 1984).

One of the innovative techniques of such policy advocacy has been the use of "accountability sessions," a practice emerging from Alinsky's era and refined by the IAF and others. An accountability session usually takes the form of a community meeting with an elected official (Bobo et al., 2001; Wood, 2002). It is ideally held on the community organization's turf. The purpose of the meeting is to express the position of one's organization on a particular issue; it is not a time to garner everyone's diverse opinions about an issue. Testimony is given by leaders of one's group and allied organizations, and then the elected official is asked to respond to very specific demands put forth by a panel of leaders. The ultimate purpose of the accountability session is to get the official to yield to the group's demands. Such techniques can play an important role in a campaign focused on specific policy reforms.

LEGAL AND REGULATORY SUITS

Exploiting legal systems and regulatory policies and agencies to further an agenda or campaign of a constituency can be an effective social reform tactic. This often takes the form of filing lawsuits and confronting governmental agencies. Some organizations are solely focused on such approaches, while other organizations may ally themselves with attorneys or organizations that specialize in this kind of engagement in the criminal and civil justice systems.

Utilizing existing legal mechanisms to hold governments, corporations, and individuals accountable can be an extremely effective organizing tactic. For example, the Freedom of Information Act can be used as a tool to uncover governmental misconduct and help fuel campaigns. These data can then be used to get media coverage and galvanize activists.* Examples include revealing the environmental impact of policies, uncovering military recruiting data, and revealing violations of the constitution.

Environmentalist Bob Spiegel was called to action by a chemical waste disposal company's unsafe and careless practices in New Jersey, in particular by the fact that rabbits in his neighborhood were actually turning green from the toxic chemicals leaking from drums buried underground. Emphasizing the persistence and determination it takes to engage in such legal and regulatory advocacy, Ivins and Dubose (2003) write about Spiegel's efforts:

---

* See, for example, http://www.centeronconscience.org.

In order to become the hero/pain in the ass of an environmental saga, it is only necessary to be obsessive, compulsive, and workaholic, to have the instincts of a trained investigator, the disposition of a bloodhound, and the skill of a research librarian. It takes a pain in the ass to get the bureaucrats off their butts and moving.... Combining plodding research and investigation with gonzo activism, he is part Ralph Nader and part Abbie Hoffman. He damn near drove the New Jersey Department of Environmental Protection, not to mention the United States EPA, out of their bureaucratic minds. Spiegel filed innumerable Freedom of Information requests for government documents. He studied the laws and regulations. He called and wrote both elected officials and regulators.

Proceeding through official channels is necessary but not sufficient in these cases, so Spiegel also took to holding impromptu press conferences on the ... site. He led television-news crews to toxic hot spots. He mailed the EPA videotapes of children playing in arsenic-laced brooks and sent stuffed green bunnies to members of Congress. (pp. 101–102)

As the authors note, engaging in these kinds of tactics requires the ability to conduct research, think creatively, and be persistent. Though interesting and inspiring, it is a rare case for one person to champion and shepherd a cause in the way Spiegel did. Instead, engaging a diverse group of the constituency is likely to be more effective and better suited to the ends of empowerment.

ASSET-BASED COMMUNITY DEVELOPMENT

In their influential book, *Building Communities from the Inside Out: A Path toward Finding and Mobilizing a Community's Assets*, Kretzmann and McKnight (1997) argue for what they call asset-based or capacity-focused development. This type of community development emphasizes the process of locating available local assets in a community, including individuals, associations, and institutions, and connecting them with one another in a way that can multiply their power and effectiveness. The authors argue that the traditional path of community development is a "needs-driven dead end." Community issues are presented as needs such as unemployment, truancy, child abuse, slum housing, etc. These needs assessments determine how problems are to be addressed through deficiency-oriented policies and programs. They point out that the intervention community, including the international development community as exemplified through the work of some nongovernmental organizations (NGOs), teaches people the nature and extent of their problems and the value of services as the answer to their problems. As a result, many lower-income urban neighborhoods are now environments of service where behaviors are affected because residents come to believe that their well-being depends upon being a client. The people in these communities begin to see themselves as people with special needs that can only be met by outsiders. This deficiency orientation, i.e., seeing the community as an endless list of problems and needs, leads to fragmentation of efforts and denies the basic community wisdom that regards problems as tightly intertwined. This orientation targets funds toward service providers, not to residents, and can have negative effects on the nature of local leadership. Kretzmann and McKnight (1997) believe communities have been invaded and colonized by professionalized services that have disempowered citizens and interfered with ways people can engage one another.

By shifting the focus from taking back power, which was at the crux of Alinsky's tactics, to focusing on the assets that already exist in a community, people have a different kind of opportunity to realize their own power. The alternative path, asset-based or capacity-focused community development, can lead toward the development of policies and activities based on the capacities, skills, and assets of lower-income people. Significant community development happens only when local community people are committed to investing themselves in the effort. The key to neighborhood regeneration is to locate all of the available local assets to begin connecting them with one another in ways that multiply their power and effectiveness and then to begin harnessing those local institutions that are not yet available for local development purposes (Kretzmann & McKnight, 1997).

It is important to keep in mind that engaging in asset-based community development does not imply that the community does not need additional resources from the outside. It means that outside resources will be used more effectively if the community is fully invested and if it can define the agendas for which additional resources must be obtained. Some basic principles to keep in mind are

1. To start with what is present in the community, not with what is absent or what is problematic
2. To be internally focused, centering on the agenda-building and problem-solving capacities
3. To be relationship driven—to constantly build and rebuild the relationships between and among local residents, local associations, and institutions

It should be clear that the asset-based approach to community development is philosophically commensurate with a strengths perspective (Saleebey, 1997) and an empowerment approach (Gutierrez, Parsons, & Cox, 1998). The strengths perspective was developed from a similar critique of deficiency-oriented interventions to individual problems. Rather than understanding a person as a list of problems and diagnoses, the strengths perspective emphasizes the resources that people naturally have within and around them. It is a reconstruction of a narrative that views communities and populations as a laundry list of problems.

Direct Action

Depending on the person, engaging in a direct-action campaign may be an exciting or scary thought. Direct action is an activity that counters the normal flow of everyday society. It conjures up acts of civil disobedience engaged in by the likes of Rosa Parks and Gandhi. In many minds, these are the actions of extreme people in extreme circumstances. In fact, direct action has somewhat of a negative connotation for many people. Because direct action tends to go against the grain of everyday society, it is not surprising that people find it distasteful or somehow feel threatened by direct-action organizers. Activists who engage in direct action may be initially marginalized by society and only later appreciated. Consider, for example, that Rosa Parks, arrested for her act of civil disobedience, is on a postage stamp now.

Direct-action tactics were a key component of the civil rights movement in the 1960s. One of these early tactics utilized was the sit-in, a practice pioneered by the Congress on Racial Equality (CORE), which combined Gandhian nonviolence with the sit-down strikes of the United Auto Workers (UAW) (Eskew, 1997). During the civil rights movement, the sit-in was a peaceful tactic whereby African-Americans entered traditionally segregated public places such as parks, restrooms, and restaurants in direct defiance of what they perceived to be unjust laws.

Bobo et al. (2001) present a useful framework developed by the Midwest Academy for planning direct-action campaigns. Their strategy chart is useful because it helps organizers analyze strategy into meaningful components. The first consideration is *goals*, i.e., the goals of the campaign, including long-term, immediate, and short-term goals. This consideration is absolutely necessary for any campaign and should not be divorced from organizational frames and issue-development processes. Elucidating goals is particularly helpful for those concerned with formal evaluation of their practices or those considering the use of a logic model. The second category is *organizational considerations*. These include many of the resources that groups invest in direct-action campaigns, including money and staff time. Other factors may include what the organization wants to get out of the campaign, such as developing new constituents and other aspects of ally-building. The third consideration is *constituents, allies, and opponents*, i.e., developing a list of potential allies and constituents. Depending on the type of organization (utilitarian or transformative), the types of activities that this entails may vary. In this process, campaign organizers should consider what groups might actively oppose the campaign. The fourth consideration is *targets*, whereby organizers can consider both primary and secondary targets. This process should include an analysis of the types of power mechanisms that are at play, such as consumer power or strike/disruptive power, keeping in mind that targeting specific individuals can be very effective. So, rather than targeting, for example, the House Ways and Means Committee of the state legislature, target the chair of the committee or specific members. Finally, *tactics* are the actual activities that the organization or coalition will engage in. This may include media hits, hearings, lobby days, one-on-one accountability sessions, etc. Like other aspects of organizing practice, this kind of strategizing is a group process, just as the assessment or issue-identification process is.

The purpose of direct action is some form of interference in the status quo. This disruption may be the disruption of entrenched ways of thinking about issues or the disruption of the operations of an institution, including a business or governmental institution. Saul Alinsky famously proposed what he called a "shit-in," where activists would occupy every single bathroom at Chicago's O'Hare airport to pressure the mayor. The mayor was attempting to renege on promises he had made to The Woodlawn Organization (TWO). Thus, TWO decided to wreak havoc at O'Hare, Daley's pride and joy of an accomplishment. Daley's staff got wind of the action and intervened, knowing that Alinsky would most certainly follow through, and thus conceded to all of TWO's demands.

A new era of activism has brought with it a new "ethos" as well as new technologically influenced organizing methods (Shepard & Hayduk, 2002). While marches and media campaigns continue to be tried-and-true methods of direct action, techniques such as "hactivism" and "fax jams" are new technologically inspired techniques. Creativity and innovation have always been hallmarks of direct action and other forms of organizing.

One of the promising findings of Gamson's (1990) study of the efficacy of social movements was that disruptive tactics in general are correlated with successful outcomes. An obviously controversial finding of Gamson's is that a subtype of disruptive tactics, namely violent action, is also correlated with success. Interestingly, other studies have reached the opposite finding, i.e., that violence is counterproductive to social movement ends (Taft & Ross, 1969). Many people associated the actions of the civil rights movement with nonviolence; however, this is somewhat of a myth, as there was successful and significant organizing in the context of this movement that utilized violence (Hill, 2004). Of course, groups and individuals have to reflect on the ethics of such tactics to determine if the ends do indeed justify the means. From a transformative organizing perspective, the means are always as important as the final goal, and thus these organizers operate in a way that is commensurate with the kind of world they are trying to create.

St. Augustine Church is a 164-year-old African-American church, located in the historic African-American Treme neighborhood in New Orleans. The building was damaged by Hurricane Katrina, and the members dispersed to places all over the country. Thus, the archdiocese determined that there were not enough parishioners to maintain the mission of the church. Many people believed that this was a wrong decision and that something had to be done. After disrupting a local church service in what was seen as one of the most conflictual events in the church in recent memory, protesters occupied the church's rectory for 20 days. Even more controversial was the fact that most of the protesters were not local parishioners and were not even local residents. These activists were mostly young white individuals affiliated with a progressive community organization. Nonetheless, the tactic appeared to work, because the Archbishop announced a reopening of the historic St. Augustine parish for 18 months, giving its parishioners a chance to meet recovery benchmarks they and the archdiocese worked out in two days of behind-the-scenes meetings. The agreement was praised by both sides as a "win/win."

Negotiation

Sometimes, either in response to a direct action or in lieu of a direct action, a negotiation with one's target may be in order. The literature on conflict resolution and win-win approaches to negotiation provides some guidelines about how to attend to relationships that are in conflict. Too often, organizers may fail to see that individual relationships are the essence of change or that the welfare administrator that one is negotiating with is a worthy subject of change, worthy of one's attention to the processes of how one interrelates. Everyone has equal value and worth, every action is connected, and the attention one takes to listen and to heal is critical. The act of listening to another's position who we "just know is wrong" is an act that can transform consciousness while simultaneously transforming policy. This practice is relevant for a variety of tactics, including direct action, legal and regulatory suits, and policy advocacy.

Eichler (2007) has argued for a consensus approach to organizing building on the mutual self-interest that diverse individuals share. Marshall Rosenberg (2004) developed a practice known as Non-Violent Communication (NVC). NVC is grounded in an understanding of conflict as occurring when individuals are not getting their basic needs met. Through compassionate listening and dialogue, conflict can be transformed into understanding. Finding common ground where everyone's needs can be met is the goal. Such approaches are challenging for groups that have been historically marginalized by systems and other political actors. Trust will always be a challenge in these situations, and if it is not present on both sides, then these approaches are not appropriate.

Most organizers are constantly faced with contradictions between their positions on issues and the positions of policy makers, corporate executives, or landlords. Faced with contradictions between "my" position and "their" position, practitioners may become befuddled and angry, and either retreat or try to impose one's position. The progressive community organizer may be able to see the paradoxes and strive for synthesis. McLaughlin and Davidson (1994) have observed that:

> Compromise is distinct from synthesis. It usually includes some of this position and some of that and can be seen as the midway point on a line between two polarities. But true synthesis is different. In synthesis we have to go to a higher level and transcend the polarities.... Just as hydrogen and oxygen need a spark to create water, so two opposites require the spark of higher consciousness to create synthesis of the best of both at a higher level. (p. 88)

ALTERNATIVE COMMUNITY AND CULTURAL DEVELOPMENT

Alternative community and cultural development has been embraced by feminist organizers, environmentalists, anarchists, mental health consumers, and many others. While advocacy within the system is one part of social change work, another part is to resist oppressive structures and create new ways of doing things both socially and culturally. Consumer-run homeless drop-in centers in Philadelphia, organic farms in India, anarchist relief efforts in post-Katrina New Orleans, and peer-led support for battered women in Thailand are all examples. Such efforts seek to create spaces where regular people come together in their communities in a way that resists traditional social service models and cultures of control, creating what Armstrong (1996) has called "communities of the heart."

Cooperative economics, also known as the solidarity economy, has been a way to engage in an alternative approach to resist the oppressive conditions of mainstream economics and development, emphasizing a more equitable, economic life. Cooperatives may engage in a wide variety of economic activities, including quilting bees, peer lending groups, and worker-owned housecleaning services. The Somali Bantu Women's Cooperative in San Diego, California, consists of a small group of immigrant Somali women who make and sell handicrafts. Their endeavor has a clear economic benefit for the women as well as the added benefits of preserving traditional knowledge and offering a more flexible schedule to take care of family and children while doing their craft.

Cooperatives promote equality among workers, thereby eliminating management and the time and money excesses that hierarchical companies require; thus, there is less discrepancy across worker wages. One of the challenges of cooperatives is that group decision making may be time consuming or unclear. However, this is challenging not necessarily because group process is in and of itself impossible, but because people have lost touch with their indigenous ability to share in decision-making activities. Professional organizers can support the work of cooperatives by organizing members and building the capacities of cooperatives in the areas of multilingual communication, group process, and other business-related supports.

Cultural activism represents an alternative form of community development that has historically been a key component of social change work. This type of activism often includes the arts, such as performance art like theater or singing, the literary arts such as poetry, and the visual arts such as painting. For many groups, this includes resistance to mainstream forms of culture that perpetuate oppression. According to Shepard (2005):

> While organizers emphasize a model of education that depends on analysis, challenging systems requires emotional as well as intellectual shifts in attitude. Cultural production, from music to poetry to storytelling, makes social breakthroughs possible … public performance, dance, and ritual provide the transformative ingredients that unleash "cognitive liberation" necessary to view the world from alternate perspective. (p. 448)

Music has been an important element of protest and social change across the globe. Songs of protest played an important role in the struggle against apartheid in South Africa. Union songs in the United States in the 1930s later influenced the folk music of the 1950s and 1960s during the time of the civil rights movements. Contemporary musicians such as Rage Against the Machine, Ani Di Franco, and Michael Franti are among those who use music as a form of activism. Raising consciousness and creating solidarity are key outcomes of cultural activism. The Lilith Fair, an all-women's music tour in the late 1990s, was an example of activism through music. The musicians gave some of their proceeds of that tour to local battered women's programs and other women's centers.

Groups such as Art in Action support youth who engage in social-justice-oriented expression such as photography, spoken word poetry, music, and digital storytelling. The HIV/AIDS activist group known as ACT UP held their first demonstration on Wall Street utilizing a combination of media work, civil disobedience, and guerilla theater (Shepard & Hayduk, 2002). Eve Ensler's *The Vagina Monologues* is an example of feminist art that attempts to question fundamental assumptions about femininity, resist violence against women, and create solidarity among women. Ensler has questioned why "vagina" was a word that is whispered and why euphemisms are often used in its place (Baumgardner & Richards, 2005). The *Vagina Monologues* phenomenon has facilitated the empowerment of women to reclaim their bodies, which have been objectified and abused throughout human history.

REFLECTING ON ORGANIZING TACTICS

Determining the appropriate organizing tactic to use in what context is a perennial challenge for organizers. It is important to consider not only an organization's frame, but also the type of power that organizers wish to break through and what resources are available to organizations and coalitions. Some organizations are better situated to engage in a particular tactic. Completely understanding one's group is a most important part of choosing tactics. *How* a group goes about deciding what tactic to use is equally critical. Such considerations include whether everyone in the organization has a say in the process of choosing tactics and the role of leadership in the overall campaign. Determining tactics should be made through the lens of the same values as any other aspect of organizing, emphasizing empowerment, social change, and accountability. Like Jane Addams did, it is also relevant to consider not only the practical outcomes of a tactic, but also the moral effects on all people involved—organizers, targets, and bystanders.

The outcomes of organizing tactics are fairly complex. Social movements exist on a wide spectrum ranging from radical to more moderate. Sociologists have argued that there is a radical-flank effect that may benefit moderate sectors of a broad social movement. McAdam (1992) describes it in this way:

A movement tends to benefit when there is a wide ideological spectrum among its adherents. The basic reason for this seems to be that the existence of radicals makes moderate groups in the movement more attractive negotiating partners to the movement opponents. Radicalness provides strong incentives to the state to get to the bargaining table with the moderates in order to avoid dealing with the radicals. (p. 3)

When groups understand their own strengths, such as whether they have negotiating skills or whether they are better suited to engage in direct actions, they are better able to determine where they can be most effective.

THE RIGHT TO RETURN CAMPAIGN, PART IV: TACTICAL DIVERSITY

Anne Dienethal and Loretta Pyles

Iberville Public Housing Development was one of the first public housing projects built in the United States. Situated just blocks from New Orleans's French Quarter, the development was opened in 1941 after passage of the 1937 Housing Act, which pledged to provide affordable public housing to those in need across the country (Mahoney, 1990). The development was one of two in New Orleans that was first designated for Caucasian servicemen and their families. When the 1964 Civil Rights Act was passed, Iberville's 858 one-, two- and three-bedroom apartments were opened to low-income African-American families for the first time (Arena, 2005). In the 2000 census, residents of the development had a reported median annual household income of $7,279, making Iberville one of the poorest areas of the city (Greater New Orleans Community Data Center, 2007b). However, located in one of the most historically wealthy areas of New Orleans, Iberville sits atop land that has been scouted for real estate development since the 1980s (Mahoney, 1990).

Despite suffering from unmet needs such as access to nutritious food as well as adequate health care and education, residents of public housing developments such as Iberville have historically been able to draw from multiple strengths, including close bonds between neighbors and families and the existence of churches and other civic organizations within close proximity. Strong resilience is also exhibited on the part of residents, and among them are many activists who utilize various organizing tactics to push for change in their environments.

C3/HANDS OFF IBERVILLE

One organization that has been instrumental in the fight for housing equity in New Orleans is C3/Hands Off Iberville. Taking multiple cues from the civil rights movement, the organization has a history of working with residents of public housing using grassroots, direct-action strategies both before and after Hurricane Katrina. Formed in 2001, C3 consists of a collaboration of New Orleans citizens, including public housing residents, whose 3 "C's" advocate community, concern, and compassion. Members of the organization came together in the wake of 9/11 to protest the occupations of Afghanistan and Iraq, and they broadened its focus in response to increasing efforts by the Housing Authority of New Orleans (HANO) to redevelop and privatize the Iberville area. In 2004, citing the link between U.S. government aggression abroad and locally, organization members added Hands Off Iberville to C3's name and began working with housing residents to keep the development from being demolished. Members of C3/Hands Off Iberville and other community members rallied together in June 2005 to defeat a plan for redevelopment by bringing the community together to publicly denounce HANO plans at its annual meeting.

In the aftermath of Hurricane Katrina, when residents were barred from returning to public housing, C3/Hands Off Iberville served as a support to residents ready to take action. Connecting with displaced residents around the country was done through telephone trees, e-mail lists, and word of mouth between residents and neighbors. Declaring a "housing state of emergency," C3/

Hands Off Iberville began formally meeting in November 2005 to assess the situation, discuss possible tactics for assisting residents, and begin lobbying local officials to reopen Iberville and other habitable developments. The first organized demonstration took place in front of the Iberville development on December 3, 2005, with subsequent demonstrations in the next two years taking the form of reoccupying public housing apartments without HANO permission, public demonstrations, and direct confrontation of government officials. Demonstrations focused on increasing solidarity among residents of public housing, but they also worked to engage community members outside of the developments to emphasize that cutbacks in public services affect not only public housing residents, but also every resident of New Orleans.

On April 4, 2006, over 250 residents of public housing entered the boardroom during a HANO meeting and vocally demanded the reopening of public housing. Later that month, public housing resident activists and other local activists worked together to put together the Iberville Neighborhood Association Recovery Plan, which was then presented to members of HUD (U.S. Department of Housing and Urban Development) and HANO at their monthly meeting. The plan called for immediate reoccupation of habitable apartment units at the Iberville development and resumption of all utilities. By mid-2006, apartments at the Iberville development had begun to be reopened to residents, signifying one of the first victories in the fight for post-Katrina public housing.

THE INNER WORKINGS OF DIRECT ACTION

The primary components of the above direct-action demonstrations are time and commitment from stakeholders. When an important issue is identified by community members in neighborhood meetings and through key contacts, organizers and activists begin organizing residents to take action on their own behalf (Minkler, 2005). Brainstorming of possible strategies ensues, and phone calls are made to encourage attendance and to assign tasks such as creating and circulating flyers, carpooling, and spreading the word. Planning meetings are scheduled and transportation is arranged for those who need it. In addition, alerting the media is often important in order to increase exposure of the issue to the broader community. Finally, a spectacle is created through banners and voices and a critical mass of people in attendance with the purpose of disrupting business as usual, increasing awareness of the chosen issue, and increasing pressure upon the power structure to respond. Behind the scenes in such direct-action efforts are the many people working together to make those voices heard.

SURVIVORS' VILLAGE

Another use of direct action in post-Katrina New Orleans can be witnessed in the construction of Resurrection City. Inspired by a vision shared by Martin Luther King, Jr., during the Poor People's Campaign of 1968, Resurrection City was erected on March 24, 2007, by New Orleans public housing residents and members of a grassroots housing movement known as Survivors' Village. Working with donated building materials and the time and commitment of resident activists, participants constructed an encampment of small wooden houses lining a chain-link fence alongside the St. Bernard housing project to symbolize solidarity among displaced residents and sending the message that residents were ready to reclaim their homes. Working with limited resources and in defiance of HANO's warning that the property was off limits, the encampment survived for 10 days when, on April 2, 2007, the encampment was bulldozed under authority of the city's administration. Members of C3/Hands Off Iberville, in partnership with housing residents and activists around New Orleans, expressed intent to rebuild Resurrection City despite the city's warning that efforts to do so would result in immediate demolition. A year later, residents—known as Homeless Pride after having been kicked out of a park across the street from city hall—have been camped out in tents under the overpasses near downtown.

LEGAL SYSTEM TACTICS

In addition to the use of direct action, efforts to challenge the power structure in post-Katrina New Orleans have also taken the form of legal action. On June 27, 2006, attorneys from the Advancement Project, Loyola University of New Orleans' School of Law, and the NAACP Gulf Coast Advocacy Center filed a class action lawsuit in the U.S. District Court of New Orleans on behalf of the over 5,000 public housing residents displaced by Hurricane Katrina (*Anderson v. Jackson*, 2006). The defendants in the suit are U.S. Department of Housing and Urban Development (HUD) secretary Alphonso Jackson and HANO on allegations of violating the Fair Housing Act and the U.S. Housing Act of 1937 by denying public housing residents their right to return home without advanced notice. The lawsuit seeks the immediate reopening of habitable public housing units, and despite HANO and HUD's January 2007 request for reconsideration, a trial date has been set for November 26, 2007 (*Anderson v. Jackson*, 2006).

The lawsuit is the result of collaboration on the part of multiple civil rights attorneys and organizations in different cities responding to persistent contacts from displaced New Orleans public housing residents asking the question: "Why can't I go home?" Residents have played key roles in garnering attention and building support for the case, including 50 residents embarking on a February 2007 bus ride to Washington, D.C., to meet with legislators and to share their personal stories.

Similar to direct-action demonstrations, the investment of time and commitment has been key to the success of the legal process; however, it also remains one of the greatest challenges. Due to the lengthy nature of the legal process, the benefits are not immediate and involve a considerable risk of participants becoming discouraged and losing momentum. However, there are multiple strengths that result from the process, including increased unity among residents and the broad exposure received by the widely publicized lawsuit. Although the verdict of the lawsuit remains undecided, the collaborative efforts of New Orleans residents and legal professionals across the country have served as an additional source of hope for residents wanting to return home.

POLICY ADVOCACY

Advocating for policy change in post-Katrina New Orleans has been ongoing and can be seen on multiple fronts, from the lobbying of city council for a moratorium on rent increases to advocating for displaced residents' right to return. In March 2007, public housing residents and activists experienced a great success when the House of Representatives passed H.R. 1227, the Gulf Coast Hurricane Housing Recovery Act of 2007 (House Report [H.R.] 1227, 2007). Introduced on February 28, 2007, by California congresswoman Maxine Waters, who visited the devastation after the storm, H.R. 1227 has united many public housing residents and nonresidents with the shared goal of welcoming everyone home, regardless of race or class. If passed by the Senate, H.R. 1227 will require HANO to make a minimum of 3,000 public housing units available to former residents by the end of 2007. Section 203 of the bill specifically prohibits the demolition of any public housing operated under HANO without a plan for its replacement (H.R. 1227, 2007).

The desire to ensure Senate passage of H.R. 1227 has prompted activists to concentrate efforts upon urging Louisiana senators to take leadership and support the bill. In response to presumed reluctance by U.S. senator Mary Landrieu of Louisiana, protestors marched to the home of her brother Lieutenant Governor Mitch Landrieu on June 4, 2007, to call upon the senator to formally sponsor the bill. In response to Senate Bill 1668, a separate bill supported by Senator Landrieu and introduced later in June 2007, activists engaged in a side-by-side comparison of the two bills, cautioning supporters of Senate Bill 1668 that its passage could increase the risk of demolition of public housing.

One of the greatest challenges in advocating for policy changes has been the need to maintain pressure on power structures, requiring ongoing capacity building and vigilance on the part of residents and activists. In addition, interpreting the differences in language among various proposals has been a complicated and sometimes frustrating challenge, as many residents want to see a bill passed as quickly as possible. Members of C3/Hands Off Iberville together with residents of public housing have incorporated direct action into advocating for policy changes by staging repeated demonstrations demanding passage of H.R. 1227 or an amended version of Senate Bill 1668. Citing the importance of keeping the proposed bill fresh in the minds of Louisiana residents, activists continue to raise awareness to ensure that no political action is taken without the knowledge of those who will be most impacted.

The various tactics used to increase access to public housing in New Orleans have often overlapped and intermingled. Direct-action strategies are continuously planned and executed as the legal process and advocacy for policy changes continue. While there is no one "right" tactic, the benefits of multiple tactics used at the right times and as a result of people uniting to effect change can be witnessed firsthand in New Orleans from day to day.

QUESTIONS FOR REFLECTION

1. Discuss a recent public organizing tactic (protest, lawsuit, etc.) in your community that you or others participated in and evaluate it. What was the goal and was it achieved? What could have been done differently?
2. What are the most important factors to consider when choosing an organizing tactic?
3. Discuss the opportunities that exist for growing constituencies, including individuals and allies, through the course of a campaign.
4. What strengths would you bring to a negotiation process? What would you find challenging about it?
5. How does the practice of "alternative community and cultural development" benefit individuals and families? Groups and organizations? A larger social change agenda? What might be the challenges for its practitioners?

SUGGESTIONS FOR FURTHER INQUIRY

BOOKS

Addams, J. (1910). *Twenty years at Hull-House*. New York: Penguin.

Baumgardner, J., & Richards, A. (2005). *Grassroots: A field guide to feminist activism*. New York: Farrar, Straus and Giroux.

Kahn, S. (1994). *How people get power* (rev. ed.). Washington, DC: National Association of Social Workers Press.

Salomon, L. R. (1998). *Roots of justice: Stories of organizing in communities of color*. San Francisco: Jossey-Bass.

Shepard, B., & Hayduk, R. (2002). *From ACT-UP to the WTO: Urban protest and community building in the era of globalization*. New York: Verso.

WEB

Highlander Research and Education Center. http://www.highlandercenter.org

Industrial Area Foundations. http://www.industrialareasfoundation.org

Labor/Community Strategy Center. http://www.thestrategycenter.org

Movement Strategy Center. http://www.movementstrategy.org

The Ruckus Society. http://www.ruckus.org

KEY TERMS

Consensus organizing: Philosophically distinct from conflict-oriented approaches to organizing, this perspective emphasizes the common ground and shared needs of all parties, including those with more power and those with less power in society. Tactics emphasize negotiation, nonviolent communication, and win-win decision making.

Cooperative economics: A community-revitalization strategy that may draw from indigenous wisdom and socialist economics. It focuses on democratic decision making and worker control over labor practices and production, with attention beyond profit making to include the holistic well-being of communities.

Devolution: The legal conferring of powers from the central government of a state to governments at the regional and local levels. For organizers, this means that social welfare policies and practices may vary from community to community, and advocacy for change with regional and local governments is necessary.

Disruptive tactics: A social-movement term that refers to direct-action strategies that are intended to disrupt the normal functioning of social institutions.

Freedom of Information Act: This vital tool of organizers is consistent with the belief that citizens have "the right to know." This act of 1966 expresses the legal requirement that all U.S. governmental agencies disclose previously unreleased information, records, and documents requested by any person.

Section III

Enduring and Emergent Issues in Organizing

In this final section I address some of the persistent issues confronted by organizers in their practices. Organizers face these issues at the personal, interpersonal, sociocultural, and institutional levels. This personal work entails grappling with the personal barriers that all organizers face, particularly those at the emotional, cultural, and spiritual levels, aspects of organizing that are often ignored in the literature. While much is known and has been written about organizing constituencies, running a campaign, and evaluating actions, less is known about the complex inner workings of community organizing in a global context. These issues might be considered the cutting-edge issues facing contemporary progressive organizers today.

There are many reasons that organizers become inspired to organize. These reasons may be existential or spiritual. Others may organize because they are inspired to preserve their personal or cultural identities. Some of these issues can get fairly complicated for organizers, and identities can come into conflict with other people's identities. Religious and spiritual perspectives can potentially be in conflict with secular agendas. Too often, though, these conflicts are ignored in community-practice settings because they are too controversial. The insights of contemporary global justice organizing offer innovative strategies to address social change. By offering a window into and critical reflection on these perennial issues faced by organizers, the practice of progressive organizing can be advanced to higher ground, offering practitioners the opportunity to actualize the ideals of social change.

10 Toward Solidarity
Understanding Oppression and Working with Identity Politics

We have been taught to either ignore our differences or view them as causes for separation and suspicion rather than as forces for change. Without community, there is no liberation, only the most vulnerable and temporary armistice between an individual and her oppression. But community must not mean a shedding of our differences, nor the pathetic pretense that these differences do not exist.

Audre Lorde (1981, p. 99)

The phrase *identity politics* is often used pejoratively and may invoke negative ideas about political correctness, conjuring images of diverse groups of people battling against each other about who is the most oppressed. Rhoads (1998) has made a case that, because of this impression, a counterinterpretation of the term is necessary. One may wish to think of identity politics, instead, as diverse groups of marginalized individuals forging their own place in the public sphere, authentically expressing the vision of a participatory democracy. These groups of individuals are participating in a forum where political and economic rights get fleshed out and actualized. Because oppression is so painful and complex, this process can appear to be a distasteful experience to the outsider; however, it seems to be a necessary practice for anyone interested in undoing histories and experiences of marginalization, violence, and slavery.

Identity politics refers to a wide range of political activity and theorizing founded in the shared experiences of injustice of members of certain racial, ethnic, and other social groups. Rather than organizing solely around ideology or party affiliation, identity politics typically concerns the liberation of a specific self-identified constituency marginalized within the larger societal context. Members of that constituency assert or reclaim ways of understanding their distinctiveness that challenge dominant oppressive characterizations, with the goal of greater self-determination. Such constituencies may include people of African origin, lesbian women, indigenous people, immigrants, etc. To what degree engagement in identity politics helps and hinders progressive community organizing efforts is one of the main purposes of this chapter. By gaining greater insight into the literature on oppression and the research on identity politics, a strategy for community organizing grounded in the cultivation of solidarity is offered.

As a white woman who "came up" in the battered women's movement, working with issues of my own power and differences in the movement has always been a central feature of social justice work for me. It has been an enlightening and sometimes painful journey. Operating in a feminist collective, we, as the women in the organization I worked for, identified ourselves in solidarity with each other as women. That was an important part of the work that we did, and it brought home the belief that violence against women could happen to any woman regardless of her location in society. Living in a patriarchal culture that privileges men and masculine traits, we knew this to be true from our own experiences and analyses. And yet, I had power within the organization based on my own social standpoint—having white skin, being in a heterosexual intimate relationship, and having formal education. Our collective was very diverse, consisting of African-American women, Asian women, Native American women, lesbian women, bisexual women, women with disabilities, as well as women who had multiple identities.

It was during that time that I began to learn about how power and privilege manifested itself not only in society, but within social movements and organizations. I was learning what being an ally to individuals who were members of marginalized groups meant. Though through my words and actions I attempted to demonstrate solidarity with my "sisters" in the many struggles for social justice, the reality was that I had a great deal of privilege that the larger society afforded me. And this could often manifest itself within the organization and in the larger community. In practice, it meant attending to my own intentions, the multiple meanings of verbal and body language, and constant critical inquiry into the policies and practices of the organization. Though it was not easy, with the support of others within the collective, I was able to work at being accountable to all women, forging the trust and attention that is necessary for solidarity.

THINKING ABOUT OPPRESSION AND LIBERATION

Philosopher Iris Marion Young (1990) has identified "five faces of oppression": exploitation, marginalization, powerlessness, cultural imperialism, and violence. This oppression happens to people who are perceived to be "other," different from individuals who fit into the dominant paradigm. One may be inclined to think that the solution to this problem would be to erase such differences, an argument for a sort of colorblind society. Young has critiqued a narrative and ideal of justice that conceptualizes liberation as the transcendence of difference, or the ideal of assimilation. Instead, the idea of democratic cultural pluralism affirms equality among differentiated groups, who respect each other and affirm differences.

Feminist thinker Patricia Hill Collins (1999) has noted that these oppressions often take on an interlocking form, meaning that for women of color, for example, the issues they may face as a result of their gender is never separate from those which they face because of their race or ethnicity, and vice versa. Not only do the hegemonic mechanisms of sexism and racism operate similarly, but their interaction creates new problems and the need for innovative intervention strategies.

The concept of internalized oppression can be useful for understanding some of the realities of the manifestation of oppression within individuals and across groups (Dominelli, 2002; Pharr, 1996). Accepting the names and negative ascription that dominant groups place on marginalized groups can result in internalized oppression. This can manifest itself in negative ways in a person's personal as well as organizational life. For a lesbian woman who has been called names and told that she was "less than" her whole life, the possibility that she will internalize this is great. Such oppression can be transformed into the liberating practices of social change, but because coping with these negative feelings can also result in a variety of problems, including depression or substance abuse, it is necessary to actively address internalized oppression. Dominelli (2002) articulates how these issues can be addressed by groups organizing themselves for social change:

> Moreover, by constructing alternative discourses around their identity attributes, oppressed groups have been able to tackle the internalization of oppressive relations amongst their own members who have accepted the "naming" of their traits as inferior by the dominant group.... Self-affirming activities re-author dominant discourses by challenging the view that it is not possible for oppressed people to ameliorate their situation. Placing affirming role models in the public domain, developing individual self-confidence, promoting positive images of the group and endorsing self-directed programs of action for part of the repertoire for building confidence in who they are. Through this process, individuals who have previously been excluded and are unable to participate in expressions of citizenship in public arenas have found their voice and capacity to act in accordance with their own interests. (p. 113)

UNDERSTANDING THE DIVISIONS

Activist Suzanne Pharr (1996) discusses the idea of "horizontal hostility," which manifests itself as the fighting that sometimes occurs between oppressed groups. Rather than work in solidarity, sometimes marginalized groups may perceive each other as the enemy. Horizontal hostility occurs when one marginalized group turns against another marginalized group; thus, internalized oppression is projected onto other people of similar social status, resulting in this horizontal hostility. This can happen through competition for political acknowledgment and resources and is perpetuated by social structures, the media, and funders. One of the obvious negative consequences of the phenomenon, known as horizontal hostility and internalized oppression, is that it has the effect of "divide and conquer" and can pit people against themselves and each other.

Corporations and politicians often have worked to divide and conquer the working class by emphasizing racial differences, often nurturing feelings of resentment against immigrants that they are "taking our jobs." Many activists have argued that attention to race and ethnicity divides the working class and that the most important conflict to transform is between the owners and workers, arguing for the unity that all workers from different races (and genders) have in common (Kaufman, 2003). The new wave of labor movements has been focusing more and more on attending to racism within the labor movement as a way to achieve unity amongst diversity.

Sometimes, divisions within progressive organizing occur between people with privilege and people with less privilege. Baumgardner and Richards (2005) discuss what they call a "fundamental conflict of progressive organizing":

> Poor or otherwise oppressed people are perceived as natural allies. Conversely, rich or otherwise privileged people are challenged before they are welcomed as activists. While we should never generalize that poor people are lazy, we shouldn't assume that rich people are insensitive, clueless and selfish. Most social justice work is about providing resources so that people who are poor or victimized can have comforts, education, basic health care—"privileges" that are currently available only to those who can afford them. The problem is that as soon as someone is successful, he or she is often accused of as being too privileged to be radical. I don't fall prey to that critique anymore because I know from my own experience that I am using what privilege I have to expand resources to others. (p. 184)

People of color may become bitter and suspicious of white people because of the ways in which they have been marginalized in organizations and social movements by people with more power. Phrases such as diversity, tolerance, multiculturalism, and inclusion become watered-down attempts to do social justice work. "Inclusivity has therefore come to mean that we start with an organizing model developed with white, middle-class people in mind, and then simply add a multicultural component to it" (Smith, 2006, p. 68).

Collins (1990) writes: "In a system of interlocking race, gender, class and sexual oppression, there are few pure oppressors or victims" (p. 194). Thus, the idea that "the system" (e.g., the welfare system) somehow consists of people who are pure oppressors is false. For example, some welfare administrators, whom organizers and advocates may view as "the enemy" or "the oppressor," actually may be trying to survive domestic violence themselves in their own homes, just as perpetrators of domestic violence work in the battered women's movement. Also, many organizers who work for nonprofits view government funding agencies as "the other." However, the relationship between nonprofits and government agencies is clearly one of interdependence, as nonprofits are often funded by such government agencies, even though government agencies have been constructed as entirely separate, and vice versa. What follows is a need within social movement culture to mend the divisions between "us" and "them" (Pyles, 2003). This may be accomplished through practices that help organizers unpack the underlying philosophy, which is likely a false construction from the outset.

Clarke (1996) attributes this fragmentation of social justice movements to the "postmodernist story" which "stresses a cultural transition from monolithic to diverse" and includes "greater diversity; the proliferation of difference; de-differentiation; indifference; the plural, contradictory, fragmented subject" (p. 41). This has translated to what some call identity politics or what Clarke calls "the politicization of difference" (p. 42). Alternatively, some postmodern scholars have challenged notions of identity, deconstructing ideas such as race and gender. At any rate, the conflict and differences that arise within the milieu of identity politics may be considered a good thing. According to Gutierrez and Lewis (1994):

> Conflicts will inevitably arise within those organizations that have been successful in reaching a diverse group, as well as between the organization and a larger community which may be threatened by the absence of expected boundaries. In some respects, the emergence of conflict is an indication that meaningful cross-cultural work is taking place. (p. 39)

A PATH TO SOLIDARITY

In the feminist literature, Roman (1993) argues for a shift from identity politics to a "politics of coalition," i.e., unity that is grounded in difference, rather than sameness, advocating for a relational politics of dialogue, or what Morales (1998) calls a "politics of inclusion." This vision can attend to problems of individual and group oppression without the fragmentation that has often been associated with it. By looking into the misconstruction of other movements, advocacy causes, and social systems themselves as "other" or even "lesser" than its own, movements can find ways to make linkages that will "expand the visions of both their movements and our own until we find the point of collaboration" (Morales, 1998, p. 125).

Standing in solidarity with everyone comes from "the deep recognition of our most expansive self-interest" (Morales, 1998, p. 125). Poet and activist Audre Lorde was concerned with precisely this idea, of "learning how to take our differences and make them strengths" (1981). Hartsock (1996) has argued that it is necessary for theorists to construct theoretical bases for coalition building that, while they are no substitute for action, are a necessary addition to action. Some activists have argued for a politics of recentering rather than inclusion:

> It is not enough to be sensitive to difference; we must ask what difference the difference makes. Instead of saying, how can we include women of color, women with disabilities, etc., we must ask what our analysis and organizing practice would look like if we centered them in it. By following a politics of re-centering rather than inclusion, we often find that we see the issue differently, not just for the group in question, but for everyone. (Smith, 2006, p. 69)

Some authors have identified the idea of "strategic essentialism" (Spivak, 1995) or "tactical fixedness" (Dominelli, 2002), pointing out that, while identity is obviously socially constructed and fluid, it can be tactically fixed to achieve specific aims. Even though a group has many differences among the members such as class or sexual orientation, the group recognizes that there is wisdom in allying themselves together. The term *women of color* was coined by diverse women, including African-American, Native American, Latina, and Asian women, in 1977 at the National Women's Conference in Houston (Silliman, Fried, Ross, & Gutierrez, 2004) and has been an organizing framework ever since. Globalization has served to make visible the common interests of Third World women that can serve as the basis for organizing across racial/ethnic differences and national boundaries. There is a real benefit to publicly present themselves as a group with commonalities and similar interests. Though privately there may be differences, publicly the group chooses to present themselves as similar. This expression of solidarity can boost the morale and power of individuals to forge change initiatives. An example of the strategic use of group identity as mothers is the CO-MADRES in El Salvador (Stephen, 2005). According to Stephen:

> Being a "mother" and "motherhood" were constantly changing concepts which were expansive in the sense that being a mother came to represent a wide range of issues within the organization—bearing and rearing children, defending them and oneself against state repression, having the right to free

speech and being heard as a full citizen, having control over one's body and its physical integrity within marriage, within families, in prison, and in any state institution, and recognizing and controlling one's sexuality. This range of meanings of motherhood was not equally experienced or shared by all women in the CO-MADRES but was the discursive field within which motherhood came to be represented and contested. (p. 69)

Feminist theorists have argued against essentializing women as some kind of nondiverse group. Indeed, it was one of the earliest feminist philosophers, Simone de Beauvoir, who argued against defining women as something so limiting as "housewife," arguing instead for an existentialist perspective that permits women to create unique definitions of themselves. Later feminists began to argue for embracing traditionally feminine qualities of caring and cooperation. One can argue that this kind of essentializing has also objectified and silenced women.

Below, I discuss some venues where promising practices are taking place in terms of working with the complexities of race, class, gender, and other issues of identity. Here I discuss campus organizing and activities in the movement for reproductive justice.

CAMPUS ORGANIZING

Social change and other organizing endeavors have an important history on college campuses. Indeed, some of the most vital organizing work during the civil rights movement and antiwar movement was spearheaded and flourished on college campuses. Some have argued that the civil rights movement failed to address interlocking oppressions and the power imbalances within its own movement. There is promising evidence that college students today may be willing to grapple with some of those difficult issues. In the diverse environments of college campuses, where more students of color and international and immigrant students are attending universities, students are seeing the importance of addressing the difficult issues of interlocking oppressions, diversity, and identity politics within the work that they do. Students engaged in organizing around global justice, violence against women, immigration issues, and LGBT (lesbian, gay, bisexual, transgender) issues have been confronting the challenges of doing antioppression work as an integral component to their organizing practice.

A group known as the Sexual Assault Task Force (SATF) at a small liberal arts college confronted issues of sexism in their organizing work. However, they found it difficult to discuss the connections between sexism and racism (Martell & Avitabile, 1998). Researchers studying this group write:

> The group members were resistant to the discussion of diversity, stating that consciousness raising related to their own racial, cultural, and sexual diversity was not a priority for them.... This attitude created a barrier to the involvement of many women students of color and international student in SATF. (p. 407)

Meyer's (2004) study of LGBT organizing on a college campus identifies tensions in their organizing practices, including unity and difference, commitment and apathy, and empowerment and disempowerment. The first tension is most relevant to the discussion on identity politics. On this particular campus, there are three different organizations with varying goals and practices. Sisters of Dissent focuses on lesbian issues and engages in more radical actions on campus. Out Daily is less of a political organization and more of a space for students who are coming out. INC focuses explicitly on issues of oppression and attempts to build alliances with other groups on campus to contest homophobia, sexism, and racism. Tensions ensue within and across the groups related to identity and attention to oppression. Because people with a variety of identities are also working from a range of ideological viewpoints, uniting as a group can be challenging. One leader of Out Daily states:

In a community that celebrates diversity to the extent that the LGBT community does, it's very difficult at times to respect that diversity and cherish it and yet try to pull everyone into a group and move forward. Because so many times what's good for this particular gay man or lesbian woman isn't necessarily wonderful for a transgender or bisexual individual. The concerns of a Caucasian lesbian woman are not going to be the same concerns as an African American bisexual man. And how do we pull all that stuff together and say, this is good for all of us? (Meyer, 2004, p. 504)

One bisexual woman stated that she sometimes thinks that maybe bisexual women need their own organization, and yet, she reflects that, when there are so many difficulties coordinating the ones already, it would not be the right solution either.

Rhoads (1998) has discussed how student protest and multicultural causes played out in higher education in the 1990s, citing several examples. At Pennsylvania State University in 1992, gay, lesbian, and bisexual students held a variety of forums and other events to forge a public identity. These tactics were a way to pressure the university to add a clause concerning sexual orientation to its official nondiscrimination statement. The movement to elevate the Chicano Studies program to departmental status at UCLA was also a significant event. The marginalization of the Chicano Studies program was seen as a dismissal of the history, culture, and issues facing the people of the city of Los Angeles, which has the largest Mexican American population in the United States. After a student sit-in and 14-day hunger strike, the university eventually granted the program what was in effect departmental status. Other protests were at Michigan State University by Native American students against a proposition by the governor of the state to end the state's tuition program for Native American students. This program had emerged from the Comstock Agreement of 1934, which exchanged indigenous land for free education. Students protested by chanting "Give us the waiver or give us the land." These students were successful in their efforts to stave off the removal of the program. The protests also served as a catalyst for identity bonding for Native American students, citing the experience as a way to preserve their cultural heritage.

Labor organizing on college campuses is one venue where organizers are working on addressing issues of diversity and marginalization today. The Student/Farmworker alliance (SF) is a group that endeavors to eliminate sweatshop conditions in the fields and engages in campaigns for fair food. A recent victory included an agreement between the Coalition of Immokalee workers and Burger King to improve the wages and working conditions of Florida tomato pickers. SF understands how racism operates in capitalist systems as well as how it can manifest in community organizations. Thus, they work to address these issues by integrating antiracism and antisexism strategies into their work and organizational structures.[1] This intentional approach includes a steering committee that consists of 50% people of color and 50% women, as a way to address the reality that the voices of women and people of color are often marginalized in social change work. This structure is not in and of itself enough to address these issues. However, other mechanisms such as consensus decision-making procedures are utilized within the steering committee, with important attention given to identity politics. SF has a heightened understanding of group process that models the use of empowering language and a willingness to hold each other accountable. Utilizing the *encuentro* practice of the Zapatistas and other Latin American organizers, the SF also holds a strategy camp with Immokalee workers, with whom they work in solidarity. The *encuentro* focuses on analyzing targets and strategies as well as making connections to larger social movements, learning about the history of the Immokalee movement as well as the indigenous roots of Immokalee.

Other similar groups, such as the Student Labor Action Project (SLAP), hold the belief that intentional leadership development of students of color is a key component of antiracism work. SLAP leaders work at making their leadership development strategies sustainable, including making sure that students-of-color organizations get resources within their universities. Ross (2004) surmises the reasons for this when talking about the work of the United Students Against Sweatshops (USAS):

---

[1] Some of these ideas come from a workshop I attended at the 2007 U.S. Social Forum in Atlanta.

Perhaps as a result of the influence of a kind of seasoned feminism, USAS meetings are characterized by teaching and emulation of fairly sophisticated techniques of group discussion and leadership. Repeated observation of USAS meetings at local and regional levels demonstrated their painstaking efforts to include all participants in discussion and active care to insure that women were selected as discussion leaders or representatives and spokespersons. This is reflected substantively in USAS Code of Conduct campaigns and WRC [Worker Rights Consortium] inspections: treatment of women workers is specifically focused upon (in an industry in which the vast majority of workers are female). (p. 307)

The social standpoint of student activists is an important subject. A study of antisweatshop activists found that these students are twice as likely to come from high-income households compared with college students in general (cited in Ross, 2004). That being said, new cohorts of students are entering the picture, and growing numbers of students of working-class people and immigrant families are entering college. These groups argue that working with diverse students is important from an empowerment perspective. Students who are most affected by the issues have a great opportunity to realize personal and social transformation by the process. Students of color and working-class students are often busy working extra jobs and have an understanding of the problems faced by people struggling to make ends meet or facing some other form of oppression; hence, there is tremendous opportunity to attain solidarity with people across the globe in transnational organizing endeavors. The shared experiences of students of color can be nurtured and leveraged into powerful action. Making connections with their own families' experience and discussing manipulative advertising strategies may resonate with diverse student populations. Organizing strategies in such situations include lots of one-on-one work such as visiting student homes, taking them to lunch, as well as creating opportunities for students of color to connect with each other. Personalizing talking points rather than replicating points is important; framing the issues in a way that is engaging and accessible to people can also attract more students of color. To sustain the empowerment that is achieved on campus, many students also identify that there is an important need to foster a community that is committed to social justice work after students graduate. Some students have participated in summer internship training programs with unions, sparking an interest in carrying on economic justice organizing beyond the college years.

The use of caucuses within organizations has been a way to create a safe space for organizers to strategize with other like groups. United Students Against Sweatshops (USAS) has caucuses for women, people of color, LGBTQ (lesbian, gay, bisexual, transgender, queer) people, and working-class people.

People of color are the first to lose union jobs. When a student group could not get recognized by the student senate, they built alliances with staff to let them in the building to have meetings. One of the difficulties of organizing on college campuses is the fact that student organizations experience continual turnover (Meyer, 2004). Leadership can change every year.

REPRODUCTIVE JUSTICE

The ongoing struggle for reproductive justice can serve as another example of the inner workings of identity politics. Descriptions of the struggle for reproductive rights in the United States have been centered primarily on the efforts of white women to defend the legal right to abortion (Silliman et al., 2004). However, framing the issues as the right to choose an abortion limits the discussion for women of color, who historically have confronted many constraints to reproduction. These constraints have included "population control, sterilization, abuse, unsafe contraceptives, welfare reform, the criminalization of women who use drugs and alcohol during pregnancy, and coercive and intrusive family planning programs and policies" (Silliman et al., 2004, p. 2). Some women-of-color activists have chosen instead to frame the issue as "reproductive justice" rather than "pro-choice" or "reproductive rights," stressing the relationship between women's reproductive health and human rights and economic justice. Analyzing the white-biased language of "choice," one can consider that a woman living in poverty who decides to have an abortion for economic reasons does not experience the situation as a "choice."

The National Black Women's Health Project (NBWHP) was the first-ever women-of-color reproductive justice organization to address these discrepancies in approaches (Silliman et al., 2004). Because their voices and issues were silenced by white pro-choice organizations, it became necessary for women of color to establish their own organizations, develop their own leadership, and implement their own organizing strategies. These organizations would reflect the fact that the fertility of women of color had been continually undermined by U.S. policies (Silliman et al., 2004). In response to the question of whether this race/ethnic-based organizing approach creates unnecessary divisions, Silliman et al. write:

> To the contrary, all social movements, whether organized for the rights of people of color or gay people or workers or whomever, use identity politics in the sense that they are working on behalf of their constituencies who share an identity. Heterosexual white people have not recognized themselves as an identity group because they assumed their identity to be the universal norm. Consequently, many white women organizing for reproductive rights assume that their agenda includes all women. (p. 16)

LESSONS LEARNED

When building alliances across group differences, such as when Latina women and African-American women decide to come together to address violence in their community, there are several strategies that emerge from the lessons learned of those doing this difficult work (Martinez, 2006). Cultural expression can be a useful mechanism for bringing seemingly disparate groups together. Youth have shown this to be the case by building bridges through hip-hop, spoken word, and other performances (Martinez, 2006). Sharing such things as food, dress, music, and theater can be a way to "liberate our alliance-building energy and talents" (Martinez, 2006, p. 194). Large, public forums are often not the place to have the ongoing difficult conversations, so smaller, more intimate groups and coalitions may be the answer. Martinez offers some words from her work doing multiracial organizing with women:

> Don't be in a hurry, too impatient to listen.... We also say, stick to dialogue. Don't give up, even if it becomes difficult. It's normal. There can be enormous resistance to speaking openly about one group's issues with another. And women are often especially afraid of hurting someone's feelings, stepping on toes, or sounding racist by bringing up feelings that might sound like stereotypes.... Silences can feed the cancer of unaddressed conflict, and this has destroyed more than one project, group, or organization. This is a matter of organizational integrity: we cannot righteously continue our struggle, any struggle, without facing it.... Women of color need to act with integrity, speak with honesty, and reject any fear of our differences and conflicts. To transform the goal of unity into a reason for denying conflict, as we sometimes do, is self-defeating.... Let us create a stubborn, imaginative, honest, powerful insurgency. Let us counter the enemy forces of divide and conquer with our strategy of unite and rebel! (pp. 194–195)

The path to solidarity is long, but it is not unpaved. There are many lessons that organizers have learned in this challenging work. Organizers may consider asking themselves several important questions as they reflect on being an ally with all people across differences working in social justice struggles:

- What am I doing to develop honest relationships across barriers of race, class, gender, and cultural backgrounds?
- In what way am I acknowledging and addressing the problems within my own community with which I identify?
- How will actions of people of privilege contribute to changing society in a way that transforms oppression?

- What does commitment to solidarity with oppressed people really look like in my life? (Gelderloos, 2005)

Working with identity politics requires commitments to self-reflection and critical inquiry as well as a willingness to give up power and privilege. Going beyond cultural-competency models, which tend to downplay power differentials and systemic injustice, is vital. Attending to these issues can help in building a politics of coalition and inclusion that builds bridges across differences that can be leveraged into powerful transformations within and across communities.

SPOTLIGHT ON YOUTH ORGANIZING

More and more, young people around the world are organizing around a variety of issues and across racial, class, and other divides. Youth bring vital strengths to community organizing, including life experiences in their families and communities, creative ideas, technological savvy, passion, and integrity. They are organizing around LGBT (lesbian, gay, bisexual, transgender) issues, public education, immigration, homelessness, and environmental justice. Arguing that the civic engagement of youth can move beyond the recycling club or other service-oriented projects, youth are increasingly being viewed as relevant constituents who are capable of confronting various power structures and winning important gains.

Some of these youth organizing endeavors are actually youth-driven, while others are based on a youth–adult partnership model (Share & Stacks, 2006). In some cases, youth are able to leverage the political relationships previously developed by adult organizing groups (Dailey, 2003). In other cases, such as in the Farm Workers Association of Florida, youth organizing in immigrant communities play a significant role in getting adults involved in civic participation activities and community actions.

Regardless of the way that leadership is constructed, youth organizations are achieving meaningful gains in their geographic and identity-based communities. For example, youth leaders in Oakland, California, involved with the group Kids First! led a coalition that organized students, parents, and elected officials. The group was able to convince the regional transportation district to provide free bus passes for students who qualify for subsidized lunch programs (Hosang, 2003). They argued their case on the premise that public education should be free, pointing out that low-income students were paying $27 per month for a bus pass, a significant amount of money for poor families.

Hosang (2003) has identified some commonalities that cut across many diverse venues of contemporary youth organizing, pointing to three common components. First, a widespread characteristic in youth organizing is a holistic approach to social change that can yield multiple outcomes. Besides the traditional organizing campaign whose outcomes are long-term, they are able to engage their constituents in cultural enrichment programs, leadership development, and personal growth opportunities. Because some of the youth have unstable family and social situations, internal supports or partnerships with youth agencies that can work with youth to address emotional, legal, and material issues can be very helpful (Dailey, 2003).

Second, another common characteristic is the value that is placed on political education of the youth. Trainings are conducted on topics such as capitalism, racism, and other issues central to developing a critical consciousness about oppression and social change. Sisters and Brothas United (SBU) grew out of the Northwest Bronx Community and Clergy Coalition (NWBCCC), a community organization that has won successful campaigns in housing and public education. While some attempts at education reform have focused on mobilizing parents, several factors made organizing the high school students themselves a more appropriate choice. SBU has been more focused on political education than some adult groups, especially regarding topics on identity and race. According to Dailey (2003):

In addition, the "C" group, a core subset of core leaders, meet to talk radical politics and link their campaigns to movement history. SBU's willingness to embrace these issues has challenged NWBCCC as a whole to increase structured political education for its adult membership and contributed to a number of shifts in staff and leadership training, issue selection and message. (p. 100)

Third, youth organizers do tend to rely on paid staff member organizers, "many of whom are in their 20s or early 30s—who can successfully balance roles as mentors, political strategists, trainers, and fundraisers" (Hosang, 2003, p. 68). These staff members, like any professional staff members engaging constituencies, can work in solidarity with young people, emphasizing empowerment and leadership development.

Besides the obvious practical social justice and policy and program outcomes of youth organizing, the positive benefits of community organizing have been studied by researchers (Gambone, Yu, Lewis-Charp, Sipe, & Lacoe, 2006). Such studies have focused on identity development and personal growth impacts that organizing can have on young people. The HOPE Girls Project is a youth-driven project founded in 1997 in California for girls between the ages of 14 and 18 with the help of Asian and Pacific Islanders for Reproductive Health (APIRH) (Silliman et al., 2004). The project focuses on developing the organizing capacity of young women to take action focusing on reproductive freedom and other social justice issues such as welfare rights, school safety, and teen pregnancy prevention.

Whether its participants learn their own history, set out their vision of reproductive freedom, or get schools to improve sexual harassment policies, HOPE's ultimate goals are to empower API girls and develop a new generation of activists with a political perspective that uses reproductive rights as a framework for analyzing the issues that affect their lives. (Silliman et al., 2004, p. 186)

Utilizing participatory action research (PAR), a HOPE group of young women in Long Beach conducted a survey to determine the degree of sexual harassment, an issue identified by the young women themselves. Using the PAR model was a way to make the investigation centered on the girls and empowered them to inquire into the problem and take action. HOPE utilizes popular education, leadership development strategies, PAR, and community-building practices as essential components of their work (Silliman et al., 2004). The staff of APIRH offer support to the youth through tutoring, counseling, a stipend program, and grassroots organizing training.

Issues of global justice have also recently captured the interests of youth organizers. A group of students in San Jose, California, working with Californians for Justice, organized a campaign to change the way the schools deal with race/ethnicity, culture, and language. Attending school in a context where one out of three students speaks a language other than English in his or her home and one in four was born in a country outside the United States, the students face struggles related to culture, language, ethnicity, and race (Bass, Chace, Chow, et al., n.d.). Understanding the importance of making demands, the group came together to demand the following improvements:

1. Training on antiracism for teachers
2. Increase the number of high school graduates and improve college access
3. Bilingual certification

Organizing youth represents a tremendous hope for social change for the future. By raising consciousness, fostering organizing skills, and supporting youth activist agendas, the seeds of sustainable social change work are being planted for the future.

QUESTIONS FOR REFLECTION

1. Explore your own personal identity, including your gender, class, race/ethnicity, sexual orientation, ability, etc.
2. Discuss the concept of internalized oppression. How have you seen this manifest in yourself, family members, and people in the wider community?
3. Identify some examples of horizontal hostility that you have seen historically or in organizing campaigns you have participated in. What are some strategies for addressing this?
4. Discuss some of the ways that culture can be used to connect different identity groups to build social movement.
5. What are some ways in which a person with privilege can express her or his solidarity with marginalized individuals?

SUGGESTIONS FOR FURTHER INQUIRY

BOOKS

Anner, J. (Ed.). (1996). *Beyond identity politics: Emerging social justice movements in communities of color.* Cambridge, MA: South End Press.
Collins, P. H. (1999). *Black feminist thought: Knowledge, consciousness, and the politics of empowerment.* Boston: Unwin Hyman.
Moraga, C., and Anzaldua, G. (Eds.). (1983). *This bridge called my back: Writings by radical women of color.* New York: Kitchen Table: Women of Color Press.
Stout, L. (1997). *Bridging the class divide and other lessons for grassroots organizing.* Boston: Beacon Press.
Young, I. M. (1990). *Justice and the politics of difference.* Princeton, NJ: Princeton University Press.

WEB

Center for Third World Organizing. http://www.ctwo.org
Incite! Women of Color Against Violence. http://www.incite-national.org
Sister Song. http://www.sistersong.net
Women of Color Resource Center. http://www.coloredgirls.org
World beyond Capitalism: International Multiracial Alliance Building Peace Conference. http://www.aworldbeyondcapitalism.org/awbc.html

KEY TERMS

Ally: A person or group that stands in solidarity with another group that may experience oppression or marginalization. Allied actions may be expressed in a variety of ways, including through formal coalition work, support of direct actions, and personal attention to one's own internalized oppressions.

Internalized oppression: A manifestation of systemic oppression in one's personal, particularly emotional, life. Negative societal messages are turned inward and may impact self-esteem or other facets of personal functioning.

Intersectionality: A perspective that rests on the premise that oppressions, such as those based on gender, race/ethnicity, disability, or sexual orientation, do not act independently, but instead intersect to create a system of oppression.

Privilege: The unearned advantage that some people in society have by virtue of their gender, race/ethnicity, etc. Privilege allows a person from dominant classes greater access to societal institutions. Progressive organizers may choose to foster personal and organizational awareness of privilege in their practices.

Solidarity: Usually based on the notion that oppressions are interlocking. The term also describes efforts to work as an ally with diverse groups on diverse issues. This term is often associated with union work or socialist activities.

11 Religious and Spiritual Aspects of Organizing

> I didn't come from a background of activism, but when I first saw what was happening to the ancient redwoods in California, I fell to the ground and started crying and immediately got involved. It changed my life.
>
> **Julia Butterfly Hill, environmental activist**
> *(cited in Zinn, 2003, p. 595)*

Recently, when a longtime African-American female neighborhood activist in New Orleans was asked why she did the work that she did, she replied that she was inspired by biblical scripture. She said, "To whom much is given, much is required" (Pyles, 2006). Of humble means herself, she believed that she had abundant resources in her life, including the gifts of being able to connect with people and being willing to speak out when necessary, to commit to community organizing. And, she believes she has a duty to God to so engage.

Many activists like her are inspired to do the work they do by explicit religious teachings. Others are inspired by a spiritual calling, such as the environmental activist Julia Butterfly Hill, who feels called by Nature. Mahatma Gandhi was inspired by his Hindu faith and the writings of the Bhagavad Gita (song of the blessed one), which taught him to not be attached to physical comforts and not be attached to the outcomes of his actions. Martin Luther King, Jr. (1997), was inspired to civil disobedience based on his religious beliefs and his belief in an "inescapable network of mutuality." Dorothy Day, pioneer of the Catholic Worker movement, adhered to the tenets of pacifism as an expression of the teachings of Jesus. Other organizers, who may have a more secular orientation, may come to find that their community organizing work comes to have spiritual or existential meaning for them. The experiences of consciousness-raising and the feelings of group identity and solidarity have, for some people, constituted a religious or spiritual experience or awakening.

Recently, people in the helping professions and other community practitioners have been reclaiming some of their early spiritual and religious roots (Canda & Furman, 1999). Activists, social workers, and other helpers have had historical ties to religion, from the Charity Organization Society to the Catholic Worker movement. Religion and spirituality have also played an important role in organizing and social movements. Churches in the United States were critical institutions involved in the civil rights movement, the anti-Vietnam War movement, and the sanctuary movement. Throughout the world, faith groups have been a part of Solidarity's resistance to the Polish community state and the anti-apartheid movement in South Africa (Smith & Woodberry, 2001).

Scholars have noted that, historically, religion has provided the following supports and resources to social movements and community organizing efforts (Smith & Woodberry, 2001):

1. Legitimation for protest rooted in sacred and moral teachings, icons, and music, including love, justice, and peace
2. Self-discipline and sacrifice
3. Resources, including money and leadership
4. Institutionally based communication channels, hierarchical structures, and social control mechanisms

5. Common identification and solidarity, including shared transnational identities beyond nations and languages

Recent studies have documented the role and efficacy of religious institutions in social movements and community organizing. Resource-mobilization scholars have noted that religion serves as a viable conduit for mobilizing resources, particularly institutional supports (McAdam, 1982; Wood, 1999). Religious institutions can also be a source of social capital and a place where democratic skills are developed (Warren, 2001; Wood, 2002). Wood has posed an important question of whether religion itself, i.e., the religious culture as distinctive from the institution, has added anything unique to social movements. His research interestingly reveals that the content of a religious group's culture is relevant for political action; some forms of religious culture enable participation, and others constrain it. He writes, "A culture that understands good and evil complexly, as potentials in every person, lends itself to sophisticated interpretation of the political world, whereas conceptualizing good and evil in absolute terms as 'us' and 'them' tends strongly toward simplistic political interpretation" (Wood, 1999, pp. 328–329).

In this section, I focus on various approaches to community organizing from a religious or spiritual perspective. First, I discuss some of the literature on the significance of faith-based organizing, highlighting accomplishments and analyzing some strengths. These approaches include faith-based organizing, with a focus on urban efforts of racially diverse groups usually coming from various Christian traditions. Next, I focus on the philosophical and theological roots of various approaches to social change community organizing that may be useful to organizers. These approaches are:

1. Gandhian approaches to social change, which include Hindu religious and philosophical perspective to civil disobedience and other forms of resistance
2. Environmental spiritual approaches, as exemplified by the philosophy and practice of deep ecology
3. Jewish theological perspectives on organizing
4. The engaged Buddhist movement, which includes Buddhist practitioners, use of Buddhist principles, and meditative techniques to enhance their community organizing endeavors
5. Catholic social justice perspectives

This chapter concludes with some analysis and lessons learned from the five religious and spiritual traditions covered here.

FAITH-BASED ORGANIZING

Members of religious congregations represent some of the most powerful groups of community organizations. A great deal of religious social welfare efforts focus on charity-oriented service projects such as soup kitchens, clothing drives, or social service delivery such as substance abuse programs or child development centers. However, some congregations focus specifically on mobilizing its constituencies to directly impact changes in social and political issues. Faith-based groups have been effective because of their ability to draw from a legacy of well-trained community organizers. Alinsky drew from the strength of the church, building relationships with parish leaders in the Catholic Church. Chambers and Cortes followed suit but went further with the strategy, organizing lay members of the church community with an eye to leadership development of the congregation. Many of these organizing projects are long-term, interfaith endeavors. Some issues that have been successfully addressed by faith-based organizers have been public school reform, community policing, welfare rights, public transportation, expansion of state-funded health insurance, and support for hate crime legislation (Wood, 2002). Many of these organizations are affiliated with national organizing networks such as the Industrial Areas Foundation (IAF); the Pacific Institute for Community Organization (PICO); the Gamaliel Network; and Direct Action, Research, and Training (DART) (Wood, 2002).

DART engages over 400 local religious congregations, providing support for a variety of campaigns. These congregations include Catholic, Protestant, nondenominational churches, Jewish synagogues, and Muslim mosques. DART organizations have a wide range of victories to their credit, including those related to affordable housing, neighborhood revitalization, health-care provision, crime and drug reform, and public education improvement. In 2006, members of Faith and Action for Strength Together (FAST) achieved a key victory regarding transportation for older adults. Because of their organizing efforts, they were able to pressure the Metropolitan Planning Organization to create a phone number where seniors could call 24 hours a day to secure transportation services (DART, n.d.).

The New Orleans-based All Congregations Together (ACT) and its local and national partners won a significant victory through their organizing activities—a commitment from Mayor Ray Nagin to close the controversial Chef Menteur landfill. This controversial landfill had been closed prior to Katrina but was reopened after Hurricane Katrina to dump storm debris and other hazardous materials from gutted homes that had flooded due to breached government-controlled levees. This was a major victory for local churches and residents of New Orleans East, who had fought for months on this issue.

Many of the tactics used in faith-based organizing are similar to tactics used in secular-based organizing, including union organizing and environmental organizing. Through "one to ones," organizers seek to build solidarity with potential members (Wood, 2002):

By engaging in research, organizers attempt to gain power through information

Through actions, organizers exemplify their power in numbers

Through negotiations with policy makers, organizers can gain power through policy formulation

By initiating public conflict, organizers can make constructive uses of political tension

Through the process of evaluation, organizers develop leaders after critical reflection

These tactics should sound familiar to students of organizing. What is unique about faith-based organizing, however, is that they draw on an even "higher power" than what they have in their numbers. For example, groups such as PICO use prayer to invoke divine power in their efforts.

In the book *Faith in Action*, Richard Wood (2002) identifies several areas of strength and weakness that faith-based organizers bring to community organizing. Some of the limits of faith-based organizing are that many critical issues may not appear on their agendas, such as the civil rights of gay and lesbian individuals, which may be viewed by leaders as too divisive. In addition, because of the nature of congregational power, the issues tend to be localized issues. Progressive faith-based community organizers have been considered weak in their ability to impact state, national, or global policies and practices. The work of the IAF in the Texas state legislature is an example of an exemption to this characterization (Warren, 2001). Recently, PICO organized what they called "Compassion Sunday/Sabbath" as an attempt to address the issue of uninsured children. With the House and Senate set to vote on children's health bills the next week, congregations in more than 50 cities across the country held Compassion Sunday/Sabbath events to encourage people of faith to make their voices heard on the moral imperative to cover uninsured children.

The organizer of migrant workers, Cesar Chavez, said that every organization needs an ideology to be able to sustain itself. For his United Farm Workers, it was Christianity. And such has been the case for Cortes and constituents in Texas, where the Catholic Church is the center of the community. They explicitly utilize religious language and biblical stories to build strength and address issues such as anger (Boyte, 1984). According to one IAF trainer:

When was Christ really angry? When he found the den of thieves in the temple, he didn't ask them politely to leave. He threw them out because the people who came had very little means. They were forced to think they had to pay to use the temple. We talk about how Christ was not meek and mild, but a man with real emotions, a man who would challenge. If anger is repressed, it can be dangerous and destructive. (Boyte, 1984, p. 142)

Unfortunately, there may be evidence that the faith-based initiatives and charitable choice funding provisions at the federal level are negatively impacting traditionally progressive churches. These groups are arguably being co-opted by funding that is available for social services, focusing their energy on developing programs rather than community organizing. Thus, faith-based groups are arguably being affected by the conservative political climate that has opened up opportunities for faith-based groups to compete for funding with traditional nonprofit organizations. This influx of funding for social services may be silencing groups that have been more prone to progressive, grassroots direct action.

GANDHIAN NONVIOLENT APPROACHES TO SOCIAL CHANGE

Mohandas K. Gandhi was the leader of the Indian struggle for independence from British colonial rule who initiated the modern practice of nonviolent resistance. Believing in the complete unity and integrity of body, mind, and soul in the individual human being, his political activism was grounded in his Hindu spiritual beliefs and practices. Having no interest in spirituality by itself as an abstract virtue, he believed instead in the spiritualization of politics. Some basic principles that Gandhi brought from his Hindu tradition into Western consciousness are: (a) *satyagraha*, which can be understood as truth force or the insistence on truth; (b) *sarvodaya*, which is concern with the good of all; (c) *swadeshi*, the notion that the first level of responsibility in doing good is to those most immediate to you; and (d) *ahimsa*, or nonviolence. Overall, Gandhi believed that the pursuit of self-realization necessarily leads to the social arena; to be able to think and act nonviolently, a person must place himself or herself in situations where such behavior is called upon (Gandhi, 1957).

Gandhi believed that all social action should be governed by the same simple set of moral values, of which the main elements are selflessness, nonattachment, nonviolence, and active service. This is possible only when one identifies himself or herself more and more with an ever-increasing circle until he or she embraces all humanity and even all living beings. He judged the value and vitality of social institutions by their capacity to foster such growth. No society, state, or any other institution has any worth or importance apart from its part in contributing to the growth of the individuals of which it is composed. The state, the nation, the community, and other traditional groupings had no intrinsic value for him. In the pages of *Young India*, a newspaper he published in his earlier years, he defended the caste system as a great scheme of social and sexual discipline; but in the light of actual experience, he abandoned it as an impractical system, though to the end he believed in some kind of voluntary and ideal social groups based on qualifications and capacity for service.

From the perspective of the Gandhian nonviolent tradition, means are at least as important as, and often even more important than, ends. It is, of course, desirable that ends should be good and reasonable. But they merely give a direction to life, while the means adopted constitute life itself. Therefore, if the means are right, that is, if they conform to the tests of truth and nonviolence, even mistakes, errors, and failures aid the growth of the individual. On the other hand, means that are wrong corrupt the soul, and no good can ever come out of them. Gandhi repudiated categorically the idea that ends justify the means. This implies the rejection of war, espionage, and crooked diplomacy, even when they are adopted for the so-called noble ends of defending the country, religion, or humanity.

Gandhi cultivated respect for his antagonists, arguing that they are not enemies and that everyone needs to be liberated (Gandhi, 1957). Gandhi's direct-action tactics always involved honesty, and he never advocated deceit or lying to his "opponents." In passive-resistance efforts, Gandhi informed his opponents in advance about what he was going to do and why; he purposefully allowed his adversaries the opportunity to avert the passive-resistance action or prepare for it.

Gandhi's legacy has been far-reaching, to be sure, informing the likes of Cesar Chavez and Martin Luther King, Jr. Cesar Chavez's leadership skills were described by his coworkers as having a spiritual quality. One described him as having a "humble innocence that is the bearer of the words of another world" (DiCanio, 1998, p. 60). Chavez was influenced by the writings of Gandhi and actively practiced nonviolent civil disobedience including the spiritual practice of fasting as a direct-action tactic. King articulated several important components of nonviolent action (MacEachern, 1994). First, nonviolent action does not attempt to defeat an opponent but, rather, seeks his or her understanding. Second, nonviolent action is directed at objectionable policies and practices rather than at a particular person or persons. Third, it involves a willingness to suffer; when opponents are not able to listen to reason, suffering can awaken their consciousness. Suffering does not necessarily imply starving oneself or other forms of self-torture; it may be useful, instead, to think of suffering in terms of personal sacrifice.

DEEP ECOLOGY AND ENVIRONMENTAL ACTIVISM

The Bhopal environmental disaster occurred in December 1984 in the city of Bhopal, India, in the state of Madhya Pradesh. A Union Carbide subsidiary's pesticide plant released 40 tons of methyl isocyanate (MIC) gas, immediately killing nearly 3,000 people and ultimately causing at least 15,000 to 22,000 total deaths. Bhopal is considered to be one of the world's worst industrial disasters. Bhopal and other human-made environmental disasters, including global warming, have served as galvanizing events for the environmental movement. Some sectors of the environmental movement have drawn their inspiration from the philosophies of deep ecology, eco-feminism, and indigenous spiritual traditions (Macy). Deep ecology is "a bio- or eco-centric way of analysing issues that affords intrinsic value to all 'natural' things, so that nature as opposed to humanity forms the basis of its value system and therefore constitutes the opposite of anthropocentrism" (Lowes, 2006, p. 61).

The term *deep ecology* was coined by the Norwegian philosopher Arne Naess in 1973 (Sessions, 1995). By "deep" ecology, Naess was referring to a spiritual approach to ecology that had more depth than other more human-centered approaches and that asked "more searching questions about human life, society, and Nature" (Devall & Sessions, 1985a, p. 215). Like social constructionism and other postmodern philosophies, deep ecology maintains that the distinction between self and nature that has been reified by Western philosophy, culture, and institutions is an egregious miscon-struction. This divide between self and nature has resulted in and is related to the environmental destruction perpetrated by humans onto nature, the sexist domination perpetrated by males onto females, and the racism carried out by white people onto people of color.

One of the core concepts of deep ecology is *biocentric equality*, which means that all things in the biosphere have an equal right to their own self-realization. This is true because everything is of and from the same substance. Naess was intrigued by the philosophy of Gandhi and adopted the "monistic cosmology that emphasized the fundamental unity of all existence" (Fox, cited in Besthorn, 1997, p. 244). Deep questioning is a fundamental practice of deep ecologists; it is a process of asking "why" and "how," which can also be psychologically therapeutic, in addition to cosmo-logically healing. The aim of this deep questioning is the redirection of human consciousness. This resultant ecological consciousness has emerged in other spiritual traditions such as Christianity, Taoism, Buddhism, and indigenous spirituality (Sessions, 1995). Naess claimed that most people follow trends (i.e., social constructions and mainstream frames) and become philosophically handi-capped. However, Naess argues that one must have "enough self-confidence to follow one's intu-ition" (Devall & Sessions, 1985b, p. 221).

The process of identification of the self with others is central to self-realization. Through this process, the "self is widened and deepened. We 'see ourselves in others'" (Naess, 1988, p. 223). Self-realization involves seeing the similarities and interconnections between one's own suffering and the suffering of others. As Naess says, "Human beings will experience joy when other forms of life experience joy, and sorrow when other life forms experience sorrow" (Devall & Sessions, 1985b, p. 221). The process of identification elicits empathy and compassion and can result in solidarity. Thus, individual awakening and collective awakening are interconnected phenomena. These techniques have been utilized by environmental organizers to gain greater understanding of social issues as well as insight into determining the correct course of action.

JEWISH THEOLOGICAL APPROACHES

Tikkun olam is a Hebrew phrase that means "repairing the world." It is sometimes used by Jewish activists to refer to the concept of social justice. Drawing from the idea of solidarity and a belief that oppression hurts everyone, they recall the Jewish commandments and are reminded that they were all slaves in Egypt. According to the TIKKUN community:

> The sources of external injustice, suffering, and ecological numbness are to be found not only in economic and political arrangements, but also in our alienation from one another, in our inability to experience and recognize ourselves and each other as holy, in our inability to respond to the call of the universe which bids us to deeper levels of consciousness and love, and in our inability to overcome our own egos and see ourselves as part of the Unity of All Being.
>
> We need a spiritual consciousness along with a political consciousness if we are to heal and transform the world. Some of us in the TIKKUN Community are atheists or secularists, some of us belong to traditional religious communities, some of us are just beginning to work out our relationship to Spirit. But all of us understand that we need a movement that can address spiritual needs.
>
> It is our contention that social change and inner change go hand in hand. (http://www.tikkun.org/core_vision, ¶ 9)

The Hebrew concept of *mitvah* (meaning "fulfilling a commandment or duty") is also a guiding concept for organizers in the Jewish organizing tradition. Engaging in such worthy deeds in the world is a central part of an individual's spiritual fulfillment.

Jewish philosopher Roger Gottlieb (1999) calls for a spirituality of resistance, i.e., where spirituality must go beyond a mere feeling and must necessarily entail the resistance to the destruction of life. In his work, Gottlieb addresses issues relevant to any advocate or organizer and particularly the question of how one can maintain a peaceful approach to resistance work in a world that often makes one feel rage, grief, and fear. Gottlieb argues from a theological viewpoint which asserts that the world is imperfect and that doing the work of God involves remedying or repairing it. Gottlieb looks to the Jewish resistance of the Nazis as a model of courage and inspiration.

The Jewish Organizing Initiative (JOI) values the investigation of one's Jewish heritage as a central part of the organizing path. By drawing from the wisdom and historical traditions of Judaism, the JOI emphasizes Jewish identity and social change. One of their endeavors is a fellowship program that recruits young Jewish adults for a year of leadership training, focusing on social and economic justice, Jewish learning and community building, and training in grassroots community organizing strategies. Other organizations include Keshet, which focuses on inclusion of LGBT (lesbian, gay, bisexual, transgender) individuals in Jewish communities, and the Jewish Labor Committee, which advocates for Jewish concerns in the labor movement.

THE ENGAGED BUDDHIST MOVEMENT (EBM)

Thich Nhat Hanh founded the School of Youth for Social Service that trained people to provide direct help and relief to victims of the war in Vietnam (Hunt-Perry & Fine, 2000). He advocated a third-way approach that emphasized Vietnamese self-determination. So, Buddhist collective action emerged that was aimed at directly influencing public policies and establishing new institutional forms. As Thich Nhat Hanh brought his message to the United States, he saw how much anger there was in the antiwar movement. He came to emphasize *being* peace as an essential element of peacemakers and peacemaking; thus began the movement known as engaged Buddhism.

There are several important concepts in the engaged Buddhist movement (EBM) that may prove helpful to organizers (Pyles, 2005). First, all beings are worthy of one's attention; there is no separation. As Chagdud Tulku Rinpoche (1985) writes: "True compassion is utterly neutral and is moved by suffering of every sort, not tied to right and wrong, attachment and aversion" (p. 40). This implies that making distinctions between "us" and "them" or the "haves" and the "have-nots" or anything else that is going to spiritually separate us from others is a trap. Second, self-transformation and social transformation are mutually necessary. Indeed, social systems do not appear in a vacuum; they were created by human beings. Third, the EBM is committed to combining social justice and democracy with meditative practice.

Engaged Buddhist social action across the globe has included working with the dying in hospices, teaching meditation to prisoners and cancer survivors, providing support for victims of AIDS, advocating for a clean environment, and supporting a free Tibet. Social development has always been one of the primary activities of engaged Buddhist practitioners.

A prime example of the possibilities offered by engaged Buddhism for progressive social change is the work of the Greyston Foundation in New York City, which was founded by Bernard Glassman and the Zen Peacemaker Order. This network of businesses and nonprofits is engaged in housing and entrepreneurial activities for the homeless (Glassman, 1998). As an economic development venture, this group chose to start a bakery that was to provide employment for low-income and homeless individuals in New York. As the group was confronted with various choices to be made about the functioning of the organization, one such choice concerned how to manage the bakery. Would they choose traditional, hierarchical models under which many businesses and social welfare agencies operate, or would they choose something different, something based on the basic tenets of Buddhism, including interconnectedness, compassion, and human empowerment? Their response was self-directed management teams, which involve workers choosing who enters the organization, workers training each other, and eventually all workers having the opportunity to own shares in the business.

The Buddhist Alliance for Social Engagement (BASE), headquartered in San Francisco, provides an educational, supportive network for individuals working in social development settings. BASE provides a structured, supportive environment for individuals who are working or volunteering in social services or activism. One of the BASE programs, called HOME BASE, involves participants who work in direct service or advocacy for the homeless. All of the BASE programs are six months and include five basic program components. These five components are based on the Buddhist concepts (*pali*) of *seva* (service/social action), *panna* (wisdom/training), *samadhi* (dharma practice), *sangha* (community), and *adhitthana* (commitment).

The Sarvodaya Shramadan movement was founded in Sri Lanka in 1958 (Macy, 1983). The Sarvodaya movement is a Buddhist-inspired self-help movement that involves young pioneers working alongside extremely poor individuals, operating programs for health, education, agriculture, and local industry. The four cornerstones of Sarvodaya are respect for all life, compassionate action, dispassionate joy, and equanimity. It was founded by a high school teacher, A. T. Ariyaratna, who named his movement after the term that Gandhi had used in his movement—*sarvodaya*, meaning "everybody wakes up."

Emphasizing the interdependence of life, the Sarvodaya movement is premised on the belief that through local action, and more specifically through social, economic, and political interaction, spiritual awakening can simultaneously take place (Macy, 1983). Based on a view of mutual causality, every act is seen to have an effect on the larger web of life. Joanna Macy, a Buddhist practitioner and activist, who spent a year working in and studying the Sarvodaya movement, describes it:

> One's personal awakening (*purushodaya*) is integral to the awakening of one's village (*gramodaya*), and both play integral roles in *deshodaya* and *vishvodaya*, the awakening of one's country and one's world. Being interdependent, these developments do not occur sequentially, in a linear fashion, but

synchronously, each abetting and reinforcing the other through multiplicities of contacts and current, each subtly altering the context in which other events occur. (p. 33)

CATHOLIC SOCIAL JUSTICE PERSPECTIVES

The Catholic Worker movement was a lay movement founded in New York City in 1933 as a social articulation of the teachings of the Catholic Church (Coy, 1997). Engaging in antiwar and pacifist actions as well as racial and economic justice causes, the periodical *The Catholic Worker* was a central mechanism for change. The organizing work of the Catholic Worker movement was based out of hospitality houses where food, clothing, and shelter are offered to individuals in need. Nonviolent direct actions have been the hallmark of the movement's organizing strategies. "Prayer vigils are held for those facing the death penalty, arms bazaars are picketed, economic boycotts are publicized and promoted in the movement's paper, and public fasting in behalf of peace and the rights of the poor is common" (Coy, 1997, p. 65).

Another approach grounded in the Catholic tradition is the well-documented movement known as liberation theology. Liberation theology is a theological praxis centered on the social action of Jesus, emphasizing Christ as liberator of the oppressed in this world and the world beyond (Reese, 1999). This Latin American social movement that began in the 1950s was centered in church-based communities in Brazil and other countries, adapting Freirean consciousness-raising approaches with Marxist social justice perspectives. In base communities, groups would meet for scripture reading and discussion emphasizing a Christian–Marxist framework that affirmed solidarity with the poor. Often referred to as a form of Christian socialism, a liberation theology of which those in the Jesuit tradition were its primary adherents, it was eventually theologically denounced by the powerful hierarchy of the Catholic Church in the 1980s.

TOWARD INTERSPIRITUAL SOLIDARITY

The variety of religious and spiritual perspectives on organizing should not be adopted uncritically; indeed, a problematizing approach is appropriate for any progressive organizing endeavor. Because faith is sometimes divorced from reason and critical thinking, one should be cautious when considering merging spirituality and political activity. Many of the approaches discussed in this chapter have been critiqued by philosophers and community organizers. Bookchin (1999), for example, has argued that deep ecology places too much emphasis on Nature and not enough emphasis on the importance of humans and society, arguing instead for a social ecology. Alinsky (1971) critiqued the Gandhian approach as incompatible with utilitarian direct-action approaches. Alinsky's approach considers power holders as the enemies, and the goal of organizers is to catch the enemy by surprise. Others have argued that Gandhi's situation was somewhat unique and that different circumstances call for different sorts of responses.

Interspiritual solidarity offers a unique path for pursing progressive organizing agendas in a globalizing world. Tikkun and Sojourners (a progressive Christian social justice organization) and other religiously based organizers have recognized the importance of working in interspiritual solidarity between Jewish and Christian organizers. The Network of Spiritual Progressives is a community of individuals from various traditions, including Christian, Jewish, and Muslim. The Progressive Muslim Union is a group of progressive Muslims interested in progressive social change within Muslim communities and across religious differences.

Because religious differences often separate people and perpetuate injustices across the globe, it would seem essential that progressive organizers who are working within a particular framework, e.g., deep ecologists, Christian activists, etc., are able to communicate and work together. The danger of such groups working in isolation is that bonding capital is strengthened at the expense of bridging capital (Putnam, 2000). Though progressive spiritual and religious organizers tend to see the many faces of interlocking oppressions, there is a danger that such groups may have trouble communicating with other religious groups who have a differing orientation in terms of spiritual and religious practices. As was discussed in the chapter on identity politics (Chapter 10), working in isolation can sometimes blind organizers to other groups who may be different or have more power, but may also be potential allies. I submit that there is tremendous power to be tapped into through "interfaith dialogue" and other progressive spiritual networking.

Finding common ground for dialogue is a first step toward interfaith coalition building. Some groups approach such work by focusing on issues where they may find that everyone agrees on increasing funding for public school programs. In such cases, spirituality and religion may not even be discussed in much detail nor be deemed relevant to the case at hand. For other groups, a beginning point may be to clarify values and find common theological ground in such universal concepts as love or justice. Indeed, religious and spiritually based organizing can take place on a spectrum of transformative and utilitarian frameworks.

For organizers with no religious or spiritual affiliation or inclination, the question of how to ally oneself and work with religious and spiritual organizers may appear to be a bit of a conundrum. Organizers may be concerned that working with such groups or individuals may be uncomfortable; the group may engage in group prayer, singing, meditation, or some other ritual that is not familiar to the organizer. One way to think of this situation is the same way that one would think about any form of cultural or ethnic diversity (Canda & Furman, 1999). Respecting traditions and learning about a religious or spiritual perspective is an important way to develop relationships with diverse groups of constituents across the globe. The power of spiritual people and those affiliated with religious institutions is tremendous, but can be activated only through understanding, critical reflection, and the search for common ground.

SPOTLIGHT ON ORGANIZING WITH OLDER ADULTS

Political commentators have long noted the power of older adults at the voting polls, representing the highest age demographic turnout in the United States (Andel & Liebig, 2002). Yet, when it comes to other forms of civic engagement, scholars have noted a decline. Theories of "disengagement" of older adults, which state that aging adults tend to discontinue activities that have high demands, have nurtured the notion that older adults are "unorganizable" (Minkler, 2005). In contrast, organizers and scholars have noted that older adults, particularly the so-called able elderly, are a "sleeping giant" in terms of their political power (Andel & Liebig, 2002, p. 92). Resisting social constructions of "frailty" (Grenier & Hanley, 2007) and other negative stereotypes, older adults represent a constituency with many resources for doing significant social change work. Working on issues such as housing, health care, and community development, older adults bring important strengths, such as leadership, knowledge, and strong social networks to community organizing practice.

Maggie Kuhn was the founder of the Gray Panthers, an organization that mobilized around many issues affecting older adults, including ageism and nursing home reform. Reframing the idea that old people were to be treated like children, Kuhn (1991) believed older Americans are an uptapped resource. The Gray Panthers movement went beyond issues related to older adults and viewed many issues as interconnected. They organized around poverty, civil liberties, and the Vietnam War.

Older activists may also sometimes use stereotypes of the elderly as "frail" to their advantage. According to Grenier and Hanley (2007):

> While older women often contest the image of seniors as "frail" or powerless, they are willing to make strategic use of stereotypes to serve their interests. It was not uncommon for senior members to bring canes or walkers to demonstrations to gain sympathy from politicians and the media. In some cases, preparations for demonstrations came to include the advice: "Don't forget your walkers!" (p. 221)

A group of activists in Montreal, Quebec, called The Raging Grannies and others also often use subversive strategies of parody of the granny image and note that authorities tend to avoid retaliatory action against them (Grenier & Hanley, 2007).

The so-called gray participation hypothesis states that, as the baby boom generation approaches old age, so will political activism. Older adults tend to be more informed about politics, and interest and political knowledge seems to grow with age (Andel & Liebig, 2002). When organizing with older adults, it is important to understand that they are not by any means a homogeneous group. Indeed, they may have in common their age, but beyond that, political beliefs may vary widely. A diversity of education, income, sexual orientation, and race/ethnicity clearly exists for these groups. "Senior political participation, although extensive, may lack the political substance and direction commonly generated by shared goals, interests, and attitudes" (Andel & Liebig, 2002, p. 89).

The positive outcomes of organizing with older adults are varied and go beyond policy change and new program development. Indeed, the social support and subsequent personal empowerment that can come from engaging in an organizing campaign can be very potent in themselves. Elderly individuals who may otherwise be isolated or depressed may become connected and thriving when engaged in a community organizing campaign (Minkler, 2005). Mutual aid programs among older adults have been a very useful strategy to engage this population because they can address real and specific needs. However, there can be a danger that mutual aid eclipses organizing activities because the positive effects of mutual aid can be felt more quickly (Minkler, 2005). Other positive outcomes of organizing with older adults have been health related. For example, an older adult who was struggling with mental health issues that left her disabled often did not take medications that would help her function better. After participating in a community organizing effort, she reported that she took her medication regularly because several of the group's activities relied on her leadership skills (Minkler, 2005). It is clear that developing the capacities of this "sleeping giant" promises rewards of empowerment and social change to a diverse community.

QUESTIONS FOR REFLECTION

1. What concerns do you have with bringing issues of spirituality and religion into the domain of social change? What is the origin/nature of your concerns—personal? familial? professional? societal?
2. Can and should social change work be a form of spiritual practice and/or have a religious component to it?
3. What strengths do religious institutions bring to progressive organizing? What barriers or challenges do such institutions pose?
4. Discuss the similarities and differences between the various religious/spiritual organizing perspectives discussed in this chapter, including the Gandhian nonviolent approach, deep ecological perspectives, Jewish theological approaches, engaged Buddhist movement, and Catholic social justice perspectives.
5. What are the important keys to engaging religious and spiritual communities in building interspiritual solidarity to achieve social change? How does a community organizer prepare himself or herself for such work?

SUGGESTIONS FOR FURTHER INQUIRY

BOOKS

Hinsdale, M. A., Lewis, H. M., & Waller, M. S. (1995). *It comes from the people: Community development and local theology*. Philadelphia: Temple University Press.
Lewis, H., & Appleby, M. (2003). *Mountain sisters: From convent to community in Appalachia*. Lexington: University of Kentucky Press.

Wallis, J. (2006). *Living God's politics: A guide to putting your faith into action.* San Francisco: HarperSanFrancisco.

Wood, R. L. (2002). *Faith in action: Religion, race, and democratic organizing in America.* Chicago: University of Chicago Press.

Yarnold, B. M. (Ed.). (1991). *The role of religious organizations in social movements.* Westport, CT: Praeger.

WEB

Global Alliance for a Deep Ecological Social Work. http://www.ecosocialwork.org/

Human Rights Tools. http://www.humanrightstools.org

Jewish Organizing Initiative. http://www.jewishorganizing.org

Keshet. http://www.boston-keshet.org

PICO National Network. http://www.piconetwork.org

KEY TERMS

Catholic Worker movement: Historical and contemporary organizing focusing on the alleviation of poverty and alternatives to violence. Methods have included small, decentralized communal associations.

Interspiritual solidarity: A form of coalition building that transcends the politics that separates diverse religious and spiritual practitioners.

Nonviolence: A direct-action organizing tactic that proactively uses creative strategies to effect change in a way that is consciously nonviolent. Gandhi's philosophy and practice of *satyagraha* (literally, "a firmness in the truth") has been a pioneering technique in nonviolence.

12 Global Justice
Organization and Resistance

We call for a strengthening of alliances, and the implementation of common actions.... We recognize that we are now in a better position to undertake the struggle for a different world, a world without misery, hunger, discrimination and violence, with quality of life, equity, respect and peace.... The proposals formulated are part of the alternatives being elaborated by social movements around the world. They are based on the principle that human beings and life are not commodities, and in the commitment to the welfare and rights of all.

World Social Forum (2001, p. 437)

At first glance, it may seem difficult to understand the relationship between local problems in communities and larger global economic issues. The truth of the matter is, though, that there are few people in this world who are not in some way affected by global economics. People across the globe, in both the global North and the global South, are affected in ways of which they may not even be aware. As local industries in the North are closed in favor of cheaper labor pools in the South, people experience unemployment, the need for retraining, and associated social problems. Home and neighborhood gardens are lost to chain stores selling genetically modified food high in sugar and fats, leading to significant public health issues. Family farms and indigenous land are lost to global corporate giants. When one begins to come to terms with the relationship between what happens in a local community to the larger forces of globalization, one may wonder if the work that global justice activists are doing can even have an impact. In other words, does the global justice movement really matter? Or, are the larger mechanisms of globalization negating local, transnational, and global organizing? Indeed, some would argue that the negative aspects of globalization are an inevitable process that cannot, in effect, be challenged.

A new kind of potent activism has emerged as a form of resistance to globalized capitalism. This global justice movement attempts to challenge practices and mediate the effects of globalization. Shepard and Hayduk (2002) use the term *glocalism* to describe this interface of global and local concerns. They define it as "political activism based on the insight that every local action has a global component" (p. 5). Transcending the false divide of local and global, the idea of glocalism can be thought of as an expression of the phrase, "think globally, act locally." In this chapter, I discuss and analyze the global justice movement, which has been described as the largest social movement in human history (Hawken, 2007). After discussing the effects of economic globalization on communities, I describe some endeavors being conducted in the areas of land-based organizing and transnational labor organizing, concluding with an analysis of the contemporary global justice organizing.

THE EFFECTS OF ECONOMIC GLOBALIZATION ON COMMUNITIES

Globalization is not a new phenomenon. Indeed, the first wave of globalization occurred when Europeans colonized Africa, Asia, Australia, and the Americas dating back some 1,500 years. The second wave of globalization came through the Western implementation of "development" projects in the postcolonial period over the last 55 years or so. The third and current wave began in the mid-1990s through the "free trade" movement (Shiva, 2000).

The current practices of the global economy can be understood by exploring in more detail the practices of neoliberalism via a variety of mechanisms, including debt, free trade, and privatization (Zerkel, 2001). Entities like the World Trade Organization (WTO) and the International Monetary Fund (IMF) have provided loans to developing countries. These loans come with what are called "structural adjustment programs," which means that governments in developing countries, particularly in the global South, many of whom are forever in debt now, must vow to retrench their countries' infrastructure and human services, such as health care. These loans come at a heavy price to local communities and have huge negative effects in the realm of social welfare. Activism working to resist these practices has been a key aspect of the global justice movement. Environmental activist Starhawk (2002) offers her perspective on globalization:

> It's an ideology that elevates corporate profit to the highest value and determining factor for all human activity, individual and collective. It says that corporations must be unfettered in their pursuit of profit, that all natural and human resources should be open to exploitation, that services and infrastructures once collectively provided by governments should become arenas of profit making, and that while some people will gain more than others under this regime, following this program will make everyone richer and benefit all. (http://www.starhawk.org/activism/activism-writings/trollstostone.html, ¶ 3)

A 2004 report by the National Labor Committee that focused on outsourcing by U.S. garment companies to China recounts the conditions of the people working for these U.S. companies. The appalling conditions include an average wage of 22 cents an hour for workers who are predominantly 16- and 17-year-old girls; factory temperatures over 100 degrees Fahrenheit; and workers being coached to lie to factory auditors about working conditions (Micheletti & Stolle, 2007). Many companies have argued that the minuscule wages paid to workers is socially just, given that the cost of living is so cheap. The rhetoric of globalization and development pronounces that such opportunities are lifting the developing world up and that foreign corporations are actually engaged in benevolent economic actions. However, activists and researchers have inquired more deeply into this social construction and have learned that living on $65 per month in China is actually quite difficult. The cost of living for a lower middle-class family in Shenzen, China, is approximately $350 per month, and this amount excludes transportation and health care (NLC, 2004). Researching the facts about what is happening in these contexts and deconstructing the narratives of corporations and their spin doctors is an essential element of global justice organizing. While many of these corporate practices are not illegal, they are certainly ethically dubious. The stories and frames about these practices must constantly be questioned by global justice activists.

It can be difficult to challenge and resolve such questionable corporate practices through national and international legal mechanisms, particularly because globalization seems to be diminishing the relevance of the state as corporations become the significant players. Indeed, the legal reality of "corporate personhood" gave corporations the same full rights that individual human beings have. Other innovative strategies have become necessary. And thus, this is one of the defining characteristics of the global justice movement. Because of the lack of legal accountability on such issues, new ways to hold corporations accountable and raise consumer awareness are required (Micheletti & Stolle, 2007). Just like the work that Ralph Nader and the consumer safety and rights movement started some 40 years ago, consumer awareness and activism about the ways in which products are manufactured, including personnel practices, becomes a central way to organize around such injustices.

The North American Free Trade Agreement (NAFTA), which came into effect in 1994, proposed to open trade between the United States, Canada, and Mexico. The discourse about this agreement emphasized the immense economic benefits that it would provide for all people as well as democratic institutions generally. The idea was that the obvious economic benefits to corporations would trickle down to the average worker over time. Indeed, this is the entire premise of global economic development. In Mexico, some 10 years after the passage of NAFTA, three-quarters of the population is living in poverty, real wages are lower, and unemployment is rising (Klein, 2002). And yet, it is still heralded as a success, and other more expansive agreements have been proposed such as the Free Trade Area of the Americas (FTAA), which would spread the so-called free trade zone into all of Latin America. One has to question—who is benefiting and for whom is the agreement a success?

CONTEMPORARY GLOBAL JUSTICE ORGANIZING

It is important to remember that, for many activists, globalization is a complex phenomenon, and indeed the globalization of culture, ideas, and technology offers great opportunities to build global community. Some have explained their position by making the distinction between globalization from above and globalization from below, indicating that a global justice movement is concerned with an alternative to corporate-driven globalization, or globalization from above (Lechner & Boli, 2004). Those organizing for a globalization from below have been referred to by many titles, including the antiglobalization movement; the alternative globalization movement; and, as I use in this text, the global justice movement. Because the movement is diverse, decentralized, and international, it is difficult to characterize it generally.

One of the central values of global justice movements is the reclamation of what some have called the cultural commons. The cultural commons is the intergenerational knowledge and practices in a community (Bowers, 2007). This exists in the creative arts, ceremony and ritual, food traditions, and healing practices. In the era of hypercapitalism and globalization, this kind of folk knowledge is arguably being commodified through such widespread phenomena as fast-food chain restaurants and television advertising. Many organizers view reclaiming the cultural commons to be central to their activist work. Related to this idea is the notion of the global commons, which falls outside the control of any single nation or corporation. The global commons includes information commons such as the Internet, traditional knowledge, and environmental systems such as the biosphere. The global commons are viewed as an "anathema to private and intellectual property rights" (Lowes, 2006, p. 104). The United Nations exists to help governments work together to safeguard the global commons; however, ensuring this is difficult, as implementations of agreements are at the discretion of individual signatory countries, and enforcement is relatively weak, involving political and financial pressure rather than formal legal consequences.

This frame of the commons has been crucial and has served as a common ground of values for diverse global activists. One organizing tactic employed has been to protect the public space that has more and more opened for commerce. Intellectual and property rights have become overvalued, argues the global justice activist, as seeds used to grow food have become the property of multinational agribusinesses. In fact, saving seeds has become illegal in some cases. In India, groups such as the Pattuvam Pnchayat community and the National Front for Tribal Self-Rule have utilized a variety of organizing tactics to declare their community's rights to biodiversity and control of their land (Shiva, 2000).

One of the targets of the global justice movement has been international financial institutions such as the IMF and WTO. The protests of the WTO international conference in Seattle in 1999 are considered a significant moment in the movement to resist globalization. It has variously been referred to as "the coming out party of the anti-globalization movement," "the Battle of Seattle," or just "Seattle" (Klein, 2002). The Seattle demonstrations were considered a success for several reasons. They achieved the tangible goal of affecting the WTO activities, forcing significant changes in the conference, including the cancellations of many conference meetings. The event revealed the common ground of activists organizing around a variety of issues, including labor, environmental, and many other social welfare causes. One of the unique aspects of the Seattle protests, and indeed the global justice movement generally, has been the expression of the joie de vivre and the creative elements of organizing. For example, the Earth Island Institute, an environmental organization, made over 500 sea turtle costumes for activists to wear in Seattle as symbols of the WTO's threats to environmental laws (St. Clair, 2004).

Castells (1999) has articulated the concept of a network society that explains social interrelatedness as something beyond territorial approaches. This network society creates the conditions for globalized organizing. The use of summit mobilizations has been a hallmark of the global justice movement. Such strategies are an antidote to the critique that the global justice movement is totally fragmented. The World Social Forum has been an example of such mobilizations. Summit mobilizations may fulfill at least two functions:

> The first is to send shockwaves demonstrating mass opposition with the capacity to threaten and disrupt capitalist globalization-from-above. The second is to strengthen and energize the networks and movements of our globalization-from-below. Strong summit mobilizations come out of ongoing campaigns and the culmination of movement building in our communities. (Solnit, 2006, p. 76)

LAND-BASED AND LOCALIZATION MOVEMENTS

Land rights, including water rights and the right to a local economy, have been central organizing points for global justice organizers. The EZLN, or the Zapatista Army of National Liberation, was initiated in the 1980s by a small group of Marxist revolutionaries. The Zapatista movement has been particularly concerned with how a globalizing economy has negatively affected indigenous people in Chiapas, Mexico. Like the American Indian Movement (AIM) that began in the 1960s and built solidarity among indigenous peoples of the United States, the Zapatista movement is concerned with what colonialism has done to indigenous peoples. Though Zapatista communities have not necessarily worked out a common political program, they all demand dignity, liberty, and justice. The decision-making structures developed by the Zapatistas offer many lessons to organizers across the globe. The methods for making decisions tend to combine democratic approaches with indigenous assemblies. This kind of approach to addressing social issues has also been employed in Australian aboriginal contexts as well as native Hawaiian contexts.

In 2004, the people of Uruguay voted to amend their constitution to recognize the fundamental right to water as a public good, challenging the possibility that water rights could be sold to private interests. The constitution now guarantees that piped water and sanitation be available to all Uruguayans, and it bans for-profit corporations from supplying this public good. In communities across India, where people live near Coca-Cola's bottling plants, people are experiencing critical water shortages. Such shortages are a direct result of Coca-Cola's immense extraction of water from the common groundwater source. Citizens are finding that wells have run dry and hand water pumps are no longer functioning. Other environmental problems are associated with the bottling plants, including contamination and toxic waste. Thus, an international campaign against Coca-Cola has been initiated charging that the company is creating water shortages and pollution across India. In an era when universities often have exclusive contracts with soft drink providers, including Coca-Cola, some college students have pressured university administrators in solidarity with international activists to relinquish such contracts. The No Borders Camp is part of a global movement against migration controls. Drawing from an analysis that recognizes that the NAFTA has uprooted millions of poor farmers and city dwellers in Mexico, forcing them to migrate north to survive, the No Borders Camp campaign seeks to undermine the limitations on the ability of people to move freely to seek work. The mobilization culminated in a week-long cross-border encampment near Calexico and Mexicali.

Because the expansion of the global economy has been accompanied by a retraction of local economies, much organizing and activism work has focused on building up local economic solutions as a way to attempt to rearrange the political economy. Thus community organizing in the era of globalization becomes a form of "resistance" to the large-scale economies. According to Mander (1996):

> Today's problems will eventually be solved by recognizing that local production for local consumption—using local resources, under the guidance and control of local communities, and reflecting local

and regional cultures and traditions within the limits of nature—is a far more successful direction than the currently promoted, clearly utopian, globally centralized, expansionist model. (p. 391)

Some of these localized initiatives have been diverse and far-reaching and are highlighted below:

- Community banks and loan funds
- "Buy local" campaigns
- Agricultural tool lending libraries
- Community kitchens
- Using local currency
- Bartering
- Cooperatively or collectively operated businesses
- Community food gardens

An alternative globalization agenda emphasizes mutual aid and the strengthening of the solidarity economy.

TRANSNATIONAL LABOR ORGANIZING

Transnational labor organizing has been an important tool for the global justice movement. Marx predicted that the inequities of capitalism would eventually minimize the differences among workers (race, culture, etc.), igniting the development of international labor organizing (Armbruster-Sandoval, 1999). Contemporary transnational labor organizing has included organizing in the *maquiladoras* (export assembly plants) in Latin America (Bender, 2004), antisweatshop organizing (Armbruster–Sandoval, 2005), and the development of fair-trade organizations. The United Fruit Company began exporting bananas from Latin America as early as the 1880s, operating on a colonialist plantationlike system. Today, the major fruit companies still operate in these countries, where some 400,000 banana workers work on such plantations (Frank, 2005). As a counter to poor wages and conditions, banana unions arose in the 1950s. In addition, immigrant communities in the United States are openly resisting the neoliberal attack on their home countries, such as Central Americans against CAFTA, Korean-Americans against the Korea–US FTA, and Congolese against World Bank–funded mining in Congo. What these seemingly disparate endeavors have in common is a concern with the effects of a global economy on workers' rights and an interest in using organizing strategies across borders to address them. This kind of organizing has offered an antidote to the impersonal, bottom-line aspect of globalization.

A transnational advocacy network (TAN) consists of a partnership between local unions, particularly in southern or developing nations, and allies such as international NGOs (nongovernmental organizations). The purpose of the TAN is to influence the state or some other target to change or enforce policies or initiate reforms (Armbruster-Sandoval, 2005). Some critics have argued that some perspectives of the TAN can silence or marginalize workers, particularly women of color, who are organizing on the front lines, and privilege the work of northern white activists (Brooks, 2002). Others have emphasized the importance of a dialectical relationship between workers and the TAN for a successful campaign. Whether or not the victories of such campaigns can be sustained over time remains in question (Armbruster-Sandoval, 2005).

One such example of a TAN in action has been the antisweatshop movement. The antisweatshop movement began in the late 1800s when "reformers," as they were called, began to call attention to the fact that workshops and factories were using "sweated labor" to produce goods (Micheletti & Stolle, 2007). This sweatable labor tended to consist of women immigrants and children in the garment industry in major urban areas in the United States.

Antisweatshop reformers used a variety of tactics to promote their cause. They investigated sweatshops, informed and educated the public, publicized sweatshop problems, offered "buycott" or best-practice shopping guides, pressured government to purchase "no-sweat" wear for its employees, mobilized public support for political responsibility-taking, supported unionization, entered partnerships with business, and even established a very early innovative no-sweat labeling scheme. (Micheletti & Stolle, 2007, p. 162)

One of the major tactics, though, was pressuring government to enact and enforce labor standards, which, through the New Deal, was accomplished through federal regulatory authority by promoting unions and labor standards. Corporations began to avoid standards by moving factories to the U.S. South, where unions were weak, and later began moving factories to Latin America and Asia. These events eventually led into the modern antisweatshop and strengthening of transnational labor organizing.

Even in the early days of the movement, however, the moral culpability of consumers was emphasized early on; Josephine Shaw Lowell, founder of the New York Consumers' League in 1891, argued that consumers had the obligation to investigate the conditions under which the clothing they purchased was produced and distributed. Similarly, Florence Kelley, general secretary of the National Consumer's League, argued that both the employers and consumers were responsible for the manufacturing conditions (Micheletti & Stolle, 2007).

The United Students Against Sweatshops (USAS) was founded in the late 1990s as a mechanism to support the work of college students in the United States who were working to oppose the manufacture of college apparel in sweatshop conditions. These students developed a solidarity with workers in China, Guatemala, and New York City, many of whom they discovered were people their own age working in factories. They were outraged by the long hours, low wages, and poor conditions that they were working in to make college sweatshirts, tennis shoes, and other products that they were consuming. "They were also moved by a sense that their own desires were being manipulated, that the glamorous advertising aimed at youth markets was a cover-up meant to distract from corporate wrongdoings" (Featherstone, 2002, p. 10). The sweatshop movement came to be a response to the increasing corporatization of universities as well as a raised consciousness about the ways in which consumers contribute to the problem (Featherstone, 2002).

In 1996, the Clinton administration, a coalition of garment companies, unions, and human rights groups created a monitoring body called the Fair Labor Association (FLA). This was in direct response to pressure by consumers and activists. Because the FLA ultimately proved to be weak and to be too heavily controlled by the apparel industries, such as Nike, another group was formed by organizers, labor unions, and groups throughout the globe called the Worker Rights Consortium (WRC). This organization worked to support the right to organize and investigate worker complaints rather than certifying a particular company as "sweat free," as the FLA was doing. Drawing on the influence of other global justice organizing, the students were demanding transparency and accountability in the disclosure of contractor sites (Ross, 2004).

Some of the tactics employed by students in transnational labor organizing have involved consciousness-raising about the issues, building relationships and solidarity with workers internationally, and participating in unions and living-wage campaigns at home. Direct action and confrontational techniques also came to be utilized, including the use of protests, sit-ins, and teach-ins. The work of USAS (particularly the use of the sit-in) has been compared to that of the Students for a Democratic Society (SDS), one of the strongest movement organizations of the 1960s (Ross, 2004). Other similarities include a rejection of mainstream electoral action and the emphasis on making demands of private parties (lunch counters and clothing labelers) rather than the government. Both groups were interested in internationalist issues (anti-imperialism and antiglobalization). The global nature of communication and the easy access to the Internet, e-mail, and inexpensive cell phone long distance has influenced the ability of the USAS group to be highly successful in its ability to organize across campuses.

USAS has been influenced by U.S. labor organizations, particularly the AFL-CIO, and the creation of an Organizing Institute and Union Summer opportunity that many students associated with USAS participated in. Some have critiqued the student sweatshop movement for its lack of solidarity with domestic workers and lack of attention to poverty problems in the United States (Ross, 2004).

REFLECTING ON GLOBAL JUSTICE ORGANIZING

The global justice movement is a vast movement of individuals working on a variety of issues including labor, health, agriculture, and other aspects of human welfare. Though some of the work of the global justice movement, such as health-related struggles to address HIV/AIDS and women's reproductive health, operates on social development models with the assistance of international NGOs, other projects are more grassroots in nature. These grassroots approaches emerge from local groups and focus on education campaigns, local policy reform, and empowerment. They emphasize local leadership development as a long-term, sustainable strategy for social change.

Many critiques of the global justice movement have been put forward. Some believe that members of the movement are against trade and internationalism generally. Katsiaficas (2004) offers a response to this criticism:

> The progressive antiglobalization movement is not against international ties; it wants to see ties that are fair and decent. It is against ties that force people off land, against the kinds of global economic relations that make it possible for the corporations to profit greatly from degrading the world. (p. 7)

Another critique suggested has been that the movement itself is uncoordinated. Though its hallmark has been the fact that there are many actors working on a variety of issues that are not coordinated, the World Social Forum is an example of the attempts of many of these groups to come together. Its main slogan being, "Another world is possible," it has in more recent years focused on alternatives to globalization. Creating alternatives such as fair trade endeavors is a productive response to those who criticize the movement for solely focusing on the negative.

Finally, some have argued that the global justice movement has overemphasized economic critiques and has not emphasized issues such as racism and sexism. Indeed, critiques of racism and discrimination against women within the movement are not uncommon. The Bananeras in Guatemala are an excellent example of a group of individuals who are looking beyond economic issues and exploring the intersections of gender and class issues (Frank, 2005). By organizing around a women's issue such as domestic violence (emphasizing consciousness-raising, social support, and criminal intervention), the Bananeras strengthen their own personal empowerment, seeking to effect social change on multiple levels. The global justice movement is a creative and powerful solution to a future that will continue to entail social inequities that negatively impact communities in complex ways.

Progressive Organizing in a Post-Katrina World

The events surrounding Hurricane Katrina and the activism that has ensued remind us of the global nature of social justice problems and solutions. Hurricane Katrina reminded the world that the so-called developed world struggles with issues similar to those in the undeveloped world—government neglect, poverty, racism, homelessness, etc. Like groups across the globe, citizens in New Orleans continue to struggle around a variety of issues, including immigrant rights, food security, neighborhood safety, access to mental health care, and the right to housing. Organizers continue to draw from a history of local organizing as well as taking cues from international movements making connections between Katrina and larger global issues in their analysis and practice.

The New Orleans City Council, along with federal and local housing agencies, recently made decisions to allow the demolition of most of the current public housing in New Orleans. The idea behind this decision was that the properties would be redeveloped to include some market-rate housing along with some low-income housing. Organizers continue to pressure these public agencies with particular concern around the following issues: (a) a one-to-one replacement for all of the units lost, (b) plans for these units from developers that are transparent, and (c) ensuring the rights of current public housing residents. The methods for attending to these concerns continue to be the same—working in coalition with a variety of groups, monitoring policies and practices, organizing residents, and attending and speaking out at public meetings. Indeed, the organizing work that needs to be done in post-Katrina New Orleans appears to be never ending. This is an important lesson for all organizers—the deep-seated nature of oppression and injustice warrants a long-term, sustainable organizing practice.

QUESTIONS FOR REFLECTION

1. Discuss ways in which you can "resist" globalization in your personal life.
2. Discuss the benefits of and barriers to transnational organizing.
3. What knowledge and skills are necessary to do organizing in a developing country?
4. What kinds of land-based and localization organizing is happening in your community? Have they been successful?
5. Discuss the successes and failures of the student antisweatshop movement.

SUGGESTIONS FOR FURTHER INQUIRY

BOOKS

Hamel, P., Lustiger-Thaler, H., Pieterse, J. N., & Roseneil, S. (Eds.). (2001). *Globalization and social movements*. New York: Palgrave.
Klein, N. (2002). *Fences and windows: Dispatches from the front lines of the globalization debate*. New York: Picador USA.
Moghadam, V. M. (2005). *Globalizing women: Transnational feminist networks*. Baltimore, MD: Johns Hopkins University Press.
Polet, F. (2004). *Globalizing resistance: The state of struggle*. London: Pluto Press.
Yuen, E., Burton-Rose, D., and Katsiaficas, G. (2004). *Confronting capitalism: Dispatches from a global movement*. Brooklyn: Soft Skull Press.

WEB

Alliance for Responsible Trade. http://www.art-us.org
Border Action Network. http://www.borderaction.org
Grassroots International. http://www.grassrootsonline.org
People's Health Movement. http://www.phmovement.org
Poor People's Economic Human Rights Campaign. http://www.economichumanrights.org

KEY TERMS

Alternative globalization: A philosophy and movement to connect people through cultural and community development that is grounded in the needs and actions of grassroots communities rather than global corporations.

Commodification: Assigning economic value to something not usually conceived of in economic terms. Marx was particularly concerned with the possibility that market values would come to replace social values and critiqued the social impact, naming it commodity fetishism.

Maquiladora: A location for strong local and transnational labor organizing, with particularly impactful organizing from women working in the *maquiladora* factories in North Mexico that have sprung up as sites for labor abuses in the post-NAFTA landscape.

Network society: A society whereby key social structures and activities are organized around electronic information networks. Drawing from the strength of power that these networks contain, transnational organizers can leverage this reality toward the ends of global justice.

Resistance: The intentional or unintentional opposition to major oppressive forces through various channels. For example, resisting negative globalization and its impact on food access may be done by creating a community garden instead of buying food made from seeds patented by a corporation that is shipped overseas.

References

Addams, J. (1910). *Twenty years at Hull-House*. New York: Penguin.

Alinsky, S. (1971). *Rules for radicals: A practical primer for realistic radicals*. New York: Random House.

Andel, R., & Liebig, P. S. (2002). The city of Laguna Woods: A case of senior power in local politics. *Research on Aging, 24*(1), 87–105.

Anderson v. Jackson, 06-3298, USDC. (2006).

Arena, J. (2005). *The Iberville public housing development: A short history*. Retrieved July 22, 2008, from http://minorjive.typepad.com/hungryblues/2005/09/the_iberville_p.html.

Aristotle (1962). T. A. Sinclair (Trans.), *The Politics*. London: Penguin Books.

Armbruster-Sandoval, R. (1999). Globalization and cross-border labor organizing: The Guatemalan maquiladora industry and the Phillips Van Heusen workers' movement. *Latin American Perspectives, 26*(2), 109–128.

Armbruster-Sandoval, R. (2005). Workers of the world unite? The contemporary anti-sweatshop movement and the struggle for social justice in the Americas. *Work and Occupations, 32*(40), 464–485.

Armstrong, J. (1996). Sharing one skin: Okanagan community. In J. Mander & E. Goldsmith (Eds.), *The case against the global economy* (pp. 460–470). San Francisco: Sierra Club Books.

Arnold, G. (1995). Dilemmas of feminist coalitions: Collective identity and strategic effectiveness in the battered women's movement. In M. M. Ferree & P. Y. Martin (Eds.), *Feminist organizations: Harvest of the new women's movement* (pp. 276–290). Philadelphia: Temple University Press.

Arnstein, R. (1969). A ladder of citizen participation. *Journal of the American Institute of Planners, 35*, 216–224.

Avery, M., Stribel, B., Auvine, B., & Weiss, L. (1981). *Building united judgment: A handbook for consensus decision-making*. Chicago: Center for Conflict Resolution.

Avner, M. (2002). *The lobbying and advocacy handbook for nonprofit organizations: Shaping public policy at the state and local level*. St. Paul, MN: Fieldstone Alliance.

Barnartt, S., & Scotch, R. (2001). *Disability protests: Contentious politics 1970–1999*. Washington, DC: Gallaudet University Press.

Barnett, B. M. (1997). Leadership. In *Protest, power and change: An encyclopedia of nonviolent action from ACT-UP to Women's Suffrage*. New York: Garland Publishing.

Bass, K., Chace, Z., Chou, M., Nguyen, H. Olsen, L. and Valentine, M. (n.d.). *The Need for change is now: Students demand justice in their schools*. Oakland, CA: California Tomorrow.

Bauman, J. F., Biles, R., & Szylvian, K. M. (2000). *Tenements to the Taylor Homes*. University Park: The Pennsylvania State University Press.

Baumgardner, J. and Richards, A. (2000). *Manifesta: Young Women, Feminism, and the Future*. New York: Farrar, Straus, & Giroux.

Baumgardner, J. and Richards, A. (2005). *A Field Guide for Feminist Activism*. New York: Farrar, Straus, & Giroux.

Beausang, F. (2002). Democratising global governance: The challenges of the World Social Forum. *Management of Social Transformations Discussion Paper Series, 59*, 1–27.

Beck, E. L., Dorsey, E., & Stutters, A. (2003). The women's suffrage movement: Lessons for social action. *Journal of Community Practice, 11*, 13–33.

Beilharz, P. (2005). Revolution. In G. Ritzer (Ed.), *Encyclopedia of social theory* (pp. 641–644). Thousand Oaks, CA: Sage Publications.

Bender, D. E. (2004) *Sweated Work, Weak Bodies: Anti-Sweatshop Campaigns and Languages of labor*. New Brunswick, NJ: Rutgers University Press.

Benham, R. (2007). The birth of the clinic: Action medics in New Orleans. In *What lies beneath: Katrina, race, and the state of the nation* (pp. 69–79). Cambridge, MA: South End Press.

Berger, D., Boudin, C., and Farrow, K. (2005). *Letters From Young Activists: Today's Rebels Speak Out*. New York: Nation Books.

Berkeley, K. (1999). *The women's liberation movement in America*. Westport, CT: Greenwood Press.

Besthorn, F. H. (1997). *Reconceptualizing social work's person-in-environment perspective: Explorations in radical environmental thought*. Unpublished doctoral dissertation, University of Kansas—Lawrence.

Betten, N., & Austin, M. J. (1990). *The roots of community organizing, 1917–1939*. Philadelphia: Temple University Press.

Blackburn, S. (2004). *Oxford Dictionary of Philosophy*. Oxford: Oxford Univesity Press.

Blank, M., & Terkel, S. N. (1997). ADAPT (Americans disabled for attendant programs today). In R. S. Powers & W. B. Vogele (Eds.), *Protest, power and change: An encyclopedia of nonviolent action from ACT-UP to Women's Suffrage* (pp. 11–13). New York: Garland Publishing.

Bobo, K., Kendall, J., & Max, S. (2001). *Organizing for social change: Midwest Academy manual for activists*. Santa Ana, CA: Steven Locks Press.

Boggs, C. (2002). Social capital as political fantasy. In S. L. McLean, D. A. Schultz, & M. B. Steger (Eds.), *Social capital: Critical perspectives on community and Bowling alone* (pp. 183–200). New York: NYU Press.

Bookchin, M. (1999). Whither anarchism? A reply to recent anarchist critics. In *Anarchism, Marxism and the Future of the Left* (pp. 160–259). Edinburgh: AK Press.

Bookchin, M. (2001). *What is communalism? The democratic dimension of anarchism*. Retrieved July 22, 2008, from http://dwardmac.pitzer.edu/Anarchist_archives/bookchin/CMMNL2.MCW.html.

Bookman, A. and Morgen, S. (eds.) (1988). Women and the Politics of Government. Philadelphia: Temple University Press.

Bourdieu, P. (1984). *Distinction*. Cambridge, MA: Harvard University Press.

Bourdieu, P. (1991). *Language and symbolic power*. Cambridge, MA: Harvard University Press.

Bowers, C. (2007). *The cultural commons: A guide for classroom teachers and university professors*. Retrieved July 22, 2008, from http://www.spiritualprogressives.org/article.php?story=culturalcommonsguide

Boyte, H. C. (1984). *Community is possible: Repairing America's roots*. New York: Harper & Row.

Brooks, E. (2002). The ideal sweatshop? Gender and transnational protest. *International Labor and Working-Class History, 61*, 91–111.

Buchbinder, E. (2007). Being a social worker as existential commitment: From vulnerability to meaningful purpose. *The Humanistic Psychologist, 35*(2), 161–174.

Burghardt, S. (1982). *The other side of organizing*. Cambridge: Schenkman Publishing.

Callahan, M. (2004). "Zapatismo Beyond Chiapas" in Solnit, D. (ed.) *Globalize Liberation: How to Uproot the System and Build a Better World*. San Francisco: City Lights Books.

Cancian, M. (2001). The rhetoric and reality of work-based welfare reform. *Social Work, 46*, 309–314.

Canda, E., & Furman, L. (1999). *Spiritual diversity in social work practice: The heart of helping*. New York: The Free Press.

Castells, M. (1999). *Information technology, globalization, and social development*. Geneva: United Nations Research Institute for Social Development.

Chamberlin, J. (1978). *On our own: Patient-controlled alternatives to the mental health system*. New York: Hawthorn Books.

Chambers, E. (2003). *Roots for radicals: Organizing for power, action and justice*. New York: Continuum.

Chambers, R. (1994). Participatory rural appraisal (PRA): Analysis and experience. *World Development, 22*, 1253–1268.

Chambon, A. S., Irving, A., & Epstein, L. (Eds.). (1999). *Reading Foucault for social work*. New York: Columbia University Press.

Chavez, G. R. (2005). To the young activists of tomorrow. In D. Berger, C. Boudin, & K. Farrow (Eds.), *Letters from young activists: Today's rebels speak out* (pp. 201–205). New York: Nation Books.

Chomsky, N. (2000). *Rogue states: The rule of force in world affairs*. Cambridge, MA: South End Press.

Chomsky, N. (2005). *Chomsky on anarchism*. Oakland, CA: AK Press.

Clark, D. N. (1997). Kwangju uprising. In R. S. Powers & W. B. Vogele (Eds.), *Protest, power, and change: An encyclopedia of nonviolent action from ACT-UP to Women's Suffrage* (pp. 296–298). New York: Garland Publishing.

Clarke, J. (1996). "After Social Work?" in Parton, N. (ed.) *Social Theory, Social Change and Social Work*. London: Routledge.

Cloward, R., & Piven, F. F. (1999). Disruptive dissensus: People and power in the Industrial Age. In *Reflections on community organization*. Itasca, IL: Peacock.

Cohen, M. B. (2004). Voices from an invisible movement: Mental health consumer/survivor/ex-patient activism. *Reflections, 10*(4), 50–61.

Collins, P. H. (1999). *Black feminist thought: Knowledge, consciousness, and the politics of empowerment*. Boston: Unwin Hyman.

Cowger, C. (1997). Assessing client strengths: Assessment for client empowerment. In D. Saleebey (Ed.), *The strengths perspective in social work practice* (2nd ed., pp. 59–73). New York: Longman.

Coy, P. G. (1997). Catholic worker movement. In R. S. Powers & W. B. Vogele (Eds.), *Protest, power and change: An encyclopedia of nonviolent action from ACT-UP to Women's Suffrage* (pp. 64–65). New York: Garland Publishing.

Creighton, A., & Kivel, P. (1993). *Helping teens stop violence: A practical guide*. Alamada, CA: Hunter House.

Dailey, M. (2003). Youth organizing is organizing: Case study of Sistas and Brothas United. *Social Policy, 34*(2–3), 95–100.

DART Center. (n.d.). Youth and elderly services. In *Accomplishments*. Retrieved July 22, 2008, from the Direct Action and Research Training Center Web site: http://www.thedartcenter.org/accomplishments. html#_youth.

Davis, L. V. (2001). Why we still need a women's agenda for social work. In J. K. Peterson & A. A. Lieberman (Eds.), *Building on women's strengths: A social work agenda for the twenty-first century* (pp. 1–22). New York: Haworth.

Day, D. (1981). *The Long Loneliness*. San Francisco: Harper & Row.

DeGeorge, R. (2005). Anarchism. In T. Honderich (Ed.), *The Oxford companion to philosophy* (pp. 31–33). New York: Oxford University Press.

Devall, B., & Sessions, G. (1985a). Deep Ecology. In D. VanDeVeer & C. Pierce (Eds.), *The environmental ethics and policy handbook* (pp. 215–220). Belmont, CA: Wadsworth.

Devall, B., & Sessions, G. (1985b). Interview with Arne Naess. In D. VanDeVeer & C. Pierce (Eds.), *The environmental ethics and policy handbook* (pp. 220–222). Belmont, CA: Wadsworth.

DiCanio, M. B. (1998). *Encyclopedia of American activism: 1960 to the present*. Santa Barbara, CA: ABC-CLIO, Inc.

DiCanio, M. B. (2004). Disability rights and independent living movement. Retrieved July 22, 2008, from http://bancroft.berkeley.edu/collections/drilm/introduction.html.

Dominelli, L. (2002). *Anti-oppressive social work theory and practice*. Basingstoke, Hampshire, England: Palgrave Macmillan.

Eichler, M. (2007). *Consensus organizing: Building communities of mutual self-interest*. Thousand Oaks, CA: Sage Publications.

Eskew, G. T. (1997). Civil Rights Movement. In R. S. Powers & W. B. Vogele (Eds.), *Protest, power and change: An encyclopedia of nonviolent action from ACT-UP to Women's Suffrage* (pp. 86–99). New York: Garland Publishing.

Ezell, M. (2000). *Advocacy in the human services*. Belmont, CA: Wadsworth.

Featherstone, L. (2002). *Students against Sweatshops*. London: Verso.

Featherstone, L., Henwood, D., & Parenti, C. (2004). Activistism: Left anti-intellectualism and its discontents. In E. Yuen, D. Burton-Rose, & G. Katsiaficas (Eds.), *Confronting capitalism* (pp. 309–314). New York: Soft Skull Press.

Ferree, M. M., & Hess, B. B. (2000). *Controversy and coalition: The new feminist movement across three decades of change*. New York: Routledge.

Ferree, M. M., & Martin, P. Y. (Eds.). (1995). *Feminist organizations: Harvest of the new women's movement*. Philadelphia: Temple University Press.

Figley, C. (Ed.). (2002). *Treating compassion fatigue*. New York: Routledge.

Finks, P. D. (1984). *The radical vision of Saul Alinsky*. New York: Paulist Press.

Fisher, R. (1994). *Let the people decide: Neighborhood organizing in America*. New York: Twayne Publishers.

Fisher, R., & Shragge, E. (2000). Challenging community organizing: Facing the 21st century. *Journal of Community Practice, 8*(3), 1–19.

Foucault, M. (1973). *Madness and civilization*. New York: Vintage.

Foucault, M. (1980) *Power/Knowledge: Selected Interviews and Other Writings*. New York: Pantheon Books.

Frank, D. (2005). *Bananeras: Women transforming the banana unions of Latin America*. Cambridge, MA: South End Press.

Frazer, E. J. (2005). Communitarianism. In T. Honderich (Ed.), *The Oxford companion to philosophy* (pp. 150–151). New York: Oxford University Press.

Freire, P. (1970). *Pedagogy of the oppressed*. New York: Seabury Press.

Freire, P. (1994). *Pedagogy of hope: Reliving pedagogy of the oppressed*. New York: Continuum.

Fried, A. (2002). "The Strange Disappearance of Alexis de Tocqueville in Putnam's Analysis of Social Capital" in McLean, S. L., Schultz, D. A. & Steger, M. B. (eds.) *Social Capital: Critical Perspectives on Community and Bowling Alone*. New York: New York University Press, pp. 21–49.

Fullilove, M. T. (2005). *Root shock: How tearing up city neighborhoods hurts America, and what we can do about it*. New York: Ballantine.

Gadotti, M. (1994). *Reading Paulo Freire: His life and work.* Albany: State University of New York Press.

Gambone, M. A., Yu, H. C., Lewis-Charp, H., Sipe, C. L., & Lacoe, J. (2006). Youth organizing, identity-support, and youth development agencies as avenues for involvement. *Journal of Community Practice, 14*(1/2), 235–253.

Gamson, W. A. (1990). *The strategy of social protest* (2nd ed.). Belmont, CA: Wadsworth.

Gandhi, M. (1957). *An autobiography: The story of my experiments with truth.* Boston: Beacon Press.

Gelderloos, P. (2005). A letter to the beautiful people holding hands on the day nothing went down in a big way. In D. Berger, C. Boudin, & K. Farrow (Eds.), *Letters from young activists: Today's rebels speak out* (pp. 115–120). New York: Nation Books.

Gelderloos, P. (2006). *Consensus: A new handbook for grassroots political, social and environmental groups.* Tucson, AZ: See Sharp Press.

Gergen, K. (1999). *An invitation to social construction.* London: Sage Publications.

Gibbs, L., & Gambrill, E. (2002). Evidence-based practice: Counter-arguments to objections. *Research on Social Work Practice, 12,* 452–476.

Gittell, M. Ortega-Bustamente, I. and Steffy, T. (2000). Social Capital and Social Change: Women's Community Activism. *Urban Affairs Review,* 36(2):123–147.

Giugni, M. (2004). *Social protest and policy change: Ecology, antinuclear, and peace movements in comparative perspective.* Lanham, MD: Rowman & Littlefield.

Glassman, B. (1998). *Bearing witness.* New York: Bell Tower.

Gluck, S. B. (1998). Whose feminism, whose history? In N. A. Naples (Ed.), *Community activism and feminist politics: Organizing across race, class and gender* (pp. 31–56). New York: Routledge.

Goodwin, J., & Jasper, J. (Eds.). (2003). *The social movement reader: Cases and concepts.* Malden, MA: Blackwell.

Goodwin, J., & Jasper, J. (Eds.). (2004). *Rethinking social movements: Structure, meaning and emotion.* Lanham, MD: Rowman & Littlefield.

Gordon, J. U. (2000). *Black leadership for social change.* Westport, CT: Greenwood Press.

Gottlieb, R. S. (1999). *A spirituality of resistance.* New York: Crossroads Publishing.

Greater New Orleans Community Data Center (n.d.). *Iberville development neighborhood snapshot.* Retrieved July 22, 2008, from GNOCDC Web site: http://www.gnocdc.org/orleans/4/41/index.html.

Greater New Orleans Community Data Center (2007a). *Census population estimates 2000–2006 for New Orleans.* Retrieved July 22, 2008, from GNOCDC Web site: http://gnocdc.org/census_pop_estimates.html.

Greater New Orleans Community Data Center (2007b). *St. Thomas development neighborhood snapshot.* Retrieved July 22, 2008, from GNOCDC Web site: http://www.gnocdc.org/orleans/2/59/snapshot.html.

Grenier, A., & Hanley, J. (2007). Older women and "frailty": Aged, gendered and embodied resistance. *Current Sociology, 55*(2), 211–228.

Guilloud, S., & Cordery, W. (2007). Fundraising is not a dirty word: Community-based economic strategies for the long haul. In *The revolution will not be funded: Beyond the non-profit industrial complex* (pp. 107–111). Cambridge, MA: South End Press.

Gutierrez, L. M. and Lewis, E. A. (1994). Community organizing with women of color: A feminist perspective. *Journal of Community Practice.* 1(2):23–48.

Gutierrez, L. M., Parsons, R. J., & Cox, E. O. (Eds). (1998). *Empowerment in social work practice: A sourcebook.* Pacific Grove, CA: Brooks/Cole.

Hamber, B., Maepa, T., Mofokeng, T., & van der Merwe, H. (n.d.). *Survivors' perceptions of the truth and reconciliation commission and suggestions for the final report.* Retrieved August 26, 2007, from Center for the Study of Violence and Reconciliation Web site: http://www.csvr.org.za/papers/papkhul.htm.

Harper, C. L. (1998). *Exploring social change: America and the world.* Upper Saddle River, NJ: Prentice Hall.

Hartsock, N. (1996). Theoretical bases for coalition building: An assessment of postmodernism. In H. Gottfried (Ed.), *Feminism and social change: Bridging theory and practice* (pp. 256–274). Urbana: University of Illinois Press.

Hawken, P. (2007). *Blessed unrest: How the largest social movement in the world came into being and why nobody saw it coming.* New York: Viking Press.

Healy, K., Hampshire, A., & Ayres, L. (2004). Beyond the local: Extending the social capital discourse. *Australian Journal of Social Issues, 39,* 329–342.

Hill, L. (2004). *The deacons for defense: Armed resistance and the civil rights movement.* Chapel Hill: University of North Carolina Press.

Hoggett, P. (1997). Contested communities. In P. Hoggett (Ed.), *Contested communities: Experiences, struggles, policies.* Bristol, England: Policy Press.

Honey, C. (2006). Community organizing: Past, present and future. *Comm-Org Papers Series, 12*. Retrieved August 6, 2008, from http://comm-org.wisc.edu/papers2006/honey.htm.

Hooks, B. (1984). *Feminist theory from margin to center*. Boston: South End Press.

Hornsby, J. (2005). Mary Wollstonecraft. In T. Honderich (Ed.), *The Oxford companion to philosophy* (pp. 964–965). New York: Oxford University Press.

Hosang, D. (2003). Youth and community organizing today. *Social Policy, 34*(2–3), 66–70.

House Report No. 1227. (2007). Gulf Coast Hurricane Housing Recovery Act of 2007. Retrieved August 6, 2008, from http://www.govtrack.us/congress/bill.xpd?tab=summary&bill=h110-1227.

Hunt-Perry, P. and Fine, L. (2000). "All Buddhism Is Engaged: Thich Nhat Hanh and the Order of Interbeing" in Queen, C. S. (ed.) *Engaged Buddhism in the West,* Boston: Wisdom Publications, pp. 35–66

Hunter, F. (1953). *Community Power Structure: A Study of Decision Makers*. Chapel Hill: University of North Carolina Press.

Ichiyo, M. (1994). Alliance of hope and challenges of global democracy. *The Ecumenical Review, 46*(1), 28–37.

Incite! Women of color against violence (Eds.). (2007). *The revolution will not be funded: Beyond the non-profit industrial complex*. Cambridge, MA: South End Press.

Inwood, M. J. (2005). Frankfurt School. In T. Honderich (Ed.), *The Oxford companion to philosophy* (pp. 311–312). New York: Oxford University Press.

Irving, A., & Young, T. (2002). Paradigm for pluralism: Mikhail Bakhtin and social work practice. *Social Work, 47*(1), 19–29.

Ivins, M., & Dubose, L. (2003). *Bushwhacked: Life in George W. Bush's America*. New York: Vintage Books.

Jackson, S. (2000). *Lines of Activity: Performance, historiography, and domesticity in Hull House*. Ann Arbor, MI: University of Michigan Press.

Jansson, B. S. (2008). *Becoming an effective policy advocate: From policy practice to social justice* (5th ed.). Belmont, CA: Wadsworth.

Jansson, B. S., Dempsey, D., McCroskey, J., & Schneider, R. (2005). Four models of policy practice: Local, state and national arenas. In M. Weil (Ed.), *Handbook of Community Practice* (pp. 319–338). Thousand Oaks, CA: Sage Publications.

Jasper, J. (1997). *The Art of Moral Protest*. Chicago: University of Chicago Press.

Jones-DeWeever, A. A. (2005). When the spirit blooms: Acquiring higher education in the context of welfare reform. *Journal of Women, Politics and Policy, 27*(3/4), 113–134.

Joseph, B., Lob, S., McLaughlin, P., Mizrahi, T., Peterson, J., Rosenthal, B. and Sugarman, F. (1991). *A framework for feminist organizing: Values, goals, methods, strategies, and roles*. New York: Education Center for Community Organizing.

Kahn, S. (1994). *How People Get Power*. Washington, DC: National Association of Social Workers.

Karger, H., & Stoesz, D. (2006). *American social welfare policy: A pluralist approach* (5th ed.). Boston: Allyn & Bacon.

Katsiaficas, G. (2004). Seattle was not the beginning. In E. Yuen, D. Burton-Rose, & G. Katsiaficas (Eds.), *Confronting capitalism*. New York: Soft Skull Press.

Kaufman, C. (2003). *Ideas for action: Relevant theory for radical change*. Cambridge, MA: South End Press.

Kellner, D. (2004). Frankfurt School. In G. Ritzer (Ed.), *Encyclopedia of social theory* (pp. 290–293). Thousand Oaks, CA: Sage Publications.

Kieffer, C. (1984). Citizen empowerment: A developmental perspective. *Prevention in Human Services, 3*(1), 9–36.

Kilty, K. and Segal, E. (2003). *Rediscovering the Other America: The Continuing Crisis of Poverty and Inequality in the U. S*. New York: Routledge.

Kincheloe, J. L., & McLaren, P. (2000). Rethinking critical theory and qualitative research. In N. K. Denzin & Y. S. Lincoln (Eds.), *Handbook of qualitative research*. Thousand Oaks, CA: Sage Publications.

King, M. L. (1997). Letter from Birmingham Jail. In I. Ness (Ed.), *Encyclopedia of American social movements* (Vol. 1). Armonk, NY: M. E. Sharpe Inc.

Kinna, R. (2005). *Anarchism: A beginner's guide*. Oxford, UK: Oneworld Publications.

Kivel, P. (2007). Social service or social change? In Incite! Women of color against violence (Eds.), *The revolution will not be funded: Beyond the non-profit industrial complex* (pp. 129–149). Cambridge, MA: South End Press.

Klandermans, B. (2001). Why social movements come into being and why people join them. In J. R. Blau (Ed.), *The Blackwell companion to sociology* (pp. 268–281). Malden, MA: Blackwell Publishing.

Klein, N. (2002). *Fences and windows: Dispatches from the front lines of the globalization debate*. New York: Picador USA.

Klein, N. (2007). *The shock doctrine: The rise of disaster capitalism*. New York: Metropolitan Books.

Kreps, B. (2003). Radical feminism. In C. R. McCann & S. K. Kim (Eds.), *Feminist theory reader: Local and global perspectives* (pp. 45–49). New York: Routledge.

Kretzmann, J. P., & McKnight, J. L. (1997). *Building communities from the inside out*. Skokie, IL: ACTA Publications.

Kriesi, H., Koopmans, R., Duyvendak, J. W., & Giugni, M. G. (1992). New social movements and political opportunities in Western Europe. *European Journal of Political Research, 22*, 219–244.

Krill, D. (1978). *Existential social work*. New York: The Free Press.

Kropotkin, P. (1919). *Mutual aid: A factor of cooperation*. New York: A. A. Knopf.

Kuhn, M. *No Stone Unturned: The Life and Times of Maggie Kuhn*. New York: Ballantine.

Lakoff, G. (2004). *Don't think of an elephant!: Know your values and frame the debate: The essential guide for progressives*. White River Junction, VT: Chelsea Green Publishing.

Landry, D., & MacLean, G. (1996). *The Spivak reader*. New York: Routledge.

Lechner, F. J., & Boli, J. (Eds.). (2004). *The globalization reader*. Malden, MA: Blackwell Publishing.

Libson, B. (2007). River garden: New Orleans' model for mixed-income housing? *Social Policy*, Spring/Summer. Retrieved July 22, 2008, from http://www.socialpolicy.org/index.php?id=1836.

Lorde, A. (1981). The master's tools will never dismantle the master's house. In C. Moraga & G. Anzaldua (Eds.), *This bridge called my back: Writings by radical women of color*. Watertown, MA: Persephone Press.

Lowes, D. E. (2006). *The anti-capitalist dictionary: Movements, histories and motivations*. Black Wood, Nova Scotia: Fernwood Publishing.

Luce, S. (2005). Lessons from living wage campaigns. *Work and Occupations, 32*, 423–440.

MacEachern, D. (1994). *Enough is enough: How to organize a successful campaign for change*. New York: Avon Books.

Macy, J. (1983). *Dharma and development: Religion as resource in the Sarvodaya self-help movement*. West Hartford, CT: Kumarian Press.

Mahoney, M. (1990). Law and racial geography: Public housing and the economy in New Orleans. *Stanford Law Review, 42*, 1251–1290.

Mander, J. (1996). Facing the rising tide. In J. Mander & E. Goldsmith (Eds.), *The case against the global economy and a turn toward the local*. San Francisco: Sierra Club Books.

Mann, E. (2006). Katrina's legacy: White racism and black reconstruction in New Orleans and the Gulf Coast. Los Angeles: Frontline Press.

Marcus, E. (2002). *Making gay history: The half-century fight for lesbian and gay equal rights*. New York: HarperCollins.

Markowitz, N. (2004). The Civil Rights movement. In I. Ness (Ed.), *Encyclopedia of American social movements* (Vol. 1). Armonk, NY: M. E. Sharpe Inc.

Martell, D., & Avitabile, N. E. (1998). Feminist community organizing on a college campus. *Affilia, 13*, 393–410.

Martinez, E. B. (2006). Unite and rebel! Challenges and strategies in building alliances. In Incite! Women of color against violence (Eds.), *Color of violence: The incite anthology* (pp. 191–195). Cambridge, MA: South End Press.

Marx, K., & Engels, F. (2004). *The communist manifesto*, L. Findley (Ed. & Trans.). Peterborough, Ontario: Broadview Press.

McAdam, D. (1982). Political Processes and the Development of Black Insurgency. Chicago: University of Chicago Press.

McAllister, P. (1997). Emma Goldman. In R. S. Powers & W. B. Vogele (Eds.), *Protest, power and change: An encyclopedia of nonviolent action from ACT-UP to Women's Suffrage* (p. 216). New York: Garland Publishing.

McCarthy, J. D. and Zald, M. N. (1973). *The Trend of Social Movements in America: Professionalization and Resource Mobilization*. Morristown, NJ: General Learning Press.

McCarthy, J. D. and Zald, M. N. (2003). "Social Movement Organizations" in Goodwin, J. and Jasper, J. M. (eds.) *The Social Movements Reader: Cases and Concepts*. Malden, MA: Blackwell Publishing, pp. 169–186.

McLaughlin, C., & Davidson, G. (1994). *Spiritual politics*. New York: Ballantine Books.

McLean, S. L., Schultz, D. A., & Steger, M. B. (2002). *Social capital: Critical perspectives on community and Bowling alone*. New York: NYU Press.

Menegat, R. (2002). Participatory democracy in Porto Alegre, Brasil. *Participatory Learning and Action, 44*, 8–11.

Meyer, M. D. E. (2004). We're too afraid of these imaginary tensions: Student organizing in lesbian, gay, bisexual and transgender campus communities. *Communication Studies, 55*, 499–514.

Meyers, D. T. (Ed.). (1997). *Feminist social thought: A reader.* New York: Routledge.

Micheletti, M., & Stolle, D. (2007). Mobilizing consumers to take responsibility for global social justice. *The Annals of the American Academy of Political and Social Science, 611*, 157–175.

Miley, K. K., O'Melia, M., & DuBois, B. (1998). *Generalist social work practice: An empowering approach* (2nd ed.). Boston: Allyn and Bacon.

Miller, R. (1997). Healthy Boston and social capital: Application, dynamics, and limitations. *National Civic Review, 86*(2), 157–167.

Minkler, M. (2005). Community organizing with the elderly poor in San Francisco's Tenderloin District. In M. Minkler (Ed.), *Community organizing and community building for health* (2nd ed.). New Brunswick, NJ: Rutgers University Press.

Mohan, G. and Stokke, R. (2000). Participatory development and empowerment: The dangers of localism. *Third World Quarterly, 21*(2):249–268

Mondros, J. B., & Wilson, S. M. (1994). *Organizing for power and empowerment.* New York: Columbia University Press.

Moraga, C., & Anzaldua, G. (Eds.). (1983). *This bridge called my back: Writings by radical women of color.* New York: Kitchen Table: Women of Color Press.

Morales, A. L. (1998). *Medicine stories: History, culture and the politics of integrity.* Cambridge, MA: South End Press.

Morgan, R. (1970). *Sisterhood Is Powerful.* New York: Random House.

Mott, A. (2003). *Strengthening social change through assessment and organizational learning* [Community learning project]. Retrieved February 23, 2008, from http://www.communitylearningproject.org/docs/ Gray%20Rocks%20Conference%20Report.pdf.

Murphy, P. W., & Cunningham, J. V. (2003). *Organizing for community-controlled development: Renewing civil society.* Thousand Oaks, CA: Sage Publications.

NLC (National Labor Committee). (2004). *Trying to live on 25 cents an hour: The U.S. companies say the workers do just fine.* Retrieved July 26, 2008, from http://www.nlcnet.org/campaigns/archive/chinareport/costoflivingdoc.shtml.

Naess, A. (1988). Self-realization: An ecological approach to being in the world. In D. Van De Veer & C. Pierce (Eds.), *The environmental ethics and policy handbook* (pp. 222–226). Belmont, CA: Wadsworth.

Nash, J. (2005). Introduction: Social Movements and Global Processes. In Nash, J. (ed.) *Social Movements: An Anthropological Reader.* Malden, MA: Blackwell Publishing, pp. 1–26.

Noakes, J. A., & Johnston, H. (2005). Frames of protest: A roadmap to a perspective. In H. Johston & J. A. Noakes (Eds.), *Frames of protest: Social movements and the framing perspective.* Lanham, MD: Rowman & Littlefield.

Ohmer, M. L., & Korr, W. S. (2006). The effectiveness of community practice interventions: A review of the literature. *Research on Social Work Practice, 16*(2), 132–145.

Olson, M. (1965). *The logic of collective action: Public goods and the theory of groups.* Cambridge, MA: Harvard University Press.

Padgett, D. L. (2002). Institutionalizing activism: The history of the Sherman Park Community Association. *Journal of Community Practice, 10*(4), 67–83.

Papa, M. J., Singhal, A. and Papa, W. H. (2006). *Organizing for Social Change: A Dialectical Journey of Theory and Praxis.* New Delhi: Sage Publications

Parton, N. (2007). Constructive social work practice in an age of uncertainty. In S. Witkin & D. Saleebey (Eds.), *Social work dialogues: Transforming the canon in inquiry, practice, and education* (pp. 144–166). Alexandria, VA: Council on Social Work Education Press.

Perez, A. H. (2007). Between radical theory and community praxis. In Incite! Women of color against violence (Eds.), *The revolution will not be funded: Beyond the non-profit industrial complex* (pp. 91–99). Cambridge, MA: South End Press.

Perry, E. (n.d.). Multiple styles of leadership: Increasing the participation of people of color in the nonprofit sector. Retrieved July 26, 2008, from http://www.leadershiplearning.org/system/files/Final_AECF_Web. pdf.

Peters, J. M., & Bell, B. (1989). Horton of Highlander. In *Highlander Research and Education Center: An approach to education* (pp. 34–64). New Market, TN: Highlander Research and Education Center.

Pharr, S. (1988). *Homophobia: A Weapon of Sexism*. Inverness, CA: Chardon Press.

Pharr, S. (1996) *In the Time of the Right: Reflections on Liberation*. Inverness, CA: Chardon Press.

Phillips, L. (Ed.). (2006). *The womanist reader*. New York: Routledge.

Piven, F. F., & Cloward, R. A. (1979). *Poor people's movements*. New York: Vintage Books.

Polletta, F. (2004). Culture is not just in your head. In J. Goodwin & J. M. Jasper (Eds.), *Rethinking social movements: Structure, meaning, and emotion*. Lanham, MD: Rowman & Littlefield.

Putnam, R. (2000). *Bowling alone: The collapse and revival of American community*. New York: Simon & Schuster.

Pyles, L. (2003). *Transforming the culture of advocacy for social and economic justice*. Retrieved July 26, 2008, from http://www.arte-sana.com/articles/transforming_culture_advocacy.htm.

Pyles, L. (2005). Understanding the engaged Buddhist movement: Implications for social development practice. *Critical Social Work, 6*(1). Retrieved July 26, 2008, from http://www.criticalsocialwork.com/units/socialwork/critical.nsf/8c20dad9f1c4be3a85256d6e006d1089/3e9b18c1f86ebce385256fd700634820?OpenDocument.

Pyles, L. (2006). *Understanding post-disaster community development: A study of community organizing efforts in New Orleans*. New Orleans: Tulane University.

Pyles, L., & Cross, T. (forthcoming). Community revitalization in post-Katrina New Orleans: A critical analysis of social capital variables in an African American neighborhood. *Journal of Community Practice*.

Quadagno, J. (1996). *The color of welfare: How racism undermined the war on poverty*. New York: Oxford University Press.

Quigley, B. (2006a). Bulldozing hope. *Third World Traveler*. Retrieved July 26, 2008, from http://www.thirdworldtraveler.com/Thirdworldization_America/BulldozingHope_NewOrleans.html.

Quigley, B. (2006b). Save NOLA affordable housing fact sheet. *Dollars and Sense*. Retrieved July 26, 2008, from http://www.dollarsandsense.org/blog/2006/12/save-nola-affordable-housing-fact.html.

Reese, W. L. (1999). *Dictionary of philosophy and religion*. Amherst, NY: Humanity Books.

Reichl, A. J. (1999). Learning from St. Thomas: Community, capital and the redevelopment of public housing in New Orleans. *Journal of Urban Affairs, 21*(2), 169–187.

Reinelt, C. (1994). Fostering empowerment, building community: The challenge for state-funded feminist organizations. *Human Relations, 47*, 685–705.

Reisch, M. (2005). Community practice challenges in the global economy. In M. Weil (Ed.), *Handbook of community practice* (pp. 529–547). Thousand Oaks, CA: Sage Publications.

Rhoads, R. A. (1998). Student protest and multicultural reform: Making sense of campus unrest in the 1990s. *The Journal of Higher Education, 69*, 621–646.

Rimmerman, C. A. (2002). *From identity to politics: The lesbian and gay movements in the United States*. Philadelphia: Temple University Press.

Rodriguez, D. (2007). The political logic of the non-profit industrial complex. In Incite! Women of color against violence (Eds.), *The revolution will not be funded: Beyond the non-profit industrial complex* (pp. 21–40). Cambridge, MA: South End Press.

Rogers, M. F. (2005). Feminism. In G. Ritzer (Ed.), *Encyclopedia of social theory* (pp. 268–269). Thousand Oaks, CA: Sage Publications.

Roman, L. G. (1993). White is a color! White defensiveness, postmodernism, and anti-racist pedagogy. In C. McCarthy & W. Crichlow (Eds.), *Race identity and representation in education*. New York: Routledge.

Rosenberg, M. (2004). *Speak peace in a world of conflict: What you say next will change your world*. Encinitas, CA: Puddle Dancer Press.

Ross, M. G. (1967). *Community Organization: Theory and Principles*. New York: Harper.

Ross, R. J. S. (2004). From antisweatshop to global justice to antiwar: How the new New Left is the same and different from the old New Left. *Journal of World-Systems Research, 10*(1), 287–319.

Rothman, J. (2001). "Approaches to Community Intervention" in Rothman, J., Erlich, J. L. and Tropman, J. E. (eds.) *Strategies of Community Intervention*, 6th ed. Belmont, CA: Wadsworth/Thomson.

Rubin, H. J., & Rubin, I. S. (2001). *Community organizing and development* (3rd ed.). Boston: Allyn and Bacon.

Saleebey, D. (Ed.). (1997). *The strengths perspective in social work practice* (2nd ed.). New York: Longman.

Sapp, J. (1989). Culture, the roots of community spirit and power. In *Highlander Research and Education Center: An approach to education* (pp. 303–322). New Market, TN: Highlander Research and Education Center.

Scanlon, E. (1999). Labor and the intellectuals: Where is social work? *Social Work, 44*, 590–593.

Schechter, S. (1982). *Women and male violence: The visions and struggles of the battered women's movement*. Cambridge, MA: South End Press.

Schechter, S. (1999). New challenges for the battered women's movement: Building collaborations and improving public policy for poor women. http://www.mincava.umn.edu/documents/nwchllng/nwchllng.html.

Scheyett, A. (2006). Silence and surveillance: Mental illness, evidence-based practice and a Foucaultian lens. *Journal of Progressive Human Services, 17*(1), 71–92.

Selznick, P. (2002). *The communitarian persuasion.* Washington, DC: Woodrow Wilson Center Press.

Sen, R. (2003). *Stir it up: Lessons in community organizing and advocacy.* San Francisco: Jossey-Bass.

Sessions, G. (ed.) (1995). *Deep Ecology for the 21st Century.* Boston: Shambala.

Share, R. A., & Stacks, J. S. (2006). Youth-adult partnership in community organizing: A case study of the My Voice Counts! campaign. *Journal of Community Practice, 14*(4), 113–127.

Shepard, B. (2005). The use of joyfulness as a community organizing strategy. *Peace and Change, 30*, 435–468.

Shepard, B., & Hayduk, R. (2002). Urban protest and community building in the ear of globalization. In *From ACT-UP to the WTO: Urban protest and community building in the era of globalization* (pp. 1–9). New York: Verso.

Shiva, V. (2000). Ecological balance in an era of globalization. In F. J. Lechner & J. Boli (Eds.), *The globalization reader.* Malden, MA: Blackwell Publishing.

Shor, I. (1993). Education is politics: Paulo Freire's critical pedagogy. In P. McLaren & P. Leonard (Eds.), *Paulo Freire: A critical encounter* (pp. 25–46). London: Routledge.

Silliman, J., Fried, M. G., Ross, L., & Gutierrez, E. R. (2004). *Undivided rights: Women of color organize for reproductive justice.* Cambridge, MA: South End Press.

Sinclair, U. (1906). *The Jungle.* New York: Doubleday.

Sinclair, Z., & Russ, L. (2006). Organizational development for social change: An integrated approach to community transformation. Movement Strategy Center. Retrieved August 6, 2008, from http://movement-strategy.org/media/docs/3796_ODforSocialChange_final[8].pdf.

Smith, A. (2006). Beyond inclusion: Re-centering feminism. *Left Turn, 20*, 66–69.

Smith, A. (2007). Introduction. In Incite! Women of color against violence (Eds.), *The revolution will not be funded: Beyond the non-profit industrial complex* (pp. 1–18). Cambridge, MA: South End Press.

Smith, C., & Woodberry, R. D. (2001). Sociology of religion. In J. R. Blau (Ed.), *The Blackwell companion to sociology* (pp. 100–113). Malden, MA: Blackwell Publishing.

Smith, M. K. (2001). Community. In *The encyclopedia of informal education.* Retrieved August 6, 2008, from http://www.infed.org/community/community.htm.

Solnit, D. (2006). Questions for global justice organizing. *Left Turn, 20*, 74–79.

Somerville, P., & Steele, A. (Eds.). (2002). *"Race," housing and social exclusion.* London: Jessica Kingsley Publishers.

SPAN (2005). *Building a multi-ethnic, inclusive and antiracist organization: Tools for liberation packet.* Boulder, CO: Safehouse Progressive Alliance for Nonviolence.

Specht, H., & Courtney, M. (1994). *Unfaithful angels: How social work has abandoned its mission.* New York: The Free Press.

Spivak, G. C. (1995). *The Spivak Reader.* New York: Routledge.

Staggenborg, S. (2005). Social movement theory. In *Encyclopedia of social theory* (pp. 753–759). Thousand Oaks, CA: Sage Publications.

Stalder, F. (2006). *Manuel Castells: The theory of the network society.* Cambridge, UK: Polity Press.

Starhawk (2002). Turning the trolls to stone. Retrieved August 6, 2008, from http://www.starhawk.org/activism/activism-writings/trollstostone.html.

St. Clair, J. (2004). Seattle diary. In E. Yuen, D. Burton-Rose, & G. Kastiaficas (Eds.), *Confronting capitalism* (pp. 48–71). New York: Soft Skull Press.

Stephen, L. (2005). Gender, citizenship, and the politics of identity. In J. Nash (Ed.), *Social movements: An anthropological reader* (pp. 66–77). Malden, MA: Blackwell.

Streeten, P. (2001). *Globalisation: threat or opportunity?* Copenhagen, Denmark: Copenhagen Business School Press.

Stringer, E. T. (1999). Principles of community-based action research. In *Action research.* Thousand Oaks, CA: Sage Publications.

Stroman, D. F. (2003). *The disability rights movement: From deinstitutionalization to self-determination.* Lanham, MD: University Press of America.

Survivors' Village (2006). United Front for Affordable Housing announces the opening of the Survivors' Village. *A Katrina Reader.* http://www.cwworkshop.org/Katrinareader/node/232.

Szakos, K. L. and Szakos, J. (2007). *We Make Change: Community Organizers Talk about What They Do—And Why*. Nashville: Vanderbilt University Press.

Taft, P., & Ross, P. (1969). American labor violence: Its causes, character, and outcome. In H. D. Graham & T. R. Gurr (Eds.), *Violence in America* (pp. 281–395). New York: Bantam Books.

Tait, V. (2005). *Poor workers' unions: Rebuilding labor from below*. Cambridge, MA: South End Press.

Taliaferro, J. (2005). Local welfare reform: Challenges and triumphs of the Comprehensive Support Services intervention. *Journal of Human Behavior in the Social Environment, 12*(2/3), 261–280.

Tarrow, S. (1994). *Power in movement: Social movements, collective action and politics*. Cambridge, UK: Cambridge University Press.

Tolbert, C. M., Lyson, T. A., & Irwin, M. D. (1998). Local capitalism, civic engagement and socioeconomic well-being. *Social Forces, 77*, 401–427.

U.S. Department of Housing and Urban Development (2003). HUD brokered agreement puts New Orleans housing development "back on track." Retrieved August 8, 2008, from http://www.hud.gov/news/release.cfm?content=pr03-049.cfm.

U.S. Department of Housing and Urban Development (2006). HUD Katrina accomplishments—One year later. Retrieved August 6, 2008, from http://www.hud.gov/news/katrina05response.cfm.

U.S. Department of Housing and Urban Development. (2007). HUD historical background. Retrieved August 6, 2008, from http://www.hud.gov/offices/adm/about/admguide/history.cfm.

von Hoffman, A. (1996). High ambitions: The past and future of American low-income housing policy. *Housing Policy Debate, 7*(3), 423–446.

Walker, A. (1976). *Meridian*. Orlando, FL: Harcourt Press.

Walter, U. M. (2003). Toward a third space: Improvisation and professionalism in social work practice. *Families in Society, 84*(3), 317–322.

Warren, M. R. (2001). *Dry bones rattling: Community building to revitalize American democracy*. Princeton, NJ: Princeton University Press.

Weil, M. (1995). Women, community and organizing. In J. Tropman, J. Erlich, & J. Rothman (Eds.), *Tactics and techniques of community intervention* (pp. 119–134). Itasca, IL: Peacock.

Williams, P. (1982). *Common sense: A guide to the present situation*. Retrieved August 2, 2008, from http://hipplanet.com/books/commonsense.htm.

Witkin, S. L., & Saleebey, D. (2007). *Social work dialogues: Transforming the canon in inquiry, practice and education*. Alexandria, VA: Council on Social Work Education Press.

Wood, A. (2005). Marx, Karl Heinrich. In T. Honderich (Ed.), *The Oxford companion to philosophy* (pp. 557–559). New York: Oxford University Press.

Wood, R. (1999). Religious culture and political action. *Sociological Theory, 17* (3), 307–332.

Wood, R. (2002). *Faith in action: Religion, race and democratic organizing in America*. Chicago: University of Chicago Press.

Worker, L. (2002). Politics, Psychology and the Battered Women's Movement. *Journal of Trauma Practice, 1*(1):81–102.

World Social Forum (2001). Porto Alegre call for mobilization. In F. J. Lechner & J. Boli (Eds.), *The globalization reader* (2nd ed., 2004, pp. 435–437). Malden, MA: Blackwell.

Yang, G. (2000). The liminal effects of social movements: Red guards and the transformation of identity. *Sociological Forum, 15*(3), 379–406.

Young, I. M. (1990). *Justice and the politics of difference*. Princeton, NJ: Princeton University Press.

Zack, N. (2007). Can third wave feminism be inclusive? Intersectionality, its problems and new directions. In L. M. Alcoff & E. F. Kittay (Eds.), *The Blackwell guide to feminist philosophy* (pp. 193–207). Malden, MA: Blackwell.

Zapatista Army of National Liberation (n.d.). Why we are here: The struggle of humble people. [Pamphlet].

Zerkel, M. (2001). Economics education: Building a movement for global economic justice. Chicago: American Friends Service Committee.

Zinn, H. (2003). *A people's history of the United States*. New York: HarperCollins.

Zinn, H., & Arnove, H. (2004). *Voices of a people's history*. New York: Seven Stories Press.

Index